MW00790988

 BOLLINGEN SERIES

SELECTED LETTERS OF
C.G. JUNG, 1909-1961

selected and edited by   GERHARD ADLER

BOLLINGEN SERIES   PRINCETON UNIVERSITY PRESS

Published by Princeton University Press, 41 William Street, Princeton, New Jersey 08540

Copyright © 1953, 1955, 1961, 1963, 1968, 1971, 1972, 1973, 1974, 1975 by Princeton University Press
Preface and compilation copyright © 1984 by Princeton University Press

All rights reserved
First Princeton/Bollingen Paperback printing, 1984

This abridgement consists of selections from C.G. Jung: *Letters*, Volume 1: 1906-1950 and C.G. *Jung: Letters*, Volume 2: 1951-1961, Bollingen Series XCV, published by Princeton University Press.

Some of the letters in this volume were published, with some variations, in C. G. *Jung: Briefe*, edited by Aniela Jaffé, in collaboration with Gerhard Adler, three volumes, © Walter-Verlag AG, Olten (Switzerland), 1972 and 1973. The following letters have been previously published either in Jung's original English or in R.F.C. Hull's translation. (Copyright in the letters prefixed by an asterisk has been assigned to Princeton University Press.) — To James Joyce, 27 Sept. 32, in Richard Ellmann, *James Joyce*, © by Richard Ellmann, 1959; to Emanuel Maier, 24 Mar. 50, in *The Psychoanalytic Review*, vol. 50 (1963), copyright ©, 1963, by the National Psychological Association for Psychoanalysis, Inc.; ° to Upton Sinclair, 3 Nov. 52, 7 Jan. 55, in *New Republic*, copyright 1953 and 1955 in the USA by New Republic, Inc.; to James Kirsch, 18 Nov. 52, in *Psychological Perspectives*, the letter being copyright © 1972 by Princeton University Press; to Carl Seelig, 25 Feb. 53; Anon., 19 Nov. 55; the Earl of Sandwich, 10 Aug. 60, in *Spring*, 1971, the letters being copyright © 1971 by Princeton University Press; to Gustave Steiner, 30 Dec. 57 (the present tr. by R.F.C. Hull with minor variations), in the editor's introduction to *Memories, Dreams, Reflections* by C.G. Jung, recorded and edited by Aniela Jaffé, copyright © 1961, 1962, 1963 by Random House, Inc., and published by Pantheon Books, a division of Random House, Inc.; ° to Joseph R. Rychlak, 27 Apr. 59, in Rychlak, *A Philosophy of Science for Personality Theory*, copyright © 1968 by Joseph R. Rychlak; to Miguel Serrano, 31 Mar. 60, 14 Sept. 60, in C. G. *Jung and Hermann Hesse*, © Miguel Serrano 1966; ° to William G. Wilson, 30 Jan. 61, in two issues of *AA Grapevine*, © 1963 and 1968 by AA Grapevine.

LCC 83-22904

ISBN: 978-0-691-61237-9

Princeton, New Jersey

TABLE OF CONTENTS

PREFACE

Among Jung's published writings, his letters take a unique place. Nowhere else has he expressed his feelings about all possible subjects with the same freedom and spontaneity. True, we have his wonderful *Memories, Dreams, Reflections*[1] where he allows himself to draw the curtain from many of his most private thoughts, but, as he says himself, "My life is a story of the self realization of the unconscious" and he describes the *Memories* as the story of his personal myth, and again defines the essence of the book as a report of his experiences: "the only events in my life worth telling are those when the imperishable world irrupted into this transitory one."

Reading the *Memories*, one is struck by the absolute uniqueness of Jung's personality, a uniqueness which also conveys the feeling of the great loneliness in which his genius had to exist. The report of this inner story excludes much of the richness and variety of his life, so much so that Jung can say how, compared with his inner life and his dreams and visions, "all other memories of travels, people and my surroundings have paled beside these interior happenings" and how "recollection of the outward events . . . has largely faded or disappeared."

But this is exactly why the letters are of such special value. Here Jung relates to every possible outside problem and event as it is brought to him by the innumerable letters that ask for elucidation of some very often personal problem as well as of worldly events. True, some of this is also contained in the collection of interviews and related material published as *C. G. Jung Speaking*,[2] but in the personal flavor of involvement in the problem of his correspondents, in his immediate relatedness to their enquiries, in the empathy with which he feels himself into their intimate difficulties, in the care with which he responds to more objective queries, the letters have no parallel.

Invariably we gain at the same time important glimpses into the general working of his mind. Here I want to mention only one passage of a letter to Professor Werblowsky (17 June 1952) where he defines his way of thinking and writing in an unsurpassably clear and revealing way, and stating his way of expressing himself as he has never done anywhere else:

The language I speak must be ambiguous, must have two meanings, in order to do justice to the dual aspect of our psychic nature. I strive quite consciously and deliberately for ambiguity of expression, because it is superior to unequivocalness and reflects the nature of life. My whole temperament inclines me to be very unequivocal indeed. That is not difficult, but it would be at the cost of truth. I purposely allow all the overtones and undertones to be heard, partly because they are there anyway, and partly because they give a fuller picture of reality. Un-equivocalness makes sense only in establishing facts but not in interpreting them; for "meaning" is not a tautology but always includes more in itself than the concrete object of which it is predicated.

Here we have a description which enables us to grasp the fundamental difference between Freud's clear, systematic, technical way of thinking, but in his clarity also relatively limited, and Jung's deliberately vague but more comprehensive approach. Jung's letter to Werblowsky enables one to put the differences between the two men into a pattern of complementarity in which each of them finds his appropriate place and value.

But contrast to this Jung's involvement in practical matters. Here again I would like to mention two letters, one to a politician and businessman, Gottlieb Duttweiler (4 December 1939), the other to a professor of law, Karl Oftinger (September 1957), both Swiss. In the letter of December 1939, when the people of Switzerland—proverbially freedom-loving—had mobilized against the threat of a German invasion, Jung shows himself deeply concerned with the "great difference between the social position of conscripts and of persons not liable for military service." He makes a truly revolutionary suggestion—namely that "every Swiss citizen between the ages of 18 and 60 should be counted as mobilized whether he is liable for military service or not." In that way, money should be made available to the conscripts' families, deprived of their breadwinners, and thus preventing social unrest. This proposal shows the feeling of social responsibility for the welfare of the whole nation in a way which few—if any—politicians would have envisaged. Not surprisingly Jung's suggestion was not accepted.

Again, the letter to Professor Oftinger shows Jung's concern with quite another social problem: that of noise. He replies to the request of Professor Oftinger for a contribution to a publication dealing with the problem of the public nuisance of noise on a much deeper psychological level than was probably hoped for. He puts the problem in the general context of such problems of modern "civilization" (the quotation marks are his) as pollution, the destructive effects of radio and television, the increase in radioactivity, and the threat of overpopulation. He contrasts the obsession with noise to the profound need for silence and inwardness. Only by "a radical change of consciousness" can the disorientation of modern "civilization" be cured. One could quote many other letters which show Jung's concern with and relatedness to practical political issues, but I hope that these two letters—which, of course, have to be read in full—give some ideas of his attitude.

Quite a different feeling is manifest in many of his answers to appeals for personal help. Many of these letters are extremely short, sometimes not more than a few sentences. I have included them in this collection exactly for the glimpses they allow us of Jung's empathy with the difficulties of other people. When somebody asks him about the value of prayer and he replies "I have thought much about prayer," as in his answer of 10 September 1943 to an anonymous letter; or if he responds—again to an anonymous letter—on 23 November 1945, in six lines to the request of a man awaiting trial for a petty offence; or when he tries to explain his attitude to suicide to an old lady who is deeply worried about this issue (19 November 1955), all his reactions show his total engagement and his serious concern. Yet another facet of his personality is apparent in his letter—one of my favorite ones—to a chief of the Taos Pueblo Indians, Antonio Mirabal, or "Mountain Lake" (21 October 1932), with its deep humanity and empathic simplicity.

Even more remarkable are letters containing unusually open and private statements referring to Jung's intimate feelings. They allow glimpses into a side of his personality which are completely absent from his other publications. Thus, when he writes in a letter to Aniela Jaffé (10 August 1947) how necessary and helpful it is for him to have an understanding reaction to his work ("how much one misses when one receives no response or a mere fragment, and what joy it is to experience the opposite" and how without it "a man's work remains a delicate child . . . released into the world with inner anxiety"), one suddenly realizes the loneliness and isolation in which he must have lived. In another letter to Aniela Jaffé (9 July 1957) Jung expresses how he is tormented by the ethical problem and that his only answer to it is to submit to God's verdict "for God's power is greater than my will." Perhaps his compassion and relatedness are evident most of all in the letters he wrote to friends bereaved of a beloved partner or other relative. The letter to Mrs. Oeri (23 December 1950) after her husband's death is characteristic of the depth of his emotional participation in her loss and his own loss of a friend. Such letters show how in the immediacy of an answer to a true and genuine question or crisis he has no hesitation in revealing his innermost feelings. This is exactly what makes these letters such a rich and meaningful complement to Jung's scientific work.

Finally, another vital subject playing a large part in this correspondence has to be mentioned—that of religion, which goes like a red thread through the letters. Deeply religious as Jung was, his concept of religion was not that of traditional Christianity, and this led him frequently into a controversial position and into sometimes polemical discussions with his correspondents. For one thing, God to him was not simply the "summum bonum," for another he refused to be drawn into any definition of God. He felt—and was—constantly misunderstood about his distinction between God as a metaphysical entity and the "God-image" in man. This comes out, for instance, in a letter to Dr. Paul Maag (12 June 1933), where he explicitly refused "coming up with a mixture of theology and science." But most of all did he become involved in profound misunderstandings—and consequently controversial arguments—after the publication of his "Answer to Job." to many (myself among them) his most beautiful and profound book, but to others a *petra scandali*. In a letter of 28 July 1952—not included in this selection—he mentions how he has "to steel my mind against the battering I receive from my *Hiob*, which causes the weirdest misunderstandings," and how he is all the more pleased with the relatively few reactions showing understanding of his true purpose and of the importance of what he had tried to convey in this book. But what comes out most clearly in all his references to religion is his absolute positive attitude to a divine power in the psyche—as, for instance, in the abovementioned 1957 letter to Aniela Jaffé. Well known also is his radio interview, of 22 October 1959,[3] in which he answered the question of the interviewer, "Do you believe in God?" with the words "I don't need to believe in God—I know" (cf. his letter to M. Leonard, 5 December 1959). In the deepest sense of the word, Jung was a *homo religiosus.*—But I must leave it to the readers of these letters to form their own judgment on this matter.

*

One short word about this selected edition of Jung's letters. The two original volumes already represent a selection from about 1600 letters which I had received as a response to my original request, and to reduce this selection to 140 letters presented me with sometimes painful decisions and with considerable doubts about what to print and what to leave out. I have tried to convey Jung's personality as it manifests itself in his correspondence. No doubt another editor might have made a completely different selection, and I do not claim to have achieved an ideal solution, influenced as it must be by my own personal preferences. But whatever the shortcomings of this selection may be, I hope they will give people who have found the two volumes, encompassing over 1300 pages, either too cumbersome or too expensive, the possibility to get some impression of the richness of Jung's mind and the scope of his immense knowledge, of his profound sense of responsibility and commitment, and of his deep compassion and reverent humanity.

London, 1983   GERHARD ADLER

NOTES

1. *Memories, Dreams, Reflections by C. G. Jung,* recorded and edited by Aniela Jaffé (New York and London, 1962), pp. 3-5/17-19.

2. *C. G. Jung Speaking; Interviews and Encounters,* edited by William McGuire and R.F.C. Hull (Princeton, 1977; shortened edn., London, 1978).

3. "The 'Face to Face' Interview," 1959, by John Freeman, in *C. G. Jung Speaking,* pp. 424 ff. (London edn., pp. 410 ff.).

FROM THE INTRODUCTION TO
THE ORIGINAL EDITION

As far as humanly possible, I, with the help of Mrs. Aniela Jaffé, tried to obtain permission for publication from every single addressee after the year 1930. Since the earlier letters date back many decades, some degree of liberty had to be taken with letters to people who we knew had died. In some cases, arrangements were made through friendly relations with families or estates of addressees; in others, where the contents seemed to justify and allow it, we had to take personal responsibility for publication. As far as living addressees are concerned, we tried to consult every one who could be identified. . . . Some of the addressees requested anonymity, or the omission of certain passages, or the anonymity of some person mentioned in a letter. . . .

The annotations are intended to provide the reader with facts it might prove difficult for him to find out for himself. . . . Some notes which may appear unduly elaborate or unnecessary are included for personal or historical interest: the more time passes, the more difficult it will become to elicit the information given in them. . . . A special problem is that of giving details concerning addressees. This has been done wherever possible in a preliminary note designated with a □; in some cases, discretion precluded such annotation, and in many more cases the addressee could not be located. It should be borne in mind that many of the letters Jung received were from people completely unknown to him.

As a matter of principle and in order to prevent the notes from becoming too bulky, publications by addressees are included chiefly in the □ notes referring to analytical psychologists (and even here occasionally only in selection; generally only published books are cited). However, a few exceptions are made where it seems desirable for the understanding of the correspondence. . . . While the notes are as concise as possible, abbreviations are kept to a minimum, the chief being CW for the Collected Works and *Memories* for the autobiographical *Memories, Dreams, Reflections*, by Jung in collaboration with Aniela Jaffé. As the London and New York editions of the latter differ in pagination, double page references are given.

. . .

The sources of the letters are varied. The largest group, from the files at Küsnacht, consists of carbon copies of dictated and typed letters and secretarial typed copies of handwritten letters. A second category includes letters sent to us by the recipients or their heirs, some in the original, some in xerox copies, some in the recipient's own typed copy. Handwritten letters are so indicated in the □ notes, and likewise previously published letters, but it has not been possible to give full details of the various documentary states of typed letters—originals with signature, xerox copies of the same, file carbon copies, typed copies of holograph letters, etc.

. . .

Omissions are of two kinds: of repetitive or quite unimportant passages, and of passages of a too intimate or confidential nature. All omissions are indicated by ". . .". Changes in the letters written in English are limited mainly to punctuation, obvious spelling mistakes, and corrections of secretarial errors. . . .

The original Editorial Committee consisted of three members: Mrs. Marianne Niehus-Jung, Mrs. Aniela Jaffé, and myself. It was a very sad loss when Marianne Niehus died in March 1965 after a prolonged illness. By that time the task of collecting the letters had virtually come to an end, but the work of selection and annotation was just beginning, and her co-operation was sorely missed. I would like to express my profound appreciation of her warmth and generosity, her tact and understanding, and her constant willingness to further my work. I am deeply grateful to her for all she had done right up to the end of her life.

After her death I had to carry the full responsibility with the support of Aniela Jaffé. Here again I would like to express my deep gratitude for the help she has given me all through the many years of the work. . . .

Last but certainly not least, my particular thanks are due to the Bollingen Foundation, without whose moral and financial support these letters could not have been collected, edited, and published in their present form.

London, 1971   GERHARD ADLER

Because for technical reasons the annotation of the selected letters could not be revised, there are occasional references that pertain to material in the original two-volume edition, and the □ note containing biographical information about the correspondents sometimes could not be included. Substantive notes are given in an appendix on page 211. —*Ed.*

CHRONOLOGY

1875   26 July: born to Johann Paul Achilles Jung (1842–1896), then parson at Kesswil (Canton Thurgau), and Emilie, née Preiswerk (1848–1923).

1879   The family moves to Klein-Hüningen, near Basel.

1884   Birth of sister Gertrud (d. 1935).

1895–1900   Medical training (and qualification) at Basel U.

1900   Assistant Staff Physician to Eugen Bleuler at the Burghölzli, the insane asylum of Canton Zurich and psychiatric clinic of Zurich U.

1902   Senior Assistant Staff Physician at the Burghölzli. — M.D. dissertation (Zurich U.): *Zur Psychologie und Pathologie sogenannter occulter Phänomene* (= "On the Psychology and Pathology of So-called Occult Phenomena," CW 1).

1902–1903   Winter semester with Pierre Janet at the Salpêtrière in Paris for the study of theoretical psychopathology.

1903   Marriage to Emma Rauschenbach, of Schaffhausen (1882–1955); one son and four daughters.

1903–1905   Experimental researches on word associations, published in *Diagnostische Assoziationsstudien* (1906, 1909) (= *Studies in Word-Association*, 1918; CW 2).

1905–1909   Senior Staff Physician at the Burghölzli; after that in private practice at his home, 1003 (later 228) Seestrasse, Küsnacht (Zurich).

1905–1913   Lecturer (Privatdozent) on the Medical Faculty of Zurich U.; lectures on psychoneuroses and psychology.

1907   *Über die Psychologie der Dementia Praecox* (= *The Psychology of Dementia Praecox*, 1909; CW 3). — First meeting with Freud in Vienna.

1908   First International Psychoanalytic Congress, Salzburg.

1909   First visit to U.S.A. with Freud and Ferenczi on the occasion of the 20th anniversary of Clark University, Worcester, Mass., where Jung lectures on the association experiment and receives hon. degree of LL.D.

1909–1913 Editor of *Jahrbuch für psychoanalytische und psychopathologische Forschungen.*

1910 Second International Psychoanalytic Congress, Nuremberg.

1910–1914 First President of the International Psychoanalytic Association.

1911 Third International Psychoanalytic Congress, Weimar.

1912 Another visit to U.S.A. for series of lectures at Fordham U., New York, on "The Theory of Psychoanalysis" (CW 4). — "Neue Bahnen der Psychologie" (= "New Paths in Psychology," later revised and expanded as "On the Psychology of the Unconscious"; both CW 7). — *Wandlungen und Symbole der Libido* (= *Psychology of the Unconscious,* 1916; for revision, see 1952) leading to

1913 break with Freud. — Fourth International Psychoanalytic Congress, Munich. Jung designates his psychology as "Analytical Psychology" (later also "Complex Psychology"). — Resigns his lecturership at Zurich U.

1913–1919 Period of intense introversion: confrontation with the unconscious.

1916 "VII Sermones ad Mortuos"; first mandala painting. — *Collected Papers on Analytical Psychology.* — First description of process of "active imagination" in "Die transzendente Funktion" (not publ. until 1957; in CW 8). — First use of terms "personal unconscious," "collective/suprapersonal unconscious," "individuation," "animus/anima," "persona" in "La Structure de l'inconscient" (CW 7, App.). — Beginning of study of Gnostic writings.

1918 "Über das Unbewusste" (= "The Role of the Unconscious," CW 10).

1918–1919 Commandant of camp for interned British soldiers at Château d'Oex (Canton Vaud). — First use of term "archetype" in "Instinct and the Unconscious" (CW 8).

1920 Journey to Algeria and Tunisia.

1921 *Psychologische Typen*; first use of term "self" (= *Psychological Types,* 1923; CW 6).

1922 Purchase of property in village of Bollingen.

1923 First Tower in Bollingen. — Death of mother. — Richard Wilhelm's lecture on the *I Ching* at the Psychological Club, Zurich.

1925   Visit with Pueblo Indians in New Mexico. — First English seminar at the Psychological Club, Zurich.

1925–1926   Expedition to Kenya, Uganda, and the Nile; visit with the Elgonyi on Mt. Elgon.

1928   Beginning of encounter with alchemy. — *Two Essays on Analytical Psychology* (= CW 7). — *Über die Energetik der Seele* (various essays, now in CW 8).

1928–1930   English seminars on "Dream Analysis" at the Psychological Club, Zurich.

1929   Publication, with Richard Wilhelm, of *Das Geheimnis der goldenen Blüte* (= *The Secret of the Golden Flower*; Jung's contribution in CW 13). — *Contributions to Analytical Psychology*.

1930   Vice-President of General Medical Society for Psychotherapy, with Ernst Kretschmer as president.

1930–1934   English seminars on "Interpretation of Visions" at the Psychological Club, Zurich.

1931   *Seelenprobleme der Gegenwart* (essays in CW 4, 6, 8, 10, 15, 16, 17).

1932   Awarded Literature Prize of the City of Zurich.

1933   First lectures at the Eidgenössische Technische Hochschule (E.T.H.), Zurich (Swiss Federal Polytechnic), on "Modern Psychology." — *Modern Man in Search of a Soul.* — Eranos lecture on "A Study in the Process of Individuation" (CW 9, i). — Visit to Egypt and Palestine.

1934   Founds International General Medical Society for Psychotherapy and becomes its first president. — Eranos lecture on "Archetypes of the Collective Unconscious" (CW 9, i). — *Wirklichkeit der Seele* (essays in CW 8, 10, 15, 16, 17).

1934–1939   English seminars on "Psychological Aspects of Nietzsche's *Zarathustra*" at the Psychological Club, Zurich.

1934–1939   Editor of *Zentralblatt für Psychotherapie und ihre Grenzgebiete* (Leipzig).

1935   Appointed Professor at the E.T.H., Zurich. — Founds Schweizerische Gesellschaft für Praktische Psychologie. — Eranos lecture on "Dream Symbols of the Individuation Process" (expanded to Part II of *Psychology and Alchemy*, CW 12). — Tavistock Lectures at the Institute of Medical Psychology, London (not published until 1968: *Analytical Psychology; Its Theory and Practice; CW* 18).

1936   Receives hon. doctoral degree from Harvard U. — Eranos lecture on "Ideas of Redemption in Alchemy" (expanded as part III of *Psychology and Alchemy*); "Wotan" (CW 10).

1937   Terry Lectures on "Psychology and Religion" (CW 11) at Yale U., New Haven, Conn. — Eranos lecture on "The Visions of Zosimos" (CW 13).

1938   Invitation to India by the British Government on the occasion of the 25th anniversary of Calcutta U.; hon. doctorates from the universities of Calcutta, Benares, and Allahabad. — International Congress for Psychotherapy at Oxford with Jung as President; he receives hon. doctorate of Oxford U. — Appointed Hon. Fellow of the Royal Society of Medicine, London. — Eranos lecture on "Psychological Aspects of the Mother Archetype" (CW 9, i).

1939   Eranos lecture on "Concerning Rebirth" (CW 9, i)

1940   Eranos lecture on "A Psychological Approach to the Dogma of the Trinity" (CW 11).

1941   Publication, together with Karl Kerényi, of *Einführung in das Wesen der Mythologie* (= *Essays on a Science of Mythology*; Jung's contribution in CW 9, i). — Eranos lecture on "Transformation Symbolism in the Mass" (CW 11).

1942   Resigns appointment as Professor at E.T.H. — *Paracelsica* (essays in CW 13, 15). — Eranos lecture on "The Spirit Mercurius" (CW 13).

1943   Hon. Member of the Swiss Academy of Sciences.

1944   Appointed to the chair of Medical Psychology at Basel U.; resigns the same year on account of critical illness. —*Psychologie und Alchemie* (CW 12).

1945   Hon. doctorate of Geneva U. on the occasion of his 70th birthday. — Eranos lecture on "The Psychology of the Spirit," expanded as "The Phenomenology of the Spirit in Fairy Tales" (CW 9, i).

1946   Eranos lecture on "The Spirit of Psychology" (expanded as "On the Nature of the Psyche," CW 8). — *Die Psychologie der Übertragung* (= "The Psychology of the Transference," CW 16); *Aufsätze zur Zeitgeschichte* (= *Essays on Contemporary Events*; in CW 10); *Psychologie und Erziehung* (CW 17).

1948   *Symbolik des Geistes* (essays in CW 9, i, 11, 13). — Eranos lecture "On the Self" (expanded to ch. IV of *Aion*, CW 9, ii). — Inauguration of the C. G. Jung Institute, Zurich.

1950   *Gestaltungen des Unbewussten* (essays in CW 9, i and 15).

1951   *Aion* (CW 9, ii). — Eranos lecture "On Synchronicity" (CW 8, App.).

1952   Publication, with W. Pauli, of *Naturerklärung und Psyche* (= *The Interpretation of Nature and Psyche*; Jung's contribution "Synchronicity: An Acausal Connecting Principle," CW 8). — *Symbole der Wandlung* (= *Symbols of Transformation*, CW 5: 4th, greatly revised edition of *Psychology of the Unconscious*). — *Antwort auf Hiob* (= "Answer to Job," CW 11).

1953   Publication of the 1st vol. of the American/British edition of the *Collected Works* (tr. by R.F.C. Hull): *Psychology and Alchemy* (CW 12).

1954   *Von den Wurzeln des Bewusstseins* (essays in CW 8, 9, i, 11, 13).

1955   Hon. doctorate of the E.T.H., Zurich, on the occasion of his 80th birthday. — Death of his wife (27 November).

1955–1956   *Mysterium Coniunctionis* (CW 14); the final work on the psychological significance of alchemy.

1957   *Gegenwart und Zukunft* (= "The Undiscovered Self (Present and Future)," CW 10). — Starts work on *Memories, Dreams, Reflections* with the help of Aniela Jaffé (pub. 1962). — BBC television interview with John Freeman.

1958   *Ein moderner Mythus* (= "Flying Saucers: A Modern Myth," CW 10). — Publication of initial vol. in Swiss edition of Gesammelte Werke: *Praxis der Psychotherapie* (Bd. 16).

1960   Hon. Citizen of Küsnacht on the occasion of his 85th birthday.

1961   Finishes his last work 10 days before his death: "Approaching the Unconscious," in *Man and His Symbols* (1964). — Dies after short illness on 6 June in his house at Küsnacht.

Selected Letters of C.G. Jung, 1909-1961

To Sandor Ferenczi

Dear Colleague,   6 December 1909

Your letter has certainly hit the mark. These things were in the air. You can well imagine that I often felt a proper fool when, because of your position, I found myself thrust into the role of a usurper. But I don't feel like a usurper at all, rather one of the workers who is doing a special bit of work. Whether I am recognized or not recognized as the "crown prince"[1] can at times annoy me or please me. Since I gave up my academic career[2] my interest in science and knowledge has become purer and amply compensates for the pleasures of outward esteem, so that it is really of greater importance to me to see clearly in scientific matters and work ahead for the future than to measure myself against Freud. No doubt my roving fantasy caters to this and particularly the unconscious, but that must be so and is the necessary undercurrent of all creativity. I believe that if we succeed in putting the work above ourselves (so far as this is possible at all) we free ourselves from a lot of unnecessary encumbrances and unwanted responsibilities brought by ambition, envy, and other two-edged swords. What does one want actually? In the end it is always the one who really is or was the strongest that remains king, even if only posthumously. As always, we have to submit trustingly to this natural law, since nothing avails against it anyway. Ambition is for the most part the same as jealousy, and therefore crippling and nonsensical. Haven't we seen that with the American mania for setting up records? All beauty gets lost in the process—a grave loss which our science can hardly afford.

Won't you translate your lectures into German? They would surely be accepted by Bresler, for instance. Have you anything in mind for the 2nd half of *Jahrbuch* II?

Congratulations on Freud's recognition!!![3]

Best greetings, JUNG

☐ (Handwritten.)

[1] Freud had frequently suggested to Jung that he should become his successor (cf. *Memories*, p. 157/154, and Freud's letter of 16 Apr. 09, ibid., p. 361/333: "my successor and crown prince"; also in the Freud-Jung Letters).

[2] Cf. Freud, 5 Oct. 06, n. 5.

[3] In the autumn of 1909 Ferenczi published a paper on "Introjection und Uebertragung" (cf. Ferenczi, 6 Jan. 09, n. 2) which met with Freud's warm approval. Ferenczi put together a volume of collected papers for which Freud wrote a preface. It was published in Hungarian in 1910 in Budapest under the title *Lélekelemzés* ("Psychoanalysis"). Later translated into German and English (*Contributions to Psychoanalysis*, 1916).

To Hans Schmid

Dear friend, 6 November 1915

. . .

In the meantime, and after long reflection, the problem *of resistance to understanding* has clarified itself for me. And it was Brigitta of Sweden[1] (1303–1373) who helped me to gain insight. In a vision she saw the devil, who spoke with God and had the following to say about the psychology of devils:

"Their belly is so swollen because their greed was boundless, for they filled themselves and were not sated, and so great was their greed that, had they but been able to gain the whole world, they would gladly have exerted themselves, and would moreover have desired to reign in heaven. A like greed is mine. Could I but win all the souls in heaven and on earth and in purgatory, I would gladly snatch them."

So the devil is the devourer. Understanding = *comprehendere* = κατασυλλαμβάνειν,[2] and is likewise a devouring. Understanding swallows you up. But one should not let oneself be swallowed if one is

□ (Handwritten.) Hans Schmid or Schmid-Guisan, M.D., (1881–1932), Swiss psychotherapist, friend and pupil of Jung's with whom he exchanged a lengthy correspondence 1915/16 on the question of types, more specifically the (later abandoned) equation of thinking with introversion and feeling with extraversion. At the end of his foreword to *Psychological Types* (CW 6, p. xii) Jung pays the following tribute to Schmid: "I owe a great deal of clarification to this interchange of ideas, and much of it, though of course in altered and greatly revised form, has gone into my book. The correspondence belongs essentially to the preparatory stage of the work, and its inclusion would create more confusion than clarity. Nevertheless, I owe it to the labours of my friend to express my thanks to him here." The correspondence was brought to light again by Schmid's daughter, Marie-Jeanne Boller-Schmid, Jung's secretary from 1922 to 1952, in 1966. The Editors of CW concurred with Jung's view that its inclusion, as an Appendix, in CW 6, "would create more confusion than clarity," and held it to be too technical and prolix for inclusion in CW 18, a volume of miscellaneous and posthumous writings, some hitherto unpublished. The passage reproduced here forms a wholly unexpected personal codicil to Jung's long letter of 6 Nov. 15, too valuable and moving to pass into oblivion. Jung's obituary for Schmid in the *Basler Nachrichten* (23 Apr. 32) and his foreword to Schmid-Guisan's *Tag und Nacht* (1931) are in CW 18.

[1] St. Bridget, the most famous saint of the Northern Kingdoms. She had eight children, one of whom became St. Catherine of Sweden. *Ca.* 1346 St. Bridget founded the Order of Brigittines (Ordo Sanctissimi Salvatoris).
[2] Cf. *Symbols of Transformation*, par. 682.

4

not minded to play the hero's role, unless it be that one really is a hero who can overpower the monster from within. And the understander in turn must be willing to play the role of Fafner and devour indigestible heroes. It is therefore better not to "understand" people who might be heroes, because the same fate might befall oneself. One can be destroyed by them. In wanting to understand, ethical and human as it sounds, there lurks the devil's will, which though not at first perceptible to me, is perceptible to the other. Understanding is a fearfully binding power, at times a veritable murder of the soul as soon as it flattens out vitally important differences. The core of the individual is a mystery of life, which is snuffed out when it is "grasped." That is why symbols want to be mysterious; they are not so merely because what is at the bottom of them cannot be clearly apprehended. The symbol wants to guard against Freudian interpretations, which are indeed such pseudo-truths that they never lack for effect. With our patients "analytical" understanding has a wholesomely destructive effect, like a corrosive or thermocautery, but is banefully destructive on sound tissue. It is a technique we have learnt from the devil, always destructive, but useful where destruction is necessary. But one can commit no greater mistake than to apply the principles of this technique to an analysed psychology. More than that, all understanding in general, which is a conformity with general points of view, has the diabolical element in it and kills. It is a wrenching of another life out of its own course, forcing it into a strange one in which it cannot live. Therefore, in the later stages of analysis, we must help people towards those hidden and unlockable symbols, where the germ lies hidden like the tender seed in the hard shell. There should truly be no understanding in this regard, even if one were possible. But if understanding is general and manifestly possible, then the symbol is ripe for destruction, as it no longer conceals the seed which is about to break from the shell. I now understand a dream I once had, which made a great impression on me: *I was standing in my garden and had dug open a rich spring of water that gushed forth. Then I had to dig another deep hole, where I collected all the water and conducted it back into the depths of the earth again.* So is healing given to us in the unlockable and ineffable symbol, for it prevents the devil from swallowing up the seed of life. The menacing and dangerous thing about analysis is that the individual is apparently understood: the devil eats his soul away, which naked and exposed, robbed of its protecting shell, was born like a child into the light.

That is the dragon, the murderer, that always threatens the newborn divine child. He must be hidden once more from the "understanding" of humanity.

True understanding seems to be one which does not understand, yet lives and works. Once when Ludwig the Saint[3] visited the holy Aegidius[4] incognito, and as the two, who did not know each other, came face to face, they both fell to their knees before each other, embraced and kissed—and *spoke no word together.* Their gods recognized each other, and their human parts followed. We must understand the divinity within us, but not the other, so far as he is able to go by himself and understand himself. The patient we must understand, for he needs the corrosive medicine. We should bless our blindness for the mysteries of the other; it shields us from devilish deeds of violence. We should be connivers at our own mysteries, but veil our eyes chastely before the mystery of the other, so far as, being unable to understand himself, he does not need the "understanding" of others.

[UNSIGNED]

[3] Louis I, the Pious (778–840), Holy Roman Emperor, King of France, third son of Charlemagne (d. 814).
[4] St. Giles (? 8th cent.), reputedly an Athenian of royal descent who fled to France, where he lived as a hermit. One of the most popular saints in the Middle Ages, he was invoked as the patron of cripples, beggars, and lepers.

To Marianne Jung

Dear Marianne,   London,[1] 1 July 1919

It was sweet of you to write me a letter. It has made me so happy that I am writing you a letter too. If you can't read it, Mama will read it to you. I have bought a doll here. It is carved from brown wood and comes from India. But it is for Mama. I shall bring it with me in my trunk. I am staying here in a big house. About fifty thousand cars

☐ (Handwritten.) Jung's third daughter Marianne (Frau Niehus-Jung; 1910–65). Co-editor of Jung's Gesammelte Werke until her death; also member of the Editorial Committee for the Selected Letters.
[1] Jung spent the first part of July 1919 in London, where he read several papers to various learned societies. Cf. "Instinct and the Unconscious" and "The Psychological Foundation of Belief in Spirits" (CW 8), and "The Problem of Psychogenesis in Mental Disease" (CW 3).

go by every day. Every morning at half past ten the Guardsmen ride past in golden breastplates with red plumes in their helmets and black cloaks. They are going to the King's castle and guard the King and the Princes and Princesses. The King has his golden throne and his golden sceptre in another castle, in a high tower. It has windows with thick bars and iron doors. By day the crown is in the tower on top and you can see it, in the evening it sinks down with the sceptre into a deep cellar which is shut with iron plates. So no one can steal it. In the crown are precious stones as big as pigeon's eggs. Round the castle are three walls and moats and soldiers stand at the gates. London lies on a big river where the seaships go. Every day the river flows downwards for 6 hours and then upwards for 6 hours. When it flows downwards, the ships that are going away float out into the sea, and when it flows upwards the ships that have waited outside come into the city.

Just think, more than twice as many people live in London as in the whole of Switzerland. Chinamen live here too.

Many loving greetings to you and Lilli,[2]

from your Papa

[2] Jung's youngest daughter Hélène (Frau Hoerni-Jung).

To Hermann Hesse

Dear Herr Hesse,   3 December 1919

I must send you my most cordial thanks for your masterly as well as veracious book: *Demian*.[1] I know it is very immodest and officious of me to break through your pseudonym; but, while reading the book, I had the feeling that it must somehow have reached me via Lucerne.[2]

☐ (Handwritten.) See Hesse, 28 Jan. 22, n. ☐.

[1] Berlin, 1919 (tr. 1965). The novel appeared originally under the pseudonym of its hero-narrator "Emil Sinclair." H. borrowed the name from Isaak von Sinclair (1775–1815), diplomat and author, and a friend of the poet Hölderlin, whom H. greatly admired. — The true author was generally unknown until June 1920, when Hesse officially acknowledged authorship. (The editor is indebted to Professor Ralph Freedman, Princeton U., for this information.)

[2] In 1916 H. had a serious breakdown, for which reason he went to the Sanatorium Sonnmatt, near Lucerne. There he was advised to consult Dr. J. B. Lang, a medical psychotherapist and pupil of Jung's. The therapeutic relationship soon developed into a close friendship. The analytical interviews went on from May

7

Although I failed to recognize you in the Sinclair sketches in the *Neue Zürcher Zeitung*,[3] I always wondered what sort of person Sinclair must be, because his psychology seemed to me so remarkable. Your book came at a time when, once again, I was oppressed by the darkened consciousness of modern man, and by his hopeless bigotry, as Sinclair was by little Knauer.[4] Hence your book hit me like the beam of a lighthouse on a stormy night. A good book, like every proper human life, must have an ending. Yours has the best possible ending, where everything that has gone before runs truly to its end, and everything with which the book began begins over again—with the birth and awakening of the new man. The Great Mother is impregnated by the loneliness of him that seeks her. In the shell burst[5] she bears the "old" man into death, and implants in the new the everlasting monad, the mystery of individuality. And when the renewed man reappears the mother reappears too—in a woman on this earth.

I could tell you a little secret[6] about Demian of which you became the witness, but whose meaning you have concealed from the reader

---

1916 to Nov. 1917, altogether about seventy sessions, each lasting up to three hours. The fruit of these interviews was *Demian*, written explosively in 1917 (and to a lesser degree H.'s *Märchen*, 1919 [tr. *Strange News from Another Star*, 1972]).—This information is taken from Hugo Ball, *Hermann Hesse, sein Leben und sein Werk* (Berlin, 1927). Also cf. Maier, 24 Mar. 50.

[3] E. Sinclair, "Der Europäer; Eine Fabel," *Neue Zürcher Zeitung*, 4 and 6 Aug. 1918 (nos. 10026, 10032); tr. "The European," in *If the War Goes On . . .* (1971).

[4] A fellow-student of Sinclair's, a lost creature, looking for the saviour in Sinclair.

[5] Sinclair, as a soldier in the first World War, has a vision of "a mighty, godlike figure with shining stars in her hair . . . and the features of Frau Eva [Demian's mother]" giving birth to thousands of stars. One of the stars seems to seek him out: "The world was shattered above me with a thunderous roar": he is hit by a shell splinter. In a field hospital he finds himself lying beside the mortally wounded Demian.

[6] As this letter came to light only after the present volume was in page proof, nothing definite has as yet been ascertained about the allusions in this and the following paragraph. More research is needed. But it is probable that the "small token of my great respect" was a copy of Jung's *Septem Sermones*, where the Gnostic figure of Abraxas plays a key role. The "passage in your book" may refer to the beginning of ch. 5 of *Demian*: "The bird is breaking its way out of the egg. The egg is the world. He who wishes to be born must first destroy a world. The bird flies to God. The name of the god is Abraxas." The winged egg and Abraxas appear in a Gnostic mandala painted by Jung in 1916: *The Archetypes and the Collective Unconscious*, CW 9, i, frontispiece and p. xi. Cf. also Theodore Ziolkowski, *The Novels of Hermann Hesse* (Princeton, 1965), pp. 111 ff.

and perhaps also from yourself. I could give you some very satisfying information about this, since I have long been a good friend of Demian's and he has recently initiated me into his private affairs—under the seal of deepest secrecy. But time will bear out these hints for you in a singular way.

I hope you will not think I am trying to make myself interesting by mystery-mongering; my *amor fati* is too sacred to me for that. I only wanted, out of gratitude, to send you a small token of my great respect for your fidelity and veracity, without which no man can have such apt intuitions. You may even be able to guess what passage in your book I mean.

I immediately ordered a copy of your book for our Club library.[7] It is sound in wind and limb and points the way.

I beg you not to think ill of me for my invasion. No one knows of it.

Very sincerely and with heartfelt thanks, C. G. JUNG

[7] The Psychological Club of Zurich.

To Hans Kuhn

Dear Hansli,   Bunambale Bugisu, Uganda, 1 January 1926

I promised to write you a letter from Africa.[1] We left England on 15 Oct. for Lisbon, Malaga, Marseille, Genoa. On 7 November we were in Egypt, in Port Said. Then we went through the Red Sea, desert on both sides, high cliffs and not a blade of grass. At night the temperature was 30° [86° F.] and by day 32° [nearly 90° F.]. On 12 Nov. we reached Mombasa, East Africa. Before sunrise it was already 28° [82° F.]. The whole town consists of huts which are thatched with grass, Negroes and Indians everywhere. Tall coconut palms. Two days later we took the train (narrow gauge) up into the interior, where the great plains are. We travelled for 24 hours. The earth there is quite red, and red dust swirled about the train so that our white clothes turned all red. We saw wild Masai with long spears and

☐ (Handwritten.) Hans Kuhn was a boy of 16, living in Bollingen, on the Upper Lake of Zurich. Jung met him by chance in 1922 when he landed there with his sailboat. Later he assisted Jung in the construction of the "Tower" (cf. *Memories*, ch. VIII), and helped him with gardening, cooking, and sailing.
[1] Cf. ibid., ch. IX:iii, "Kenya and Uganda."— For snapshots from the African trip, see pl. IV in the present vol.

9

shields, they were quite naked and had only an ox skin draped on. They had bored through the lobes of their ears and hung such heavy brass rings in them that the lobes were 10 cm. long. The women wear iron rings round their ankles, sometimes up to the knee. We travelled through jungle where monkeys were sitting in the trees, then we came on unending plains where we saw whole herds of antelope and zebra —two ostriches raced the train. Finally we were in Nairobi, capital of Kenya. There we bought two guns and 400 cartridges. We also hired four black servants and a cook. Then we went on by train for a whole day until the line ended. We hired a truck for all the baggage, tents, utensils, etc. and drove 100 km. We came into the jungle and then into the land of the Kavirondo. Then we marched 5 days with 48 bearers until we reached the foot of an extinct volcano. This mountain is called Elgon or Masaba, it's 4300 metres high and about 60 km. wide from base to top. We trekked our way up for about 12 km. until we came to huge and impenetrable forests. There we camped. Almost every night we heard lions, often leopards and hyenas prowled round the camp. We stayed there for 3 weeks and climbed the mountains and took a look at the wild natives. I learned their language. We slaughtered an ox. Immediately great eagles came to steal the meat. We shot at them. Then the natives came and begged us for the guts and feet of the ox. They at once put them on sticks, made a fire, waggled the guts through the flames and ate them half raw. We dried the meat in the sun. The camp was pitched at 2100 metres. I climbed up to 2900 metres. Up there the bamboo forests are full of black buffalo and rhino. These animals are very dangerous. We always had to keep our guns at the ready. We killed three big poisonous snakes. One of them suddenly came down a hill and wanted to attack Mr. Beckwith,[2] but he was able to shoot it in the head in time. It was all green and about 8 feet long. I am bringing 2 snakeskins home. A week ago we travelled westwards round the southern foot of the mountain and are now 2000 metres high. Lots of buffalo and leopard here, also giant snakes. Tomorrow we set out for Lake Victoria. It is so big that it takes a steamer 13 days to go round it. On 15 Jan. we journey up the river for 6 weeks as far as Egypt. I am coming home at the beginning of April and shall soon be in Bollingen again.

Many greetings to you, your parents and brothers and sisters,

DR. C. G. JUNG

[2] George Beckwith, a young American friend of Jung's and an excellent shot. The party also included H. G. Baynes (cf. Baynes, 6 Mar. 37) and Ruth Bailey.

To Frances G. Wickes

[ORIGINAL IN ENGLISH]

My dear Mrs. Wickes,   6 November 1926

Nobody, as long as he moves about among the chaotic currents of life, is without trouble. So I say again: Don't worry about myself. I am on my road and I carry my burden just as well as I can do. You got worries enough—more than enough. Thus, inasmuch as it is not for your own sake, don't worry about the things I have to deal with. There is no difficulty in my life that is not entirely myself. Nobody shall carry me as long as I can walk on my own feet.

If you are troubled about me, ask yourself what the thing is in you that troubles you, but don't assume that *I* trouble you. I am doing my best to be up to myself. Nobody can do it for me.

Yours cordially, C. G. JUNG

To J. Allen Gilbert

[ORIGINAL IN ENGLISH]

My dear Dr. Gilbert,   2 January 1929

Please be kind to your fellow beings! Don't think that they are all damned fools, even if they say excitingly foolish things, even if they are the most inconsistent idiots. Allow for one grain of wisdom in all their foolishness. Can't you conceive of a physicist that thinks and speaks of atoms, yet is convinced that those are merely his own abstractions? That would be my case. I have not the faintest idea what "psyche" is in itself, yet, when I come to think and speak of it, I must speak of my abstractions, concepts, views, figures, knowing that they are our specific illusions. That is what I call "non-concretization." And know that I am by no means the first and only man who speaks of anima, etc. Science is the art of creating suitable illusions which the fool believes or argues against, but the wise man enjoys their beauty or their ingenuity, without being blind to the fact that they are human veils and curtains concealing the abysmal darkness of the Unknowable. Don't you see that it is life too to paint the world with divine colours? You never will know more than you can know, and if you proudly refuse to go by the available "knowledge" (or whatever you like to call it) you are bound to produce a better "theory" or "truth," and if you should not succeed in doing so, you are left on the bank high and dry and life runs away from

11

you. You deny the living and creative God in man and you will be like the Wandering Jew. All things are *as if* they were. *Real* things are *effects* of something unknown. The same is true of anima, ego, etc. and moreover, there are no real things that are not *relatively real*. We have no idea of absolute reality, because "reality" is always something "observed." And so on. I am sure all this stuff gets your goat, but that's not the point. The point is that if you create a better theory, then I shall cock my ears.

Cordially yours, c. g. jung

☐ (Handwritten.)

To Walter Robert Corti

Dear Herr Corti,   30 April 1929

It doesn't surprise me that you were rather offended by my letter. I had to write to your father and tell him honestly what my "diagnosis" is. "Diagnosis" does not mean saying someone is pathological; it means "thorough knowledge," that is to say of your psychological state. "Hypertrophy of intellectual intuition" is a diagnosis I would apply also to Nietzsche and Schopenhauer and many others. I myself am one-sided in this respect. One compensates for it with a feeling of inferiority. Diagnoses like this merely hurt our vanity. But we must see where we stand, otherwise we are immoral illusionists. This isn't to say that a person is pathological, let alone mad. Your medical man is a stupid shitbag who ought to become a psychiatrist so that he can get better acquainted with X., whose sister I saved from the madhouse. There is too much of this sorry medical rabble running around Switzerland judging me without knowing me.

I expected my letter would dismay you, because you don't yet have the distressing capacity of seeing yourself from outside. You must hasten to acquire it without letting it upset you. Jesus said to the man who was working on the Sabbath: "Man, if indeed thou knowest

☐ (Handwritten.) Walter Robert Corti, Ph.D., Swiss writer, philosopher, and teacher, founder of the Pestalozzi Village for Children (1946); 1942–57, editor of the Swiss monthly *Du*; editor of the *Archiv für genetische Philosophie*; 1954, founder of the Bauhütte der Akademie, an educational institution. He met Jung in Mar. 1929 through the mediation of his father, who had been warned by a doctor of the young man's emotional state.

12

what thou doest, thou art blessed; but if thou knowest not, thou art cursed, and a transgressor of the law."[1] We live not only inwardly, but also outwardly.

O you carriers of ideas, why do you have to make buffoons of them by the idiotic life you lead? Nietzsche preached: "You should make friends with the nearest things."[2] I would hold his world-negating life responsible for this did I not know that syphilis lurked in him and that paralysis hung over him like the sword of Damocles.

Look, the Catholic priest is the most faithful, the closest to the earth. He is living history, and no Holzapfel.[3]

That you "live for God" is perhaps the healthiest thing about you —"He that is near me is near the fire,"[4] so runs a Gnostic saying of the Lord. But where God is nearest the danger is greatest.[5] God wants to be born in the flame of man's consciousness, leaping ever higher. And what if this has no roots in the earth? If it is not a house of stone where the fire of God can dwell, but a wretched straw hut that flares up and vanishes? Could God then be born? One must be able to suffer God. That is the supreme task for the carrier of ideas. He must be the advocate of the earth. God will take care of himself. My inner principle is: Deus et homo. God needs man in order to become conscious, just as he needs limitation in time and space. Let us therefore be for him limitation in time and space, an earthly tabernacle.

Jesus—Mani—Buddha—Lao-tse are for me the four pillars of the temple of the spirit. I could give none preference over the other.

Sometime I will show you some Manichean Turfan frescoes.[6]

Next Saturday I shall be at my country seat, a tower by the Upper Lake, halfway between Bollingen and Schmerikon. You can come to see me there.

With best regards, DR. C. G. JUNG

---

[1] Non-canonical saying of Jesus in Codex Bezae Cantabrigiensis (5th cent. text of the Gospels and Acts) to Luke 6:4. Cf. M. R. James, *The Apocryphal New Testament* (1924), p. 33.

[2] *Human All Too Human*, II: "The Wanderer and his Shadow," sec. 16.

[3] Rudolf Maria Holzapfel (1874–1930), philosopher and poet; his main work is *Panideal* (1901; rev. 1923). (The name contains a pun: *Holzapfel* = crab-apple.)

[4] Quoted from Origen, *Homiliae in Jeremiam*, XX, 3, referring to Isaiah 33:14. Cf. James, p. 35.

[5] Cf. opening lines of Hölderlin's "Patmos": "Near is God, and hard to apprehend. But where danger is, there arises salvation also."

[6] The Turfan oasis, where important frescoes, some dating back to the 7th cent., were discovered, is situated in Sinkiang (W. China).

To Robert Edmond Jones

[ORIGINAL IN ENGLISH]

My dear Jonah,   6 January 1931

Thank you very much for sending me a copy of the wonderful book. Having read *Ol' Man Adam and his Chillun*[1] I was quite able to appreciate the particular beauty of the play and of your share in it. I wish we could see such a thing over here. But, alas, it is not even to be seen in England. The censors[2] there must be completely possessed by the devil. No wonder, it is a piece of true religion. I once said in the seminar it would be by no means impossible that the next saviour might be a coloured man for the better humiliation of the white man's spiritual inflation.

Thank you again! My best wishes for a happy New Year.

Yours sincerely, C. G. JUNG

☐ (1887–1954), American theatrical designer.
[1] J. designed the set for Marc Connelly's play *The Green Pastures*. The play was based on Roark Bradford's stories of Negro life in the Deep South, *Ol' Man Adam an' his Chillun* (1928). Connelly's play opened in New York in Feb. 1930 and won the Pulitzer Prize for Drama, 1929/30.
[2] The Lord Chamberlain, the Earl of Cromer, refused a license for a London production. Although no reason was given, the general impression was that exception was taken to the impersonation of God by a Negro.

Anonymous

. . .   8 January 1932

I have attacks of feeling horribly inferior. I have to digest a whole span of life full of mistakes and stupidity. Anyway feelings of inferiority are the counterpart of power. Wanting to be better or more intelligent than one is, is power too. It is difficult enough to be what one is and yet endure oneself and for once forgive one's own sins with Christian charity. That is damnably difficult.

. . .

☐ This letter was sent in as printed, without beginning or end.

To A. Vetter

Dear Dr. Vetter,   8 April 1932

The chief difficulty seems to be the concept of transcendence. For me this concept is only epistemological, but for you, if I understand you correctly, it is something almost theological. Cf. the Christian concept of the Trinity, resulting from the efforts of the old theologians to push God out of the sphere of psychic experience into the Absolute. We all know that this was done for the (necessary) purpose of bolstering up the authority of the Church against continual erosion by Gnosis and heresy. Thus man was most effectively separated from God and the intercession of *Ecclesia Mater* became unavoidable. It is in fact the great achievement of Protestantism that this transcendence, in practice at least, came a cropper. Actually it is not correct to say that there is no mother goddess in the Christian Trinity. The mother is simply veiled by the Holy Ghost (Sophia), which is the connecting link between Father and Son. It is the breath that moves to and fro between them, according to the Catholic view. This veiling of the mother (for the reasons mentioned above) had the result that the mother then appeared in an all the more concrete and authoritarian form as *Ecclesia*.

You are perfectly right when you say that an orthodox theologian could never equate God and the unconscious. In my opinion he cannot do so because he imagines he can make assertions about God. I don't imagine I can, so that it doesn't matter to me in the slightest whether God and the unconscious are ultimately identical or not. The mother is, I maintain, only one aspect of the unconscious. There is also a father aspect, though I wouldn't attribute to these aspects more than a necessary illusionary character, due to the mental difficulty of conceiving anything that is not concrete and the incapacity of our language to express anything that is not a verbal image. In a certain sense I could say of the collective unconscious exactly what Kant said of the *Ding an sich*—that it is merely a negative borderline concept, which however cannot prevent us from framing . . .[1] or hypotheses about its possible nature as though it were an object of human experience. But we do not know whether the unconscious *an sich* is

---

[1] Lacuna in file carbon copy. Most likely a Greek word handwritten by Jung, a frequent procedure in his letters.

unlimited, whether it is experienceable in part or not at all. It could be absolute, i.e., inexperienceable. At all events it is absolutely necessary for us to give up the anthropomorphism of the Christian concept of transcendence if we do not want to commit flagrant transgressions. I grant you that I am on the best way to delivering up the Christian concept of the spirit to the chaos of Gnosis again, from which it was so carefully insulated. But in my view the spirit is alive only when it is an adventure eternally renewed. As soon as it is held fast it is nothing but a man-made expression of a particular cultural form. Of course the cultural form owes its very existence to the intervention of a true and living spirit, but once it is fixed it has long ceased to be. In my view the woolliness of our present-day thinking comes from our illegitimately granting it prerogatives which appear to endow thinking with faculties it doesn't really possess. Hence my function theory.

I hope we can meet again sometime and that we can then [continue] our discussion by word of mouth.[2]

. . .

[2] The end of the letter is missing.

Anonymous

Dear Frau N.,   20 June 1932

Sincerest thanks for kindly sending me the mandala.

Please forgive me if I don't go into your questions, lack of time unfortunately makes it quite impossible for me to write long letters. I would only remark that our proper life-task must necessarily appear impossible to us, for only then can we be certain that all our latent powers will be brought into play. Perhaps this is an optical illusion born of inner compulsion, but at any rate that is how it feels. With best regards,

Yours sincerely, C. G. JUNG

☐ Germany.

Anonymous

Dear Frau N.,   23 June 1932

Unfortunately I am so very busy at the moment that I can see you only today week, Thursday, June 30th, at 11 in the morning.

☐ Switzerland.

16

The rumour that I do not recommend analytical treatment for elderly people is quite erroneous. My eldest patient—a lady—has reached the stately age of 75. The psyche can be treated so long as a person has a psyche. The only people you can't treat are those who are born without one. And of these there are not a few.

Hoping the appointed time will suit you also, I remain, dear lady,

Yours sincerely, c . g . j u n g

Anonymous

[ORIGINAL IN ENGLISH]

Dear Mr. N.,   5 July 1932

You will realize the extraordinary difficulty of telling anything about dreams of people one doesn't know. Your dream[1] has interested me indeed. The second part of it, the secretary-bird and the snake, has been correctly interpreted, in spite of the fact that the snake is not exactly Kundalini[2] because the Kundalini serpent actually dissolves into light. But sure enough the two animals represent a pair of opposites, which represent spirit and matter, or the spiritual and chthonic principle. Yet the fact that they are represented by two animals means, according to the rules of dream interpretation, that this peculiar conflict does not take place in a human consciousness, but outside it in the collective unconscious. Since olden times the bird and the snake are the symbols which typify this conflict. It is a peculiarity of our Western mind that we can think such a conflict consciously without having it. This is rather a peculiar fact which, I find, is most difficult to explain to the said Westerner. It's rather a curse to be able to think a thing and to imagine one possesses it while one is miles away from it in reality.

So this dream has a peculiar introduction which you omitted completely in attempting an interpretation. You behave exactly as if you were possessing the two opposites, like any good Westerner. What happened in reality was the following thing: you did try some Yoga stunt,[3] and then the dream said, "Look out, that lovely young lady

___

□ Eastern U.S.A.

[1] A secretary-bird (*Serpentarius secretarius*) swallows a snake.

[2] Concerning the Kundalini serpent cf. Avalon, *The Serpent Power*; also Jung, "The Realities of Practical Psychotherapy," CW 16 (1966 edn.), pars. 558ff., and "The Psychology of the Transference," ibid., par. 380.

[3] The (unanalysed) dreamer wrote of some Yoga exercises "for the unfoldment of the Golden Flower" which he had tried a few hours before the dream.

17

is threatened by the presence of the gila monster,[4] pregnant with sensuality!" You see, in spite of being a man in advanced age,[5] you still have a young soul, a lovely anima, and she is confronted with the dangerous lizard. In other words, your soul is threatened by chthonic poison. Now this is exactly the situation of our Western mind. We think we can deal with such problems in an almost rationalistic way, by conscious attempts and efforts, imitating Yoga methods and such dangerous stuff, but we forget entirely that first of all we should establish a connection between the higher and the lower regions of our psyche. Such a connection exists in Eastern man, while we are cut off from our earth through more than a thousand years of Christian training. Thus the Western man has to develop that connection with his unconscious first, and then only he will understand really what the Eastern methods aim at. If he can't establish the connection, then the conflict between bird and snake remains a sort of vicious circle that turns round and round in his mind and never even touches our reality, it remains a mere fantastical pastime which as a rule creates an unwholesome inflation.

Now watch what the bird is doing: he plunges his head backward, out of your sight, which is a very unusual thing for the secretary-bird to do. Now that is a hint of what one really ought to do: if you look down in front of you, you are in the sphere of your consciousness, but if you look backward, you look into the region of your unconscious which is always there where we haven't got the eyes of our consciousness. So the bird tells you, you ought to look behind your back and then you would discover the means by which you can attain your end. Your aim is to kill the lizard that threatens the anima. You are the secretary-bird that should protect the anima. You can't protect your anima by Yoga exercises which only procure a conscious thrill, but you can protect her by catching the unconscious contents that well up from the depths of yourself. Try to see what your fantasies are, no matter how disreputable they seem to be; that is your blackness, your shadow that ought to be swallowed. The serpent is the bird, and the bird is the serpent.

You know, Eastern Yoga is based upon man as he really is, but we have a conscious imagination about ourselves and think this is our

---

[4] *Heloderma suspectum.* "With its relative *H. horridum* of Mexico, the only lizards known to be poisonous . . . inhabits deserts in the southwestern United States" (*Enc. Brit.*). In the dream it endangered "a lovely young lady."
[5] The dreamer reported he was 64, "virile and in good health."

18

Self, which is an appalling mistake. We are also our unconscious side, and that is why the bird swallows the black snake, namely to show what you ought to do in order to be complete. Not perfection, but completeness is what is expected of you.

Yours sincerely, C. G. JUNG

To James Joyce

[ORIGINAL IN ENGLISH]

Dear Sir,   27 September 1932

Your *Ulysses* has presented the world with such an upsetting psychological problem that repeatedly I have been called in as a supposed authority on psychological matters.

Ulysses proved to be an exceedingly hard nut and it has forced my mind not only to most unusual efforts, but also to rather extravagant peregrinations (speaking from the standpoint of a scientist!). Your book as a whole has given me no end of trouble and I was brooding over it for about three years until I succeeded in putting myself into it. But I must tell you that I'm profoundly grateful to yourself as well as to your gigantic opus because I learned a great deal from it. I shall probably never be quite sure whether I did enjoy it, because it meant too much grinding of nerves and of grey matter. I also don't know whether you will enjoy what I have written about *Ulysses*[1] because I couldn't help telling the world how much I was bored, how I grumbled, how I cursed and how I admired. The 40 pages of non-stop run in the end is a string of veritable psychological peaches. I suppose the devil's grandmother knows so much about the real psychology of a woman, I didn't.[2]

Well, I just try to recommend my little essay to you, as an amusing

□ Joyce (1882–1941) was then living in Zurich. — This letter is published in Richard Ellmann, *James Joyce* (rev. edn., 1982), p. 629, and also in his *Letters of James Joyce*, III (1966), p. 253. — For Joyce's encounter with Jung cf. Patricia Hutchins, *James Joyce's World* (1957), pp. 181ff., reprinted in *C. G. Jung Speaking*, ed. W. McGuire and R.F.C. Hull (1977), pp. 239ff.; also cf. Jung's letter to Patricia Graecen (Hutchins), 29 June 55, in his *Letters*, vol. 2.

[1] Jung's essay on *Ulysses* was originally published in *Europäische Revue*, VIII:2/9 (Sept. 1932); now in CW 15, where this letter is also published.

[2] Concerning Joyce's reaction to Jung's letter, Ellmann wrote (*James Joyce*, rev. edn., 1982, p. 629): "Joyce proudly displayed this tribute to his psychological penetration, but Nora [Joyce] said of her husband, 'He knows nothing at all about women.' " (From Ellmann's interview with Samuel Beckett, 1953.)

attempt of a perfect stranger who went astray in the labyrinth of your *Ulysses* and happened to get out of it again by sheer good luck. At all events you may gather from my article what *Ulysses* has done to a supposedly balanced psychologist.

With the expression of my deepest appreciation, I remain, dear Sir,

Yours faithfully, c. g. j u n g

To Antonio Mirabal

[ORIGINAL IN ENGLISH]

My dear friend Mountain Lake, 21 October 1932

It was very nice of you indeed that you wrote a letter to me. I thought you had quite forgotten me. It is very good that this woman Schevill[1] from California has come to see you and to remember you of myself. It is good that she could give you my address. I often thought of you in the meantime and I even talked of you often to my pupils. And whenever I had the opportunity to talk to Americans, I tried to give them the right idea about your people and how important it would be for them to give you all the rights of the American Citizen. I believe that things are getting better in the future.

I'm glad to hear that your crops were good. I wish you would write to me once, what your religious customs are in order to secure a good harvest. Have you got corn-dances, or other ways by which you make the wheat and the corn grow? Are your young men still worshipping the Father Sun? Are you also making occasionally sand-paintings[2] like the Navajos? Any information you can give me about your religious life is always welcome to me. I shall keep all that information to myself, but it is most helpful to me, as I am busy exploring the truth in which Indians believe. It always impressed me as a great

---

□ Antonio Mirabal = Ochwiay Biano (Mountain Lake), chief of the Taos Pueblo, whose acquaintance Jung made during his travels in Arizona and New Mexico, 1924–25. Cf. *Memories*, pp. 247ff./232ff.

[1] Cf. Schevill, 1 Sept. 42.

[2] Sand-paintings are traditional symbolic designs made on the ground with coloured sands and used for various ceremonial purposes, mainly by North American Indian tribes of the Southwest. Several examples are reproduced in Schevill, *Beautiful on the Earth* (1945). Cf. J. King, M. Oakes, J. Campbell, *Where the Two Came to Their Father* (with a portfolio of Navaho pollen-paintings; 2nd edn., 1969) and G. A. Reichard, *Navaho Religion* (1950). Cf. also "Concerning Mandala Symbolism," figs. 45 and 46, and *Psychology and Alchemy*, fig. 110.

truth, but one hears so little about it, and particularly over here, where there are no Indians. Times are very hard indeed and unfortunately I can't travel as far as I used to do. All you tell me about religion is good news to me. There are no interesting religious things over here, only remnants of old things. I will send you something which is still alive in this country of the old beliefs.

I was glad to hear that you are in better health than when I saw you. I'm sure your tribe needs you very much, and I wish that you will live still many happy years.

If you ever see Mrs. Schevill again, please give her my best greetings.

As ever your friend, c . g . j u n g

Anonymous

Dear Dr. N.,   28 January 1933

I understand your difficulties, but I have to tell you that it fares with every civilized man as it formerly did with Doctor Faustus, who also was unable to follow the Mephistophelean advice that he live the simple life of a peasant. This for the simple reason that civilized life is no longer the simple life. The civilized man must be able to change his whole attitude accordingly. You know that Faust finally had to approach the unsavoury witches' cauldron. Today this is called analysis.

You rightly surmise that I am an expensive customer. I have to be, otherwise I would be eaten up skin, bones, and all. Therefore I wanted to give you good advice and save you a lot of money. From earlier days you naturally still have the amiable habit of expecting effects from others. You have yet to learn how one can produce effects on oneself, and you can learn that from simpler people than me. Nor, in the last resort, could I conjure them up for you as if by magic, but you would have to do the ultimate and best yourself. You must only learn how to make the effort, and that was what I meant when I once advised you to talk over your problems with my wife. I thought you would continue these discussions.

I am sorry it is not possible for me to see you for the next four weeks as I am soon going to Germany on a lecture tour. Therefore I would advise you to try once again and this time more thoroughly.

☐ Switzerland.

You know very well that what you put into something with a serious effort will always come out again.

Yours sincerely, c. g. j u n g

To Pastor W. Arz

Dear Pastor Arz,   17 February 1933
. . .
It is of little use having any convictions about the question you ask. I therefore determine the probability of certain views whenever possible by the empirical method. It is naturally quite out of the question that we shall ever be able to furnish a proof of the immortality of the soul. On the other hand, it does seem to me possible to establish certain peculiar facts regarding the nature of the soul[1] which at least do not rule out the immortality affirmed by religious belief. What is commonly understood by "psyche" is certainly an ephemeral phenomenon if it is taken to mean the ordinary facts of consciousness. But in the deeper layers of the psyche which we call the unconscious there are things that cast doubt on the indispensable categories of our conscious world, namely time and space. The existence of telepathy in time and space is still denied only by positive ignoramuses. It is clear that timeless and spaceless perceptions are possible only because the perceiving psyche is similarly constituted. Timelessness and spacelessness must therefore be somehow inherent in its nature, and this in itself permits us to doubt the exclusive temporality of the soul, or if you prefer, makes time and space appear doubtful. Every ephemeral phenomenon requires limitation in time and space, but if time and space are doubtful, then the peculiar limitation of such phenomena becomes doubtful too. It is sufficiently clear that timelessness and spacelessness can never be grasped through the medium of our intelligence, so we must rest content with this borderline concept. Nevertheless we know that a door exists to a quite different order of things from the one we encounter in our empirical world of consciousness. This is about all that science can contribute to this question. Beyond that there is still the subjective psychological experience which can be in the highest degree con-

☐ Kleinwittenberg, Germany.
[1] Cf. "The Soul and Death," CW 8, pars. 813ff., and *Memories*, ch. XI: "On Life after Death."

vincing for the individual even though it cannot be shared by the wider public.

Yours sincerely, c. g. j u n g

To Jolande Jacobi

Dear Frau Jacobi,   21 April 1933

Many thanks for your detailed letter. From what you say of him, Dr. N. seems to be the right man. If he can win over Frau S., in whose sound judgment I have the fullest confidence, he must be quite something. An ordinary idiot of a neurologist couldn't do that. X. is an extraordinarily difficult case, unfortunately far advanced in neurotic degeneration. The danger is that the treatment will get lost in trivialities. With X. one must always keep the whole in mind. He should be cured from "above," for ultimately it is a question of the great conflict for a *Weltanschauung*, which in his case has collided with an antiquated infantile attitude embodied by his wife. Hence on the one hand this great question must be considered, and on the other his infantilism and the junk shop of trivialities. No small task! I would be glad to know of an intelligent neurologist in Vienna. I have often been asked.

My wife has told me of all the garbage that has piled up round the magazine project. Oh this anima! I hope I won't need to do any more explanatory work. For instance the essence of the "famous" meeting in Munich was my *private* talk with Heyer, where only the two of us were together. I had to see what sort of programme he would commit himself to. Even then I had my private doubts, but had still to wait for the official document, the prospectus, where it was bound to come out how those gentlemen were planning the project. I then saw that *everything* would devolve upon me and that I would be boundlessly overburdened. An absolutely unworkable proposition! The stuff men talk on such occasions, sniffing around each other like dogs, is what the English call "eyewash." Everything null and void, valueless, until there's a signed contract. *That alone counts.* Everything else a capricious, deceptive anima intrigue that simply drives women crazy, because they always want to know why and how. The main thing is to know how things are *not* done.

☐ (Handwritten.)

23

Please give X. my best greetings and tell him—because his love is all too easily injured—he should meditate on Paul's words in the Epistle to the Corinthians: "Love endureth all things." With cordial greetings,

Yours ever, J U N G

To Paul Maag

Dear Colleague,   12 June 1933

Best thanks for your kind letter. You assume, unjustly, that your specifically orthodox position arouses in me a feeling of mockery. Nothing could be further from my mind. I can only emphasize yet again that I must fulfil my scientific duty as a psychologist and therefore may not go beyond the bounds proper to science without making myself guilty of intellectual presumption. I cannot under any circumstances square it with my scientific conscience to presume to make any arrogant assertions about God that spring from a belief or a subjective opinion. Even what I may personally believe about the ultimate things is, regarded as an object of science, open to scientific criticism. But that in no way prevents me from having views of my own. These views cannot possibly be known to you since I have never expressed them. When therefore you state in your estimable letter that you know exactly what kind of God I believe in, I can only marvel at your powers of imagination. In my humble opinion you would perhaps have done better to ask me first what I actually think about God outside the bounds of my science. It might then have turned out that I am a Mohammedan, or a Buddhist, or possibly even an orthodox Christian like you. Whatever my subjective opinions may be, I would consider it absolutely immoral to use them to anticipate what is scientifically knowable. My subjective attitude is that I hold every religious position in high esteem but draw an inexorable dividing line between the content of belief and the requirements of science. I consider it unclean to confuse these incommensurables. Even more, I consider it presumptuous to credit human knowledge with a faculty that demonstrably exceeds its limitations. We must admit in all modesty the limitations of all human knowledge and take it as a gift of grace if ever an experience of the Unfathomable should come our way. What men have always named God is the Unfathomable itself. Were that not so, it would be as possible for an ant to

24

know man and his nature as it is for us to know the nature of the ant.

As you see, I am wholly incorrigible and utterly incapable of coming up with a mixture of theology and science. This was, as you well know, the prerogative of the early Middle Ages and is still the prerogative of the Catholic Church today, which has set the *Summa* of Thomas Aquinas above the whole of science. It has been one of the greatest achievements of Protestantism to have separated the things of God from the things of the world. With our human knowledge we always move in the human sphere, but in the things of God we should keep quiet and not make any arrogant assertions about what is greater than ourselves. Belief as a religious phenomenon cannot be discussed. It seems to me, however, that when belief enters into practical life we are entitled to the opinion that it should be coupled with the Christian virtue of modesty, which does not brag about absoluteness but brings itself to admit the unfathomable ways of God which have nothing to do with the Christian revelation. Even though the apostles and Paul and John of the Apocalypse himself emphasize its uniqueness and exclusiveness, we nevertheless know that they were all mortal men who for that reason were also subject to the limitations of human knowledge.

Hoping I have made my standpoint sufficiently plain,

With collegial regards, C. G. JUNG

To Linda Gray Oppenheim

[ORIGINAL IN ENGLISH]

Dear Mrs. Oppenheim,   12 August 1933

A year ago I heard through a friend of Mr. Oppenheim's most unexpected death. Yes, it is true, such a death and such suffering seem to be pointless if one assumes that this life is the acme of all existence. I have seen quite a number of people who died when they had reached the most they could. Obviously then the measure of their life was fulfilled, everything said and everything done and nothing remained. The answer to human life is not to be found within the limits of human life.

Sincerely yours, C. G. JUNG

☐ Widow of James Oppenheim (1882–1932), American poet and writer on psychology. His *American Types* (1929) was based on Jung's typology.

To Poul Bjerre

Dear Colleague, 22 January 1934

I would like to express my best thanks for your willingness to take part in the reorganization of the General Medical Society for Psychotherapy. I am very glad of your help.

The main concern at present is the organization of the International Society. As you know, the German Society has been compelled by the political change in Germany to form a national group under a leader. This group has to comply with the strictest political guidelines, as you can well imagine. Its existence would have been impossible without absolute submission to the National Socialist State. I have therefore advised the Germans to submit without hesitation, for what matters above all is that psychotherapy in Germany, now gravely threatened, should survive the adversities of the time. Therefore I have also got into touch with the leading circles in order to do everything possible to ensure the continued existence and recognition of psychotherapy. All the German organizations are now under the uniform direction of Prof. Göring in Elberfeld. He is the responsible leader.

Through this founding of a national group influenced by the special political conditions, the international section of the Society has been compelled to form national groups in turn, constituting an organization within the framework of which the German group is absorbed. By means of this organization I am trying to prevent the special political currents in the German group, which is numerically the strongest, from spilling over into the Society as a whole. This is what many foreigners fear, particularly the Jews, who as you know are very numerous. If we succeed in organizing some national groups in neutral countries, this will act as a counterweight and at the same time afford the Germans a much needed opportunity to maintain a connection with the outside world in their present spiritual isolation. This connection is essential for the continued development of psychotherapy in Germany, since at present she is even more cut off than during the war.

I should be very grateful to you if you would take the initiative in Sweden for the founding of a national group which would be a member of the International Society. It would be sufficient for individual members to declare their enrolment in this Society. Naturally you are

☐ M.D., (1876–1964), Swedish psychotherapist. His attempt to form a Swedish group failed at the time. He succeeded, however, in 1936 (cf. Bjerre, 8 May 36).

26

free to organize your group in such a way that it also holds local meetings in Sweden itself, though this is not necessary. Dr. W. Cimbal is secretary-general of the whole Society and I would ask you to get in touch with him as regards both the membership fees and the subscription to the *Zentralblatt*. Perhaps there would also be an opportunity to discuss preferential terms for subscribers.

Further, I want to tell you that I would be very pleased if you could assure us of your cooperation with the *Zentralblatt*. For the present it would be a matter of your now and then bringing to our notice, either personally or through one of your co-workers, new publications of a psychotherapeutic nature by means of reviews. We should also be grateful for original contributions. Submissions to the *Zentralblatt* should be sent to the secretary-general, Dr. Cimbal. With collegial regards,

Yours sincerely, c. g. j u n g

P.S. I have just received word from Copenhagen that a Danish national group, under the presidency of Dr. Paul Reiter, St. Hans Hosp. near Roskilde, has been formed under the name "Selskab for Psykoterapi" [Society for Psychotherapy].

To Erich Neumann

Dear Colleague,   29 January 1934

It is possible that a Dr. X. will turn to you. He pants for therapy, needs it too, because he consists essentially of only an intellectual halo wandering forlorn and footless through the world. He could be not uninteresting, but there's no money in it. With best greetings,

Yours sincerely, c. g. j u n g

☐ M.D., Ph.D., (1905–1960), originally German, later Israeli. His works include *Origins and History of Consciousness* (orig. 1949), *Amor and Psyche* (orig. 1952), *The Archetypal World of Henry Moore* (1959), *The Great Mother* (1955), *Art and the Creative Unconscious* (orig. 1954), *Depth Psychology and a New Ethic* (1969), *The Child* (orig. 1963), and contributions in the *Eranos Jahrbücher XVI/XXIX*. (See pl. in vol. 2.)

To Bernhard Baur-Celio

30 January 1934

.   .   .

I cannot leave your "question of conscience" unanswered. Obvi-

☐ According to a communication from Prof. Baur-Celio, this letter reached him

ously I speak only of what I know and what can be verified. I don't want to addle anybody's brains with my subjective conjectures. Beyond that I have had experiences which are, so to speak, "ineffable," "secret" because they can never be told properly and because nobody can understand them (I don't know whether I have even approximately understood them myself), "dangerous" because 99% of humanity would declare I was mad if they heard such things from me, "catastrophic" because the prejudices aroused by their telling might block other people's way to a living and wondrous mystery, "taboo" because they are an ἄδυτον[1] protected by δεισιδαιμονία[2] as faithfully described by Goethe:

> Shelter gives deep cave.
> Lions around us stray,
> Silent and tame they rove,
> And sacred honours pay
> To the holy shrine of love.[3]

And already too much has been said—my public might be fatally infected by the suspicion of "poetic licence"—that most painful aberration!

Can anyone say "credo" when he stands *amidst* his experience, πιστεύων ὁράματι δεινῷ,[4] when he knows how superfluous "belief" is, when he more than just "knows," when the experience has even pressed him to the wall?

I don't want to seduce anyone into believing and thus take his experience from him. I need my mental and physical health in fullest measure to hold out against what people call "peace," so I don't like boosting my experiences. But one thing I will tell you: the exploration of the unconscious has in fact and in truth discovered the age-old, timeless *way of initiation*. Freud's theory is an apotropaic attempt to block off and protect oneself from the perils of the "long road"; only a "knight" dares "la queste" and the "aventiure." Nothing is submerged for ever—that is the terrifying discovery everyone makes

---

in the form reproduced here, without beginning or end. It is in answer to the question whether Jung possessed any "secret knowledge" surpassing his written formulations.

[1] Holy (numinous) precinct, sanctuary.
[2] Fear of the gods (or demons).
[3] *Faust II*, Act 5, last scene (tr. P. Wayne, p. 279).
[4] "In faith trusting the terrifying apparition."

28

who has opened that portal. But the primeval fear is so great that the world is grateful to Freud for having proved "scientifically" (what a bastard of a science!) that one has seen nothing behind it. Now it is not merely my "credo" but the greatest and most incisive experience of my life that this door, a highly inconspicuous side-door on an unsuspicious-looking and easily overlooked footpath—narrow and indistinct because only a few have set foot on it—leads to the secret of transformation and renewal.

> Intrate per angustam portam.
> Quia lata porta et spatiosa via est,
> quae ducit ad perditionem,
> Et multi sunt qui intrant per eam.
> Quam angusta porta et arcta via est,
> quae ducit *ad vitam,*
> *Et pauci sunt qui inveniunt eam!*
> Attendite a falsis prophetis qui veniunt
> ad vos in vestimentis ovium—
> *intrinsecus autem sunt lupi rapaces.*[5]

Now you will understand why I prefer to say "scio" and not "credo" —because I don't want to act mysterious. But it would infallibly look as though I were acting mysterious if I spoke of a real, living mystery. One *is* mysterious when one speaks of a *real* mystery. Therefore better not speak of it in order to avoid that evil and confusing look. Like all real life it is a voyage between Scylla and Charybdis.

. . .

[5] Matthew 7:13–15 (Vulgate).

Anonymous

Dear Herr N.,   20 February 1934

Nobody can set right a mismanaged life with a few words. But there is no pit you cannot climb out of provided you make the right effort at the right place.

When one is in a mess like you are, one has no right any more to worry about the idiocy of one's own psychology, but must do the next thing with diligence and devotion and earn the goodwill of others. In

☐ Germany.

29

every littlest thing you do in this way you will find yourself. It was no different with X. He too had to do it the hard way, and always with the next, the littlest, and the hardest things.

Yours truly, c. g. j u n g

To J. H. van der Hoop

Dear Colleague, 12 March 1934

It goes without saying that the International ("überstaatliche") Society is totally independent of the German group, which as you know cannot exist without being conformed. This necessity which has been imposed on the German group applies only inside Germany. The International Society would consist essentially of separate national groups. Since it is not possible, for political and other reasons, to form national groups everywhere, the necessity will arise of having to accept individual members who do not belong to any national group. There are no regulations about this at present, as I have purposely not yet worked out the statutes for the International Society. I want to carry through this work at the next Congress.[1]

As you will have seen from the *Zentralblatt*, the German Society considers itself an independent Society which, however, is affiliated as a unit to the International Society. This state of affairs, which is occasioned by the peculiar political conditions, does not apply to the organization of the International Society. The latter can accept any kind of member. Race, religion, and suchlike things are not taken into account, nor of course political sentiments. As a medical Society we are rather like the Geneva Convention,[2] which internationalizes doctors as politically neutral. I do not, however, disguise the fact that in individual cases all sorts of difficulties might arise for the Germans,

---

[1] The statutes of the International Medical Society for Psychotherapy, drawn up by Jung, were ratified in May 1934 at the 7th Congress for Psychotherapy in Bad Nauheim. The constitution was approved by delegates from Switzerland, Holland, Sweden, Denmark, and Germany. It contained a clause enabling German Jewish doctors to become members of the International Society. Cf. "Circular Letter," CW 10, Appendix, pars. 1035ff., and ibid., par. 1060.

[2] The Geneva Convention of 1906 (preceded by one in 1864) gave international protection to the Red Cross and secured humane treatment for wounded or ill prisoners of war.

30

for instance at Congresses if they take place in Germany. It may prove necessary under the circumstances to hold the Congresses abroad.

Certain necessities will also arise in connection with the general statutes. That is to say, in order to prevent the large number of German members from having the decisive voice in the conduct of the International Society, it is necessary that national groups be organized, or rather separate Societies which nominate some kind of representatives or delegates. In this way it will be possible to paralyze in a constitutive assembly what might be an overwhelming German influence. The Germans have a great interest in getting affiliated abroad and for this reason I do not fear that they will make special difficulties. (Errors excepted!) At any rate the experiment is worth trying.

Whether German psychotherapists can join the International Society without belonging to their own national group is a very delicate question. From our side we would naturally make no difficulties. But it is not impossible that the German political authorities would take steps against it. In that case the matter would not be in our hands. At any rate I shall suggest that individual psychotherapists be allowed membership alongside the national groups regardless of where they come from. But in the interests of the counterweight against Germany one would have to insist that these individual members are entitled to a vote for the election of the Committee only when they join a national group. For the reasons indicated above, as you can well understand, I would like the Committee to be elected by the delegates of the national groups.

The question of membership fees is a technicality to be cleared up at the ratification of the statutes at the next Congress.

With regard to the next Congress one of the major difficulties is that no general statutes yet exist and we are therefore not in a position to appear with delegates from national groups. So I would like to ask you to select a few colleagues privately, who are to take part in the constitutive assembly in Nauheim. We shall then discuss the statutes with these delegates and ratify them. We must do this with a limited number of people because experience has shown that it is quite impossible to discuss statutes properly when a Congress is in plenum. This can only be done in committee. For the rest, I think you can be assured that the Nazi outpourings of the German members are due to political necessity rather than to the religious convictions of the gentlemen in question.

31

I am very grateful to you for your positive cooperation. Without this it would be altogether impossible to cope with this insanely complicated situation in a fruitful way. If there is anything unclear in my letter I am ready to give you further information. With best regards,

Yours sincerely, C. G. JUNG

P.S. I have just heard that the Congress is fixed for May 10th in Nauheim.

Anonymous

Dear Frau N.,   13 July 1934

If X. feels particularly well when he studies religion and philosophical literature it is a sure sign that this activity is vital to him. So there is nothing for it, aside from physical treatment, but to support this tendency in his nature. It is, however, striking that a young man of 30 should have such a vital relation to ideas of this kind, a relation which even affects the body. Whatever the reason for this may be, it seems to be a matter of the greatest importance. But one question remains to be answered: is it absolutely certain that X. is not somewhere circumventing a vitally important collective demand, and that as a result an unnatural intensification of his spiritual activity has set in? If so, the impairment of his working capacity would signify a resistance from the side of instinct. Unfortunately I know far too little of X.'s personal life to presume to an opinion, but with young people one must always be careful in this respect, because the demands of instinct are only too easily covered up by deceptive spiritual interests. But if that is not the case, there is probably no alternative for him than to come to terms with the unconscious, for better or worse. I would conjecture that this is so because middle life has set in too early in consequence of a relatively short life expectancy.[1]

.   .   .

With best regards,

Yours sincerely, C. G. JUNG

☐ Berlin.
[1] In fact X. died at 55.

32

To Pastor Ernst Jahn

Dear Pastor Jahn,   7 September 1935

I am sorry that pressure of work has prevented me from answering your kind letter. Please forgive me. It is very kind of you to have gone into my work so thoroughly. With your permission, I would like to draw your attention to a few points that have struck me.

It seems to me that you approach my views too much from the angle of the theologian. You seem to forget that I am first and foremost an empiricist, who was led to the question of Western and Eastern mysticism only for empirical reasons. For instance, I do not by any means take my stand on Tao or any Yoga techniques, but I have found that Taoist philosophy as well as Yoga have very many parallels with the psychic processes we can observe in Western man. Nor do I get anybody to draw or contemplate mandala pictures as in Yoga, but it has turned out that unprejudiced people take quite naturally to these aids in order to find their bearings in the chaos of unconscious processes that come to light.

A point which theologians very often overlook is the question of the reality of God. When I speak of God, I always speak as a psychologist, as I have expressly emphasized in many places in my books. For the psychologist the God-image is a psychological fact. He cannot say anything about the metaphysical reality of God because that would far exceed the limits of the theory of knowledge. As an empiricist I know only the images originating in the unconscious which man makes of God, or which, to be more accurate, are made of God in the unconscious; and these images are undoubtedly very relative.

Another point is the relation between the psychological I and Thou. The unconscious for me is a definite *vis-à-vis* with which one has to come to terms. I have written a little book[1] about this. I have never asserted, nor do I think I know, what the unconscious is in itself. It is the unconscious region of the psyche. When I speak of psyche, I do not pretend to know what it is either, and how far this concept extends. For this concept is simply beyond all possibility of cognition. It is a mere convention for giving some kind of name to the unknown which appears to us psychic. This psychic factor, as experience shows,

☐ Berlin.
[1] "The Relations between the Ego and the Unconscious," CW 7.

is something very different from our consciousness. If you have ever observed a psychosis in a person you know intimately, you will know what a dreadful confrontation that can be. It seems to me that it is difficult for a theologian to put himself in an empiricist's shoes. What the theologian takes to be spiritual realities are for the empiricist expressions of psychic life, which at bottom is essentially unknown. The empiricist does not think from above downwards from metaphysical premises, but comes from below upwards from the phenomenal world and, conscious of the limitations of his mind, must be content with understanding the psychic processes reconstructively. And so it is with my therapy. I have chiefly to do with people in whom I cannot implant any values or convictions from above downwards. Usually they are people whom I can only urge to go through their experiences and to organize them in a way that makes a tolerable existence possible. The pastor of souls is naturally not in this position as a rule; he has to do with people who expressly demand to be spiritually arranged from above downwards. This task should be left to the pastor of souls. But those rarer people who cannot accept traditional values and convictions, who in other words do not possess the charisma of faith, must perforce seek advice from the empiricist, who for his part, in order to do justice to his task, can appeal to nothing except the given realities. Thus he will on no account say to his patient, "Your psyche is God," or "Your unconscious is God," because that would be just what the patient has fled from in disgust. Rather he will start off the psychic process of experiencing unconscious contents, whereby the patient is put in a position to experience his psychic realities and draw his own conclusions. What I described in the *Golden Flower* are simply the results of individual developments which closely resemble those arrived at through Eastern practices. Centuries ago Yoga congealed into a fixed system, but originally the mandala symbolism grew out of the unconscious just as individually and directly as it does with Western man today. I had known about the spontaneous emergence of these symbols for 17 years but deliberately published nothing on this subject so as to prevent the regrettable but undeniable imitative instinct from getting hold of these pictures. In these 17 years I had ample opportunity to see again and again how patients quite spontaneously reached for the pencil in order to sketch pictures that were meant to express typical inner experiences. Yoga, however, as we know it today, has become a method of spiritual training which is drilled into the initiands from above. It holds up the traditional pictures for contemplation and has precise rules as to how they should be executed. In this respect Yoga is directly comparable to the *Exercitia* of Loyola. But that is the exact opposite of what I do. I am therefore an avowed opponent of taking over Yoga methods or Eastern ideas uncritically, as I have stated publicly many times before.

So what I have said on these matters is the result of empirical work and does not constitute the technical principles of my therapy. Perhaps I may draw your attention to a book that has just been published (*Die kulturelle Bedeutung der komplexen Psychologie*, Jul. Springer, Berlin 1935), in which the first contribution[2] deals with my method. There you will find a philosophical basis for my whole work, which will doubtless elucidate for you any points that may still be obscure.

Yours sincerely, C. G. JUNG

[2] Toni Wolff, "Einführung in die Grundlagen der komplexen Psychologie," now in Wolff, *Studien zu C. G. Jungs Psychologie* (1959). Jung's introduction to this book is in *Civilization in Transition*, pars. 887ff.

To Abraham Aaron Roback

[ORIGINAL IN ENGLISH]

Dear Sir,   [Bailey Island, Maine?], 29 September 1936

I am sorry I cannot accept President Moore's kind invitation as I am leaving this country already Oct. 3rd.

Since we are bilingual in Switzerland my name is "Carl" as well as "Charles" (French), so there was not much of a mistake.

Concerning my so-called "Nazi affiliation" there has been quite an unnecessary noise about it. I am no Nazi, as a matter of fact I am quite unpolitical. German psychotherapists asked me to help them to maintain their professional organization, as there was an immediate danger that psychotherapy in Germany would be wiped out of existence. It was considered as "Jewish science" and therefore highly suspect. Those German doctors were my friends and only a coward would leave his friends when they are in dire need of help. Not only did I set up their organization again but I made it clear that psychotherapy is an honest-to-God attempt and moreover I made it possible for Jewish German doctors, being excluded from professional organizations, to become immediate members of the International Society at least. But nobody mentions the fact that so many perfectly innocent existences could have been completely crushed if I had not stepped in.

It is true that I have insisted upon the *difference* between Jewish and Christian psychology[1] since 1917, but Jewish authors have done the same long ago as well as recently.[2] I am no anti-Semite.

From all this I gained neither honours nor money, but I am glad that I could be of service to those in need.

Faithfully yours, C. G. JUNG

□ Ph.D., American psychologist (1890–1965). — This letter was written in the U.S.A., after Jung had lectured at the Harvard Tercentenary Conference of Arts and Sciences. Cf. Murray, 10 Sept. 35, n. 1.
[1] Cf. "The Role of the Unconscious" (orig. 1918), *Civilization in Transition*, CW 10, pars. 17ff., and "A Rejoinder to Dr. Bally," ibid., pars. 1025ff. & n. 5.
[2] Cf. Freud's letter to Ferenczi, 8 June 13, quoted in Jones, II, p. 168: "Certainly there are great differences between the Jewish and the Aryan spirit [*Geist*]. We can observe that every day. Hence there would assuredly be here and there differences in outlook on life and art." Cf. also Erich Neumann, "In Honour of the Centenary of Freud's Birth," *Journal of Analytical Psychology* (London), I:2 (May 1956).

To Heinrich Zimmer

Dear Professor Zimmer,   14 December 1936

First of all I want to thank you most heartily for your very friendly review of *The Tibetan Book of the Dead*.[1]

Secondly, I enclose letters of recommendation to various Americans.[2] I give you these letters sealed, because they also contain personal matters.

1. Prof. W. E. Clark[3] of Harvard University, whom I know personally. I had some delightful talks with him on the occasion of my visit there. He is a very introverted man who must be approached with the politeness due to animals in the bush, that is to say one must act as if one had not seen him and must talk softly and slowly so as

[1] Review of Jung's "Psychological Commentary on *The Tibetan Book of the Dead*," CW 11. The review cannot be traced.
[2] Zimmer, whose wife was partially of Jewish ancestry, had decided to leave Germany. Cf. Zimmer, 21 Nov. 32.
[3] Walter Eugene Clark (1881–1960), professor of Sanskrit.

not to scare him off. It is also advisable to whistle before going into the forest so that the rhinos won't be startled out of their slumbers but are gently and melodiously prepared for your coming and have time to make themselves scarce. He has a very nice wife who is the exact opposite.

2. I also recommend you to Prof. W. E. Hocking[4] of Harvard University. This one is "correct." He wears a stiff collar day and night. But once you have deeply acknowledged his correctness and conventionality and given him a chance to explain that he is not what he looks like, the way is paved for a useful conversation. His rebellion against American Christianity, or rather against the *Genius Agri Harvardensis*, has brought about a strong link with Taoist philosophy. A few sublimities dropped *sotto voce* from Chuang-tsu and Chu-hsi[5] should strike the right note. His wife overflows with feeling and it is very advantageous to display a certain helplessness.

3. The third recommendation is to Prof. Harry Caplan[6] at Cornell University.

4. The fourth is to Prof. Blake,[7] director of the Widener Library at Harvard. He is Gargantuan in every respect and helpful like all fat people. He is a linguist (Slavic languages).

5. Don't omit to visit my friend Leonard Bacon, the American poet, whose most important work appears to be his "Animula Vagula."[8] He lives in his private theatre where it is all tremendously noisy and diverting.

6. In New York I can recommend you to our Psychological Club, whose president is Dr. E. Henley. . . .

I should be greatly obliged if you could tell me whereabouts in Indian literature Surya[9] or the sun is described as one-footed. I think I have read it somewhere but cannot find the note. With best wishes,

Yours sincerely, C. G. JUNG

[4] Cf. Hocking, 5 May 39.

[5] Chinese philosopher (1130–1200).

[6] 1930–67 professor of classics.

[7] Robert Pierpont Blake, 1928–36 director of Harvard U. Library; linguist and Byzantinist.

[8] "Little wandering soul," the opening words of a poem by the Roman emperor Hadrian. Bacon (1887–1954), poet and formerly professor of English at Berkeley, wrote his *Animula Vagula* (1926) in Zurich while working with Jung. Pulitzer Prize for Poetry, 1941.

[9] In the *Atharva Veda*, XIII.1.32, the sun-god Rohita, synonymous with Surya, the sun, is called the "one-footed goat." Cf. *Mysterium Coniunctionis*, par. 734.

To V. Subrahamanya Iyer

[ORIGINAL IN ENGLISH]

Dear Sir,   16 September 1937

I quite agree with you that it is a noble pursuit for any philosophy to seek a way to happiness for all mankind. It is quite obvious that one cannot attain to this end without eradicating misery. Philosophy must find a way to accomplish the destruction of misery in order to attain to happiness. I should call it a pretty ambitious task, however, to eradicate misery and I'm not so optimistic as to believe that such a task could be accomplished. On the contrary, I believe that misery is an intrinsic part of human life, without which we would never do anything. We always try to escape misery. We do it in a million different ways and none of them entirely succeeds. Thus I come to the conclusion that a feasible thing would be to try to find at least a way how to enable people to endure the inevitable misery which is the lot of every human life. If anybody achieves at least endurance of misery, he has already accomplished an almost superhuman task. This might give him some happiness or satisfaction. If you call this happiness, I wouldn't have much to say against it.[1]

I sincerely hope that I shall see you again in India.[2] In the meantime I remain with every good wish,

Yours faithfully, C. G. JUNG

☐ Guru (teacher and spiritual guide) of the Maharajah of Mysore (cf. *Memories*, pp. 275/257). He came to Europe to represent India at the International Congress of Philosophy at the Sorbonne, Paris, in 1937. Jung invited him, together with Paul Brunton, English writer on Yoga and related subjects, to Küsnacht, where they discussed problems of Indian philosophy.

[1] Walther Uhsadel (cf. Uhsadel, 4 Aug. 36), in his book *Evangelische Seelsorge* (1966), p. 121, reports a conversation he had with Jung in 1938 at his house in Küsnacht. Jung, pointing to a copy of one of the glass windows in the monastery at Königsfelden, Aargau, Switzerland, representing the Crucifixion, said: " 'You see, this is the crux for us.' When I asked him why, he replied: 'I've just got back from India, and it has struck me with renewed force. Man has to cope with the problem of suffering. The Oriental wants to get rid of suffering by casting it off. Western man tries to suppress suffering with drugs. But suffering has to be overcome, and the only way to overcome it is to endure it. We learn that only from him.' And here he pointed to the Crucified."

[2] Jung had "searching talks" with Iyer on his visit to India the following year, when the British Government invited him to take part in the Indian Science Congress 25th anniversary (cf. *Memories*, pp. 274ff./256ff.).

Anonymous

Dear Dr. N.,   2 December 1937

I have the feeling that you are really going a bit too far. We should make a halt before something destructive. You know what my attitude is to the unconscious. There is no point in delivering oneself over to it to the last drop. If that were the right procedure, nature would never have invented consciousness, and then the animals would be the ideal embodiments of the unconscious. In my view it is absolutely essential always to have our consciousness well enough in hand to pay sufficient attention to our reality, to the Here and Now. Otherwise we are in danger of being overrun by an unconscious which knows nothing of this human world of ours. The unconscious can realize itself only with the help of consciousness and under its constant control. At the same time consciousness must keep one eye on the unconscious and the other focussed just as clearly on the potentialities of human existence and human relationships.

I certainly don't want to interfere, but before I go to India I would beg you to reflect on this warning. With kindest regards,

Yours, CARL

☐ Switzerland (a woman).

To Dr. S.

Dear Colleague,   10 May 1938

In the confrontation with the unconscious there are indeed a considerable number of arid patches to be worked through. They cannot be circumvented. At such time it is a good thing to have some occupation which has the character of an *opus divinum*. Something like a careful shaping of images, such as many patients paint or carve in wood or stone. These primitive methods have the great advantage that the unconscious continues to work on these patterns, is enthralled and transformed by them. Naturally I can't go into further details as you have to take your own material for a starting-point. With kind regards,

Yours sincerely, C. G. JUNG

39

To Erich Neumann

Dear Colleague, 19 December 1938

Please don't worry about having written me such a long letter. I would have liked to know long ago what you are doing. You should not imagine me enthroned above world events on snow-covered peaks. I am right in the thick of it and every day I follow the Palestine question in the newspapers and often think of my friends there who have to live in this chaos. Unfortunately I foresaw all too clearly what was coming when I was in Palestine in 1933.[1] I also foresaw bad things for Germany, actually very bad, but now that they have come to pass they seem unbelievable. Everyone here is profoundly shaken by what is happening in Germany.[2] I have very much to do with Jewish refugees and am continually occupied in bringing all my Jewish acquaintances to safety in England and America. In this way I am in ceaseless touch with contemporary events.

I am very interested in what you have told me about your plans for work. Your experiences exactly parallel those I have had in Europe for many years. But I think you should be very cautious in judging your specifically Jewish experiences. Though it is true that there are specifically Jewish traits about this development, it is at the same time a general one which is also to be found among Christians. It is a general and identical revolution of minds. The specifically Christian or Jewish traits are only of secondary importance. Thus the patient you want to know about is a pure Jew with a Catholic upbringing, but I could never with absolute certainty characterize his symbolism—in so far as I have presented it[3]—as Jewish although certain nuances occasionally seem so. When I compare his material with mine or with that of other academically trained patients one is struck only

[1] In spring 1933 Jung travelled to Egypt and Palestine with Prof. Hans Eduard Fierz-David (1882–1953). One interesting episode (reported by Fierz's son, Dr. H. K. Fierz) was that when the two men alighted at Alexandria a palmist at the port read their hands. To Jung he said: "Oh, you are one of the few great men I have ever seen. I can't say more."

[2] The pogroms organized by the Nazis on the night 9/10 Nov., the so-called "crystal night," and its consequences.

[3] Cf. the dreams commented on in "Psychology and Religion" (orig. 1937), pars. 56ff. and 108ff. The case is described in much greater detail in Part II of *Psychology and Alchemy*.

by the astonishing similarities, while the differences are insignificant. The difference between a typically Protestant and a Jewish psychology is particularly small where the contemporary problem is concerned. The whole problem is of such overwhelming importance for humanity that individual and racial differences play a minor role. All the same, I can very well imagine that for Jews living in Palestine the direct influence of the surroundings brings out the chthonic and ancient Jewish element in a much more pregnant form. It seems to me that what is specifically Jewish or specifically Christian could be most easily discovered in the way the unconscious material is assimilated by the subject. In my experience the resistance of the Jew seems to be more obstinate and as a result the attempt at defence is much more vehement. This is no more than a subjective impression.

The Zosimos essay[4] is the last thing of mine to be published. Still outstanding[5] are an article on India (written in English for an American magazine),[6] two lectures on the mother complex,[7] which will appear in the *Eranos-Jahrbuch* 1938, a long commentary on Zen Buddhism,[8] and finally an introduction to the individuation process for an American edition of my Eranos lectures.[9]

Dr. X. has apprised me of a detailed correspondence with you. It is clear that the devil has been up to his tricks again. As soon as one notices that, one should say no more but withdraw into oneself.

I was glad to hear that you are fully occupied, though it would be even more agreeable if you also had time to realize your great plan.[10] Hoping that you are keeping fit, and with friendly greetings,

Yours sincerely, C. G. JUNG

[4] "The Visions of Zosimos," CW 13.
[5] Jung used regularly to send Neumann copies of his books and offprints of his Eranos lectures.
[6] "The Dreamlike World of India" and "What India Can Teach Us," CW 10, first published in *Asia* (New York), XXXIX:1/2, 1939.
[7] Now combined as "Psychological Aspects of the Mother Archetype," CW 9, i.
[8] "Foreword to Suzuki's *Introduction to Zen Buddhism*," CW 11.
[9] "The Meaning of Individuation," intro. to *The Integration of the Personality* (tr. Stanley Dell, 1939), containing four Eranos lectures and one other essay by Jung. Revised as "Conscious, Unconscious, and Individuation," CW 9, i.
[10] Neumann planned to write a book on the psychological problem of the modern Jew. It remained an unpublished fragment.

Anonymous

Dear Herr N.,   22 March 1939

Your first dream[1] shows that you yourself are identical with an unconscious feminine figure which as you know I call the anima. So the process you are in is a real one, but it is being falsely played out on you instead of on the anima.

The second dream[2] follows from the first. Through the identity with the anima you are driven up to a steep cliff where you find yourself in a very precarious situation. You can't hold the child because it doesn't belong to you. The icy storm goes together with the heights on which no man can live: again an expression of an unnatural and dangerous situation. In Goethe, Euphorion[3] is the child of Helen, begotten by father Faust. That is a normal situation.

Obviously the processes in Faust are real. Such things cannot possibly be "wishful fantasies." They are on the contrary the material which, when it comes up in a man, can make him go mad. This is also true of the fourth stage of the transformation process,[4] the experience in the Beyond. It is an unconscious reality which in Faust's case was felt as being beyond his reach at the time, and for this reason it is separated from his real existence by death. It expresses the fact that he still had to "become a boy" and only then would he attain the highest wisdom. Euphorion stands for the future man who does not flee from the bond with the earth but is dashed to pieces on it, which means that he is not viable under the existing circumstances. Faust's death must therefore be taken as a fact. But like many a death it is really a mystery death which brings the imperfect to perfection.

The Paris-Helen-Euphorion episode is actually the highest stage that the transformation process has reached, but not in itself the highest, for the element Euphorion has not been integrated into the Faust-Mephisto-Paris-Helen quaternity as the *quinta essentia*.

☐ France.

[1] The dreamer gives birth to a child.

[2] The dreamer stands on a steep cliff, beneath him a deep abyss, in an icy storm. He has a small child in his arms but cannot hold it.

[3] *Faust II*, Act 3. Cf. *Psychology and Alchemy*, CW 12, par. 243.

[4] The fourth transformation of Faust—into Doctor Marianus—after his mystery death (*Faust II*, Act 5, last scene.) Cf. ibid., par. 558.

The connections you adduce with typology are interesting but difficult. Goethe himself was an intuitive feeling type. Faust first appears as Goethe's shadow, namely as an introverted scientist and doctor (thinking and sensation). Now comes the first transformation: he discovers his countertype ("feeling is all") and at the same time realizes the projection of the anima, as is invariably the case in the analytical process. Behind Gretchen stands the Gnostic sequence: Helen-Mary-Sophia.[5] They represent a real Platonic world of ideas (thinking and sensation on the mystic level). Here Goethe divines the fact that unconscious, undifferentiated functions are contaminated with the collective unconscious, with the result that they can be realized only in part rationally but for the most part irrationally, i.e., as an inner experience.

All the rest of Part Two is closely connected with Goethe's alchemical knowledge, which no one should underestimate. I was amazed at the amount of Hermetic philosophy I found in it. For your own clarification I would urgently recommend you to take account of the thought-processes of alchemy in relation to *Faust*. By the same post I send you two offprints of my writings, "Die Erlösungsvorstellungen in der Alchemie" and "Die Visionen des Zosimos."

. . .

Now a general remark. I don't know if I am deceiving myself, but it seems to me as though you have understood the "reality character" of Faust's experience in a rather limited psychological or perhaps psychologizing way. Forgive me if this criticism offends you. But I had a rather uncomfortable feeling when you spoke of "wishful fantasies." The idea of a wishful fantasy is an expression taken over from Freud's personalistic psychology of neurosis, which enables the doctor to break a patient of his silly megalomania or hysterical pretensions. But this only disguises the fact that the doctor does not understand in what respect such ideas are perfectly correct. They are just as incorrect as the dream in which you give birth to a child, but in a deeper sense they are just as correct as Goethe's Paris-Helen experience. When an insane person says he is the forefather who has been fecundating his daughter for millions of years, such a statement is thoroughly morbid from the medical standpoint. But from the psychological standpoint it is an astounding truth to which the broadest possible *consensus gentium* bears witness. It is expressed in the words:

[5] Cf "The Psychology of the Transference," CW 16, par. 361.

Scit et te Deum esse.[6] Freud would say: "An incestuous wish-fantasy," because he would like to save the poor patient from a bit of obnoxious nonsense. But I would say to the patient: "What a pity you are too stupid to understand this revelation properly." In the case of Goethe's *Faust*—which I consider altogether superb—I would anathematize the expression "wishful fantasy" from beginning to end.

. . .

Yours sincerely, c. g. j u n g

[6] "For He [God] doth know that . . . ye shall be as gods." Gen. 3:5.

Anonymous

[O R I G I N A L   I N   E N G L I S H]

My dear Mrs. N., 5 October 1939

If there hadn't been such a throng of things lately I surely would have written to you long ago. It is a curious thing that the closer people are to very serious issues, the calmer they seem to be. There is of course a great deal of apprehension in Switzerland and we feel the sword of Damocles hanging over our heads. But I was recently in Basel and I found that people are carrying on as usual, despite the fact that hell can break loose at any moment. I was on a point of the frontier right between the French and German lines. You could see the French and German fortifications and all was as quiet and peaceful as possible. No noise and no shots; all the villages are evacuated and nothing stirs.

My son and my sons-in-law are, with one exception, all with the army and my daughter from Paris with her children has taken refuge with us.

Young Hans[1] has been called to the army finally! He is now in a motorized unit where he has to serve as chauffeur and mechanic, as a member of the Auxiliary Service. I suppose that he has even got a uniform which will please him very much. I occasionally get an enthusiastic postcard. Up to the beginning of September he helped me in Bollingen as long as I was there. But with the mobilization he had to join the ranks.

I myself am too old to do active service, but I have been asked to

□ U.S.A.
[1] Cf. Kuhn, 1 Jan. 26, n. □.

44

"stand for Parliament."[2] That means, a large group of people seem to want me as a member of the Conseil National (which would be the House of Commons in England). I told them that I'm no politician and they say that that was exactly why they wanted me, that they had politicians enough. I said: Well, under those conditions I can do it. I don't know exactly yet what it means; at all events it means sessions of a fortnight's duration about five or six times a year, and personally no end of boredom. By great good luck it might be that I can say something reasonable. I'm told that people want representatives who mean spiritual values. It is an interesting sign of the times. I'm only on the list and I insisted upon being put practically on the last line, as I still hope that I won't be elected. The elections take place somewhere at the end of October or beginning of November. So you'd better tell nobody of this very curious new development.

If I can help you in any way to get through to Switzerland I might do so through the Fremdenpolizei.

It is not exactly the time when one could be busy with a book. The atmosphere is terribly disturbed and it is quite difficult to keep out of it. The things that happen in Germany are just incredible, and the future is full of unheard-of possibilities. The feeling is entirely apocalyptic. It is just like the time when God has allowed Satan to roam on earth for one time and a half.[3] The Germans as far as I know them are partially terrified and partially drunk with blood and victory. If ever there was a mental epidemic it is the actual mental condition in Germany. Hitler himself (from what I heard) is more than half crazy. With every good wish,

Yours cordially, C. G. JUNG

[2] Jung was asked to stand as candidate for the "Landesring der Unabhängigen" (National Group of Independents) but was not elected.
[3] A contamination of Rev. 20:7–8 and 12:14.

To Gottlieb Duttweiler

Dear Herr Nationalrat,   4 December 1939

Although I know you have more than enough to do I would like to make the suggestion that in view of the internal difficulties in

☐ (1888–1962), Swiss businessman and politician. Founder of Migros, the first

45

Switzerland all possible steps should be taken to prevent social unrest in the future.

As you know, mobilization has resulted in a great difference between the social position of conscripts and of persons not liable for military service. There are hundreds and thousands of soldiers whose families have been deprived of their breadwinners, while on the other hand foreigners and those not liable for military service can quietly go on earning a living and eventually take over the job the soldier has lost. This situation is bound to lead to the gravest disputes unless energetic action is taken right away to even out these inequalities.

In my opinion a political party should seize the initiative and introduce the following measure: *mobilization will be declared absolute, every Swiss citizen between the ages of 18 and 60 being counted as mobilized whether he is liable for military service or not.* Those who are not liable would be under the same regulations as the conscripts, the only difference being that the soldier would do his duty with a rifle and the non-conscript as a wage-earner. Every Swiss citizen would accordingly be put on the payroll and anything he earned above and beyond that would be used for the public good[1] for the duration of the mobilization. If this measure were introduced now, everything possible would have been done to prevent social unrest, and the soldier at the front need no longer have the uncomfortable feeling that on top of his risking his life for others he and his family are financially disadvantaged. If the war should last for a long time we shall be exposed to the greatest financial hardships anyway. Hence we need a magnanimous gesture now in order to cope with future difficulties.[2]

Yours sincerely, C. G. JUNG

Swiss co-operative retail trading society; member of the National Council, Councillor of State. Also founded the "Landesring der Unabhängigen" (cf. Anon., 5 Oct. 39, n. 2).

[1] In an almost identical letter, written the same day, to his old friend Albert Oeri (cf. Oeri, 11 Dec. 20), editor of the *Basler Nachrichten* and member of the National Council, Jung specified that these funds should be made available primarily to the "distressed families of the conscripts."

[2] Jung's suggestion was not accepted. Instead, the Schweizerische Lohn- und Verdienstersatzordnung (Swiss Wages and Income Compensation Order) arranged compensation for financial losses caused by the mobilization.

Anonymous

[ORIGINAL IN ENGLISH]

Dear Mrs. N.,   20 May 1940

This is just the kind of experience you needed. You trust your unconscious as if it were a loving father. But it is *nature* and cannot be made use of as if it were a reliable human being. It is *inhuman* and it needs the human mind to function usefully for man's purposes. Nature is an incomparable guide if you know *how* to follow her. She is like the needle of the compass pointing to the North, which is most useful when you have a good man-made ship and when you know how to navigate. That's about the position. If you follow the river, you surely come to the sea finally. But if you take it literally you soon get stuck in an impassable gorge and you complain of being misguided.

The unconscious is useless without the human mind. It always seeks its collective purposes and never your individual destiny. Your destiny is the result of the collaboration between the conscious and the unconscious.

I am actually in the mountains with my family and all the little grandchildren avoiding the dangers of Zurich. We all hope and pray for a British victory over the Antichrist.

Sincerely yours, C. G. JUNG

To H. G. Baynes

[ORIGINAL IN ENGLISH]

My dear Peter,   Bollingen, 12 August 1940

This is the fateful year for which I have waited more than 25 years. I did not know that it was such a disaster. Although since 1918[1] I knew that a terrible fire would spread over Europe beginning

---

□ (Handwritten.)

[1] While working on the "North Africa" chapter in his *Memories* (IX, i), Jung related to Aniela Jaffé that, soon after peace was declared in 1918, he had a "visionary dream" which continued to haunt him until the outbreak of World War II: "I was returning to Switzerland from a trip in Germany. My body was covered with burns and my clothes were burnt full of holes; for I had seen fire falling like rain from heaven and consuming the cities of Germany. I had an intimation that the crucial year would be 1940." (Communication from A. J.)—

47

in the North East, I have no vision beyond 1940 concerning the fate of Europe. This year reminds me of the enormous earthquake in 26 b.c. that shook down the great temple of Karnak. It was the prelude to the destruction of all temples, because a new time had begun. 1940 is the year when we approach the meridian of the first star in Aquarius. It is the premonitory earthquake of the New Age.

Up to the present moment Bollingen has escaped—together with Switzerland—the general destruction, but we are in prison. You don't see the walls, but you feel them. The newspapers are hushed and one hardly cares to read them, except for doubtful information about the war. For a while, just when I studied your book,[2] I went with all my grandchildren to the West of Switzerland because we expected an attack. Afterwards I was very busy because all doctors were with the army.

It is awkward to write, as the censor reads the stuff. But I must tell you how often I think of you and all my friends in England. I often complain that Mr. Chamberlain did not read my interview with Knickerbocker.[3]

Your book is quite interesting and it seems as if your interpretations hit the nail on the head. Certain points would need some discussion. But one should talk, writing is too clumsy.

It is difficult to be old in these days. One is helpless. On the other hand one feels happily estranged from this world. I like nature but not the world of man or the world to be. I hope this letter will

---

In the autumn of 1913, while actually on a journey, Jung had an "overpowering vision" of a "monstrous flood covering all the northern and low-lying lands between the North Sea and the Alps. . . . Then the whole sea turned to blood." The vision was repeated two weeks later. During the spring and early summer of 1914 he had "a thrice-repeated dream that an Arctic cold wave descended and froze the land to ice" (*Memories*, pp. 175f./169). — These dreams and visions foretold the outbreak of World War I. And in 1918 he wrote: "As the Christian view of the world loses its authority, the more menacingly will the 'blond beast' be heard prowling about in its underground prison, ready at any moment to burst out with devastating consequences" ("The Role of the Unconscious," CW 10, par. 17). Cf. also "The Fight with the Shadow," ibid., par. 447.

[2] *Mythology of the Soul.*

[3] An interview with the American journalist H. R. Knickerbocker, "Diagnosing the Dictators," *Hearst's International Cosmopolitan*, Jan. 1939. In it Jung suggested that Western civilization might be spared the horrors of Nazi terrorism by turning Hitler's aggressive libido towards Russia, as the only way to stop Hitler making war on the West. In this way Nazism could be induced to commit suicide. The interview is included in *C. G. Jung Speaking* (1977).

48

reach you and convey to you all the wishes the human heart can't suppress in spite of censors. They are human too after all.

In autumn I resume my lectures at the E.T.H. about the individuation process in the Middle Ages![4] That's the only thing with me one could call up to date. I loathe the new style, the new Art, the new Music, Literature, Politics, and above all the new Man. It's the old beast that has not changed since the troglodytes.

My dear Peter, I am with you and with old England!

Cordially yours, C . G .

[4] Alchemy I and II, Nov. 1940–Feb. 1941; May–July 1941.

To Paul Schmitt

Dear Dr. Schmitt,   Locarno, 5 January 1942

Best thanks for your New Year letter, with its welcome news that the pebbles ejected by the volcano on whose edge I am sitting have landed somewhere. It is a never-failing pleasure to hear an echo. The recognition of this bad quality in myself makes me indulgent with the vanity and sensitivity of otherwise competent authors—too long one can hear no echo, and this can easily lead to an obdurate and grim self-admiration—or the reverse. . . .

You have hit the mark absolutely: all of a sudden and with terror it became clear to me that I have taken over *Faust as my heritage*, and moreover as the advocate and avenger of Philemon and Baucis,[1] who, unlike Faust the superman, are the hosts of the gods in a

☐ (Handwritten.) Paul Schmitt, LL.D., (1900–1953), Swiss publisher and journalist, editor of the *Münchner Neueste Nachrichten* until 1933, when he had to leave Germany on account of his opposition to Naziism. Lectured at several Eranos meetings on philosophical and historical subjects.

[1] The myth of Philemon and Baucis tells how they were the only ones to offer hospitality to Zeus and Hermes when they came down to earth to test men's piety. In *Faust II* (Act 5) Faust wantonly causes the death of the couple. In his *Memories* (pp. 234f./221f.) Jung reports how the inner dichotomy between "Personality No. 1 and No. 2" (pp. 57/66) made him identify with Faust ("Two souls, alas, are housed within my breast"), and how he felt Faust's guilt as his own and that he had to expiate Faust's crime. (Cf. Keyserling, 2 Jan. 28, n. 3.) Concerning Jung's interest in the figure of Philemon cf. *Memories*, pp. 182ff./176ff.

49

ruthless and godforsaken age. It has become—if I may say so—a personal matter between me and *proavus* Goethe.[2] To the extent that I harbour a personal myth of this kind you are right in nosing up a "Goethean" world in me. Indeed it is there, for it seems to me unavoidable to give an *answer* to Faust: we must continue to bear the terrible German problem that is devastating Europe, and must pull down into our world some of the Faustian happenings in the Beyond, for instance the benign activity of Pater Profundus.[3] I would give the earth to know whether Goethe himself knew why he called the two old people "Philemon" and "Baucis." Faust sinned from the beginning against these first parents ($\phi i\lambda\eta\mu a$ and Baubo[4]). One must have one foot in the grave, though, before one understands this secret properly.

I wish you all the best for the New Year and hope to see you again soon after my return.

Yours sincerely, c. g. JUNG

[2] = Goethe the ancestor. There is a family tradition according to which Jung's grandfather, Carl Gustav Jung (1794–1864), was an illegitimate son of Goethe's. Although this tradition could not be proved, it amused Jung to speak of it (*Memories*, pp. 35/47 & n. 1). Cf. also Jung, 30 Dec. 59.

[3] *Faust II*, Act 5.

[4] $\phi i\lambda\eta\mu a$ = kiss. Baubo (= belly) is a Great Mother figure; in Greek mythology, a lewd old woman who succeeded in making Demeter, grieving over the abduction of her daughter Persephone to the underworld, laugh at an obscene gesture.

To Aniela Jaffé

Dear Frau Jaffé,   Bollingen, 22 December 1942

Heartiest thanks for the very welcome and edible Christmas present you have destined for me. I hope you haven't stinted yourself of these things! To me they come most opportunely, especially here in Bollingen where one is a bit pinched.

□ (Handwritten.) Aniela Jaffé, originally of Berlin; 1955–61 Jung's secretary and collaborator; editor of the Swiss edition of these Letters. Recorded and edited *Memories, Dreams, Reflections*. Cf. also her "Bilder und Symbole aus E.T.A. Hoffmanns Märchen 'Der Goldne Topf,'" in Jung's *Gestaltungen des Unbewussten* (1950); "Hermann Broch: Der Tod des Vergil," *Studien zur Analytischen Psychologie C. G. Jungs* (1955); *Apparitions and Precognitions* (tr., 1963; Jung's foreword is in CW 18); *The Myth of Meaning* (tr., 1970); *From the Life and Work of C. G. Jung* (tr. 1971).

Your dream¹ is very remarkable in that it coincides almost literally with my first systematic fantasy,² which I had between the ages of 15 and 16. It engrossed me for weeks, always on the way to school, which took three-quarters of an hour. I was the king of an island in a great lake like a sea, stretching from Basel to Strassburg. The island consisted of a mountain with a small medieval town nestling below. At the top was my castle, and on its highest tower were things like copper antennae which collected electricity from the air and conducted it into a deep vault underneath the tower. In this vault there was a mysterious apparatus that turned the electricity into *gold*. I was so obsessed with this fantasy that reality was completely forgotten.

It seems to me that your dream is an important contribution to the psychology of the self. Through the self we are plunged into the torrent of cosmic events. Everything essential happens in the self and the ego functions as a receiver, spectator, and transmitter. What is so peculiar is the symbolization of the self as an apparatus. A "machine" is always something *thought up*, deliberately put together for a definite purpose. Who has invented this machine? (Cf. the symbol of the "world clock"!³) The Tantrists say that things represent the *distinctness of God's thoughts*. The machine is a microcosm, what Paracelsus called the "star in man."⁴ I always have the feeling that these symbols touch on the great secrets, the *magnalia Dei.*⁵ With best greetings and cordial thanks,

Ever sincerely yours, C. G. J.

¹ "I am in a deep cellar, together with a boy and an old man. The boy has been given an electric installation for Christmas: a large copper pot is suspended from the ceiling and electric wires from all directions make it vibrate. After some time there are no more wires; the pot now vibrates from atmospheric electric oscillations."
² *Memories*, pp. 8off./86ff.
³ *Psychology and Alchemy*, pars. 307ff.
⁴ Cf. "Paracelsus as a Spiritual Phenomenon," CW 13, pars. 163, 188; "On the Nature of the Psyche," CW 8, par. 390.
⁵ Possibly a Paracelsan term, meaning "The great things of God."

To Jolande Jacobi

Dear Dr. Jacobi,   Bollingen, 26 August 1943

. . .

The mistake you are making consists in your being drawn too much into X.'s neurotic problem. This is evident from the fact, for instance,

51

that your animus is trying like mad to interpret when there is nothing to be interpreted. *Why* does he say he has other relationships? Why indeed! As though anyone knew. He just says it. That is very nice of him, inconsiderate, truthful, tactless, unpremeditated, confiding, etc., etc. If you knew the *real* reason you would also know who X. was at his birth and at his death. But we shall only find that out in the Hereafter. He has absolutely no reason he can state, it has simply happened and can be interpreted quite superfluously in a hundred different ways, and no single interpretation holds water, being merely an insistence which, once made, only has the effect of driving him into further whimsical and uninterpretable reactions. In reality his irrational behaviour represents the conscious and unconscious sides of the anima, and is absolutely necessary in order to gain insight into her, just as in general he needs a bevy of women in order to grasp the essence of this glamorous figure. Of course he is still too naïve to notice this. But you, just as naïvely, have intruded yourself as an anima figure into this witches' sabbath and are therefore caught up in the dance as though you were nothing but an anima. Wherever you stick a finger in out of "love" or involuntary participation you will burn it, for it is not involvement that is expected of you, but objective, disincarnate observation, and if you want to snatch something out of it for the heart—and no reasonable objection can be made to this—you must pay for it in blood, as was always so and always will be. At least one must keep one's head out of it so as not to be eaten up entirely by emotional ape-men. Where there are emotional ties one is always the disappointed disappointer. This one has to know if one wants, or is forced, to participate correctly.

. . .

With cordial greetings,

Yours sincerely, C. G. JUNG

Anonymous

Dear N. N.,   10 September 1943

Here I send you merely a greeting to tell you that I have understood your letter. I have thought much about prayer. It—prayer—

□ (Handwritten.)

is very necessary because it makes the Beyond we conjecture and think about an immediate reality, and transposes us into the duality of the ego and the dark Other. One hears oneself speaking and can no longer deny that one has addressed "That." The question then arises: What will become of Thee and of Me? of the transcendental Thou and the immanent I? The way of the unexpected, not-to-be-expected, opens, fearful and unavoidable, with hope of a propitious turn or a defiant "I will not perish under the will of God unless I myself will it too." Then only, so I feel, is God's will made perfect. Without me it is only his almighty will, a frightful fatality even in its grace, void of sight and hearing, void of knowledge for precisely that reason. I go together with it, an immensely weighty milligram without which God had made his world in vain. Best wishes,

Yours ever, J U N G

Anonymous

Dear Frau N.,   11 July 1944

What happens after death[1] is so unspeakably glorious that our imagination and our feelings do not suffice to form even an approximate conception of it. A few days before my sister died[2] her face wore an expression of such inhuman sublimity that I was profoundly frightened.

A child, too, enters into this sublimity, and there detaches himself from this world and his manifold individuations more quickly than the aged. So easily does he become what *you* also are that he apparently vanishes. Sooner or later all the dead become what we also are. But in this reality we know little or nothing about that mode of being, and what shall we still know of this earth after death? The dissolution of our time-bound form in eternity brings no loss of meaning. Rather does the little finger know itself a member of the hand. With best regards,

Your devoted C. G. J U N G

[1] This letter is especially significant since Jung himself had been close to death after a severe cardiac infarct at the beginning of 1944. He gives a vivid description of the visions he had during his illness in *Memories*, ch. X. The illness accounts for the long gap in the letters between Jan. and July.
[2] She died in 1935.

To H. Irminger

Dear Herr Irminger,   22 September 1944

After having been prevented from doing so by a long illness, I have now read your MS. First of all, I would like to thank you for having taken so much trouble to show me how the Catholic doctrine completes and perfects my psychological writings. You also wonder—rightly, from your point of view—why I don't declare my belief in God and return to the bosom of the Church.

It may interest you to know that I once received a letter from an "alchemist," that is, from a man who still believes in the medieval art of gold-making, who informed me that I understood nothing whatever of the true alchemy, but that if I did I would avow my faith in it. When I was in India, the philosophers there assured me that their enlightened philosophy was infinitely further advanced than mine, whereas I still languished in the darkness of Ahamkara,[1] Maya, etc. No doubt a Persian sufi[2] would find my remarks about Chadir[3] very jejune and, by thoroughly instructing me in his mysticism, would show me the way to salvation.

All critics of this kind have one thing in common: with a couple of more or less polite remarks they all without exception pass over the *facts* I have presented and verified, which do not interest them in the least, and want to convert me to their special credo.

My dear Sir! *My pursuit is science*, not apologetics and not philosophy, and I have neither the capacity nor the desire to found a religion. *My interest is scientific, yours evangelical*, therefore you write an apologia for Catholic doctrine, which I have never attacked and don't want to attack. These two standpoints are mutually exclusive so that any discussion is impossible. We talk at cross purposes and charge through open doors.

As a scientist I have to guard against believing that I am in possession of a final truth. I am therefore put in the wrong from the start, since I am not in possession of the truth, which is solely on the side of my opponent. Consequently, the only thing that matters for you is that I should emerge from my benighted error and acknowledge the truth of the Catholic doctrine. As a Christian, of

---

[1] *Ahamkara* ("I-maker"), is the world of ego-consciousness.
[2] Lit. "clad in wool." Adherents of Sufism, a mystical development of Islam.
[3] Chadir (or Khidr) is the enigmatic, immortal knower of divine secrets; he figures in the 18th Sura of the Koran and plays an important role in Sufism. Cf. "Concerning Rebirth," CW 9, i, pars. 240ff.

course, I take my stand on the Christian truth, so it is superfluous to want to convert me to that.

In my writings I naturally remain below the heights of every religious system, for I always go only as far as the psychological facts I have experienced permit me. I have no ambition to profess or support any one faith. I am interested solely in the facts.

On this empirical foundation every religion has erected its temple, and the two intolerant ones among them, Christianity and Islam, vie with each other in raising the totalitarian claim that their temple is the only right one.

Though I know little of Catholic doctrine, that little is enough to make it an inalienable possession for me. And I know so much about Protestantism that I could never give it up. This lamentable indecision is what you, with so much psychological acumen, censure as a "complex." Now with regard to this indecision I must tell you that I have consciously and deliberately decided for it. Since no man can serve two masters, I can submit neither to one creed nor to the other, but only to the *one* which stands above the conflict. Just as Christ is eternally being sacrificed, so also he hangs eternally between the two thieves. There are good Catholic and Protestant Christians. If the Church has suffered a schism, then I must be satisfied with being a Christian who finds himself in the same conflict Christendom is in. I cannot disavow my brother who, in good faith and for reasons I cannot invalidate with a good conscience, is of a different opinion. You yourself express the view that dire abuses within the Church played no small part in causing the schism. I can only agree with this and would draw your attention to the fact that a far more terrible schism has occurred in our own day, namely the Antichristian movement which *rules* Russia and Germany. The Church in both its denominations is causally implicated in this schism too. The cause, to be sure, is no longer the profligacy of the declining 15th century, but rather a loss of spiritual authority which, it seems to me, is due to the inability of the Churches to come to terms adequately with the scientific spirit. Science seeks the truth because it feels it does not possess it. The church *possesses* the truth and therefore does not seek it.

The fact of Antichristianity posits a far deeper schism which is infinitely harder to hold together than Catholicism and Protestantism. This time it is a Yes and No to Christianity as such.

When a crack runs through a house, the entire building is affected and not merely one half of it. The house is no longer as trustworthy

55

as before. A conscientious builder does not try to convince the owner that the rooms on either side of the crack are still in an excellent condition, but will set to work on the crack and seek ways and means to mend it. The splendid and costly furnishings of the rooms will interest him only in so far as he is intent on saving the rooms. He has no time to wander around admiringly, exclaiming that they are the most beautiful in the world, when there is already a creaking in the beams.

As a doctor I am interested only in one thing: how can the wound be healed? It is quite certain that the schism can never be repaired by each side extolling its advantages to the other instead of lamenting their woeful inability to establish peace. While mother and daughter bicker, there comes the enemy of both, the Antichrist, and shows these Christians who are squabbling about *their* truth what *he* can do—for in egotism he outbids everybody.

Anyone who wants to, or has to, heal this conflict is faced with the hell of a mess: he sees that the European is only half a Christian. He will become a whole one only when he can also stand on his left leg. The doctor has to treat both sides, for the whole man suffers when he is sick and not merely the half.

This is the reason why I try to establish facts *on which the two sides can unite*. (It is also the reason why I get kicks from both sides.) Every hardening of the denominational standpoint enlarges the crack and diminishes the moral and spiritual authority of Christianity, as everyone outside the Church can plainly see. But certain people are as though smitten with blindness.

It is naturally much *easier* to cling obstinately to a credo and assert its absolute validity. In this way you avoid any personal conflict but fuel the general one instead. Usually this is called egotism, but I call it blindness and bigotry when one party still believes it can finally settle the other's hash. Even the Antichrist, who is a past-master of this method, deceives himself mightily in this respect (thank God!).

As much as the Christian is bound to be convinced of the moral value of his own submission, he should not require or even expect it of others, for this totalitarian claim destroys his humility, even when it is cunningly hidden behind an impersonal mask.

As a doctor I am continually concerned with the victims of the great schism of our time. For this reason I cannot, through onesided denominationalism, throw the seekers of healing out on their necks, for they have come straight from the battlefield of the schism. The *tertius gaudens*[4] of the domestic squabble is the Antichrist, who has not by a long shot sprung only from German Protestantism or the venality of the Church of the Czars, but also from the eminently Catholic soil of Italy and Spain. Every Church must beat its breast, as must every European: *mea culpa, mea maxima culpa! None is right*, and therefore the scientifically minded man of today says: Let us go and seek the facts upon which all could unite, for opinions that have sprouted into totalitarian truths are the source of never-ending strife which no one wants to end.

I was amazed to see that you too have not understood the concept of the "self." How on earth did you come by the idea that I can replace God, and by means of a concept? As a scientist I cannot after all assert that "God" does something, for how can I prove that the specific cause is "God"? For this I would need a proof of God, which we have long known can be nothing but a begging of the question. I can, if need be, still demonstrate the existence of a wholeness supraordinate to consciousness, but of its own nature it defies description. This "self" never in all one's life takes the place of God, though it may perhaps be a vessel for divine grace. Such regrettable misunderstandings are based on the assumption that I am an irreligious man who doesn't believe in God, and to whom, therefore, one only needs to show the way to belief. These critics remind me of a certain Benedictine Father who, in the 18th century, wrote a book in which he demonstrated that Greek mythology was nothing but alchemy. The poor chap didn't know that alchemy grew out of mythology.

Thus, with commendable patience and undoubted goodwill ("He who loves his child chastises it"), and despite my stupendous and obdurate folly, you want to bring me to the goal and consummation of my life's work, and whither do you lead me? To the very spot from which I started, namely to that still medieval Christianity, which failed not only four hundred years ago but is now more of a failure than ever and in the most terrible way. The German Army is supposed to consist of Christians, and the larger half of it of Catholics at that.

Why don't people read my books conscientiously? Why do they gloss over the facts?

4 = "the third who laughs."

Germany dreams of world domination and is getting it in the neck with a vengeance. Likewise, Christianity dreams a noble dream of catholicity and is not only split up in itself but largely disowned even in its Western homeland. And people do not see that I am gathering *for tomorrow* the factual material which will be desperately needed if the European of the future is to be convinced of anything at all. The denominationalist is interested only in apologias and propaganda. Scientific responsibility means nothing to him. Nowadays he is invariably a *laudator temporis acti*. The kerygma[5] of the early centuries poured forth *new spirit* and it worked like fire. But the salt has lost its savour and salts no more. Hence that *granum salis* is also missing which my critics would need in order to correct their projections and to open their drowsy eyes wide enough to see reality: nowhere and never have I denied God. I start from a positive Christianity which is as much Catholic as Protestant, and I endeavour in a scientifically responsible manner to point out those empirically graspable facts which make the justification of Christian and, in particular, Catholic dogma at least plausible, and besides that are best suited to give the scientific mind an access to understanding. I expect no gratitude from spiritual and clerical pride, merely a little less blindness. I know, however, of a few high-ranking clerics who appreciate my labours. It is by no means in the interests of the Church if insufficient understanding ventures too far. People should read authors who take as positive a stance towards Christianity as I do rather more carefully and reflect before trying to convert them to what is already an object of their greatest concern.

Have you never noticed that I do not write for ecclesiastical circles but for those who are *extra ecclesiam*? I join their company, deliberately and of my own free will outside the Church, and should I on that account be branded a heretic, I answer: "The savourlessness of the salt serves the work of Antichrist."

In my view it is utterly wrong to criticize my scientific work, which does not claim to be anything except scientific, from any other standpoint than that which alone is appropriate to the scientific method. Confessions of faith are, as we know, not the business of science. I would be sinning against the modesty proper to science if I said anything more, or other than, what can be gleaned from the facts. I once described the archetype as an *imprint* which presup-

[5] Preaching, declaration of religious truth.

poses an *imprinter*.[6] Science can never assert that the imprinter is
"God," since that can never be proved. Just as I restrict myself to
the facts, any proper criticism that deserves a hearing must likewise
concern itself with these facts, and either prove that they do not exist
or that their interpretation runs counter to scientific principles.
Should the facts be inconvenient for any kind of creed, then they
are not to be got rid of by an authoritarian fiat or by faith. Anyone
who tries to do so immobilizes himself and remains irretrievably
behind world history. Instead of such purposeless criticism I would
far rather have a scholarly Catholic collaborator who with understanding and goodwill would correct my theologically defective mode
of expression, so that I could avoid everything that looks even
remotely like a criticism, let alone a devaluation, of Church doctrine.
I am so profoundly convinced of the immeasurable significance of
the Church that I would wish to spare her all unnecessary difficulties.

You may discern from the length of my letter the interest I evince
in your work, in spite of the fact that you have charged with ex-
cessive vehemence through a door I have long kept open.

Yours sincerely, c. g. j u n g

[6] *Psychology and Alchemy*, pars. 15f.

To Kristine Mann

[ORIGINAL IN ENGLISH]

My dear Dr. Mann,   1 February 1945

Eleanor Bertine has already given me the news of your illness[1] in a
letter I received a few days ago. I wish I could talk to you personally,
but one is so far from each other and it is such a long time we are
separated from the rest of the world that one feels quite hopeless
about a communication. We don't trust even our letters to be capable
of jumping over the abyss which yawns between us and the wide
world. Still I hope that a good star conveys my letter to you.

As you know, the angel of death has struck me down too and almost succeeded in wiping me off the slate.[2] I have been practically
an invalid ever since, recovering very very slowly from all the arrows

□ M.D., (1873–1945), American analytical psychologist, a founder of the Analytical Psychology Club of New York and of its library, now named in memory
of her. (See pl. in vol. 2.)
[1] She was dying of cancer.
[2] Cf. Anon., 11 July 44, n. 1.

59

that have pierced me on all sides. Fortunately enough my head has not suffered and I could forget myself in my scientific work. On the whole my illness proved to be a most valuable experience, which gave me the inestimable opportunity of a glimpse behind the veil. The only difficulty is to get rid of the body, to get quite naked and void of the world and the ego-will. When you can give up the crazy will to live and when you seemingly fall into a bottomless mist, then the truly *real* life begins with everything which you were meant to be and never reached. It is something ineffably grand. I was free, completely free and whole, as I never felt before.[3] I found myself 15,000 km. from the earth and I saw it as an immense globe resplendent in an inexpressibly beautiful blue light. I was on a point exactly above the southern end of India, which shone in a bluish silvery light with Ceylon like a shimmering opal in the deep blue sea. I was in the universe, where there was a big solitary rock containing a temple. I saw its entrance illuminated by a thousand small flames of coconut oil. I knew I was to enter the temple and I would reach full knowledge. But at this moment a messenger from the world (which by then was a very insignificant corner of the universe) arrived and said that I was not allowed to depart and at this moment the whole vision collapsed completely. But from then on for three weeks I slept, and was wakeful each night in the universe and experienced the complete vision. Not I was united with somebody or something—*it* was united, *it* was the *hierosgamos*, the mystic Agnus. It was a silent invisible festival[4] permeated by an incomparable, indescribable feeling of eternal bliss, such as I never could have imagined as being within reach of human experience. Death is the hardest thing from the outside and as long as we are outside of it. But once inside you taste of such completeness and peace and fulfillment that you don't want to return. As a matter of fact, during the first month after my first vision I suffered from black depressions because I felt that I was recovering. It was like dying. I did not want to live and to return into this fragmentary, restricted, narrow, almost mechanical life, where you were subject to the laws of gravity and cohesion, imprisoned in a system of 3 dimensions and whirled along with other bodies in the turbulent stream of time. There was fulness, meaning fulfillment, *eternal* movement (not movement in time).

[3] The following description is a condensation of *Memories*, pp. 289ff./270ff.
[4] Ibid., pp. 294/274.

Although your letter is dated Nov. 27th/44, I hope that my answer will reach you. Your letter arrived today and I am writing at once.

Throughout my illness something has carried me. My feet were not standing on air and I had the proof that I have reached a safe ground. Whatever you do, if you do it sincerely, will eventually become the bridge to your wholeness, a good ship that carries you through the darkness of your second birth, which seems to be death to the outside. I will not last too long any more. I am marked. But life has fortunately become provisional. It has become a transitory prejudice, a working hypothesis for the time being, but not existence itself.

Be patient and regard it as another difficult task, this time the last one.

I greet you, CARL G. JUNG

To Jolande Jacobi

Dear Dr. Jacobi,   12 June 1945

I would answer your question as follows: It is a fact that intelligence and psychological preparation in cases of schizophrenia result in a better prognosis. I therefore make it a rule to give anyone threatened with schizophrenia, or the mild or latent schizophrenic, as much psychological knowledge as possible, because I know from experience that there is then a better chance of his getting out of the psychotic interval. Equally, psychological enlightenment after a psychotic attack can be extraordinarily helpful in some circumstances. I am not convinced that schizophrenia is absolutely fatal any more than tuberculosis is. I would always recommend psychological education to patients at risk as a measure of prophylactic hygiene. Like neurosis, psychosis in its inner course is a process of individuation, but one that is usually not joined up with consciousness and therefore runs its course in the unconscious as an ouroboros.[1] Psychological preparation joins the process to consciousness, or rather, there is a chance

[1] The snake that bites its own tail (cf. *Psychology and Alchemy*, Figs. 7, 13, 20, 46, 47, 108, 147, 253). The term is used here as an image of an unconscious circular process without effect on consciousness. But the (o)uroboros as a mandala and image of the alchemical *opus circulare* can symbolize the conscious process of individuation. Cf. *Aion*, p rs. 297, 407.

61

of its being joined, and hence of the individuation process having a healing effect.

Hoping I have answered your question satisfactorily, and with best regards,

Yours sincerely, C. G. JUNG

To P. W. Martin

[ORIGINAL IN ENGLISH]

Dear Mr. Martin,   28 August 1945

I was very pleased with your kind letter of June 4th. It is long ago since I heard of you last.[1] Happily enough we have been spared in Switzerland. So easily it could have happened that the Germans would have invaded our country too. It would not have been so easy as France or Austria though. We were decided to fight.

I'm glad to know that you are still interested in the psychology of the unconscious. I know it is exceedingly difficult to write anything definite or descriptive about the progression of psychological states. It always seemed to me as if the real milestones were certain symbolic events characterized by a strong emotional tone. You are quite right, the main interest of my work is not concerned with the treatment of neuroses but rather with the approach to the numinous. But the fact is that the approach to the numinous is the real therapy and inasmuch as you attain to the numinous experiences you are released from the curse of pathology. Even the very disease takes on a numinous character.

I hope it won't take so long any more until travelling becomes possible again. We have been secluded from the rest of the world for about 5 years. In the days before the radio it would have been very bad indeed, but the radio was very helpful in this war. One always could keep in touch with the decent world beyond that infernal hovel of lies and crimes.

Please remember me to Mrs. Martin!

Yours cordially, C. G. JUNG

---

[1] Cf. Martin, 20 Aug. 37.

62

Anonymous

Dear Herr N.,   23 November 1945

When moral weakness[1] is coupled with a relatively good intelligence, as seems to be the case with you, one must use this intelligence when the ethical sense fails. This trite bit of wisdom cannot teach you any psychotherapy, but you must understand it and simply apply it yourself. If you can make this minimal use of your intelligence, you are saved. If not, not.

Yours truly, C. G. JUNG

☐ Switzerland.

[1] N., who was awaiting trial for a petty offence, asked for advice as to how not to succumb to similar temptations in the future (he was at the time on probation for a similar offence committed two years before).

To Pastor Fritz Buri

Dear Pastor Buri,   10 December 1945

Very many thanks for kindly sending me your book, *Die religiöse Ueberwindung der Angst.*[1] I have been waiting for a rejoinder to Pfister's book[2] from theological quarters. I myself cannot agree with Pfister. First and foremost because fear is a fundamental reaction of nature. Kierkegaard's view that animals have no fear is totally disproved by the facts. There are whole species which consist of nothing but fear. A creature that loses its fear is condemned to death. When "cured" by missionaries of their natural and justified fear of demons, primitives degenerate. I have seen enough of this in Africa whatever the missionaries may say. Anyone who is afraid has reason to be. There are not a few patients who have to have fear driven into them because their instincts have atrophied. A man who has no more fear is on the brink of the abyss. Only if he suffers from a pathological excess of fear can he be cured with impunity.

Second, where the religions are concerned, they deliver from fear

☐ Bern.

[1] Bern, 1945.

[2] Pfister, *Das Christentum und die Angst* (1944). (Concerning Pfister cf. Ferenczi, 25 Dec. 09, n. 5.)

63

and at the same time create fear, even Christianity, and that is right because one person has too much, another too little. Absolute deliverance from fear is a complete absurdity. What about the fear of God? Doesn't God ordain fearful things? Has Pfister no fear if both legs are broken for him and in the end he must dangle from a meat-hook through his chin? Does no fear warn him of danger to body and soul? Has he no fear for the life of his sick child? A man without fear is a superman. I don't like supermen. They are not even likeable. If Christ in Gethsemane had no fear, then his passion is null and void and the believer can subscribe to docetism![3]

Third, religions are not by any means mere fear-constructs. Far be it from me to deny the existence of apotropaisms, but like all religious phenomena, they go back to something that the biologist can only describe as a basic instinct of human nature. His science does not entitle him to assert that religions are revelations of the divine spirit, which they very easily might be although we are unable to prove it. In this sense I must describe every religious idea as a "fiction" since, formally at any rate, it is a conflation of imaginative possibilities. On the other hand, we can be sure that it is not motivated by any conscious intention, rather it "happens" to man on an unconscious level (unconscious = unknown). That is the utmost science can establish. The wonder does not lie in the content of the "fiction" but in the existence of the fiction, even if it should be a conscious device used for illegitimate purposes (e.g., banishing fear). But it is putting the cart before the horse to explain all dogmas and rites as apotropaic fear-constructs. It is not only a scandal if theologians entertain such notions, but psychologically false as everyone knows who has had a religious experience, and as is also proved by the investigation of primitive rites. It verges directly on atheism to try to reduce the religious function to anything other than itself. . . .

Fourth, as a psychotherapist I do not by any means try to deliver my patients from fear. Rather, I lead them to the reason for their fear, and then it becomes clear that it is justified. (I could tell you a few instructive stories in this respect!) If my patient understands religious language, I say to him: Well, don't try to escape this fear which

[3] Docetism, a heresy of the early Christian Church, taught that Christ was born without any participation in physical matter and that accordingly his body and his suffering were not real but only apparent.

God has given you, but try to endure it to the end—*sine poena nulla gratia!*[4] I can say this because I believe I am a religious man and because I know with scientific certainty that my patient hasn't invented his fear but that it is preordained. By whom or what? *By the unknown.* The religious man calls this *absconditum*[5] "God," the scientific intellect calls it the unconscious. Deriving fear from repression is a neurotic speculation, an apotropaism invented for cowards; a pseudo-scientific myth in so far as it declares a basic biological instinct unreal and twists it into an *Ersatz*-formation. One could just as well explain life as a flight from death or love as an evasion of the hate which one hasn't the courage to muster. They are neurotic artifices with which one diddles hysterics out of the only meaning they have (which lies precisely in their neurosis), naturally with the best but unendurably shallow intentions.

I hope you will not take it amiss if I hazard the conjecture that you may have read rather too little of me. I infer this from the difficulties which my manner of expression seems to cause you. *Fictio* and *imaginatio* have for me their original, full meaning as important activities that concern not only man but God. (*Deus imaginatur mundum. Trinitas imaginata in creatura.*)[6] Formal dogma is *fictio s. imaginatio*; but its origin, its very existence, is a *revelation* of hidden contents which are not in accord with the *mundus sensibilis*. (Hence Tertullian's unsurpassable paradox.[7])

In the hope that it will make my standpoint somewhat clearer to you I am taking the liberty of sending you my little book *Psychology and Religion*, as a token of gratitude for the rich stimulation your book has afforded me.

Yours sincerely, C. G. JUNG

[4] "Without punishment no grace."
[5] The hidden (God).
[6] "God imagined the world. The Trinity is imaged in the creature." In spite of exhaustive inquiries the source remains unidentified. But cf. von Franz, *Aurora Consurgens: A Document Attributed to Thomas Aquinas*, p. 186, n. 141: "God created all visible things through imagination ($\phi\alpha\nu\tau\alpha\sigma\acute{\iota}\alpha$) and manifests himself in everything. . . . Thus the creative fantasy of God is contained in the visible world" (paraphrase of Scott, *Corpus Hermeticum*, I, p. 158). Cf. also *Psychology and Alchemy*, pars. 396, 399.
[7] Cf. Wegmann, 20 Nov. 45, n. 2.

To the owner of this book: Dr. Jürg Fierz

Writing a prefatory note to these *diversa* gives me a peculiar feeling. A collection of my essays from various times and situations of life is rather like a grasshopper with type on its feet jumping through the world of ideas, leaving occasional traces behind it; and it requires a considerable effort of imagination to reconstruct from the zigzag track of these footprints the nature of the animal that produced them. I envy no one this task, as I myself have a distaste for autobiography. The immense expanse of vaguely recognizable objects in the world has lured me forth to those twilit border zones where the figure I have meanwhile become steps towards me. The long path I have traversed is littered with husks sloughed off, witnesses of countless moultings, those *relicta* one calls books. They conceal as much as they reveal. Every step is a symbol of those to follow. He who mounts a flight of steps does not linger on them, nor look back at them, even though age invites him to linger or slow his pace. The great wind of the peaks roars ever more loudly in his ears. His gaze sweeps distances that flee away into the infinite. The last steps are the loveliest and most precious, for they lead to that fullness to reach which the innermost essence of man is born.

Küsnacht, 21 December 1945   C. G. JUNG

☐ A dedication which Jung wrote for a bound volume of his own offprints prepared by F., literary editor of the *Weltwoche* (cf. Fierz, 10 Apr. 42, n. ☐). Although, strictly speaking, not a letter it is included here for the sake of its personal expression and human interest.

Anonymous

Dear Sir,   10 July 1946

By parental power is usually understood the influence exerted by any person in authority. If this influence occurs in childhood and in an unjustified way, as happened in your case, it is apt to take root in the unconscious. Even if the influence is discontinued outwardly, it still goes on working in the unconscious and then one treats oneself as badly as one was treated earlier. If your work now gives you some joy and satisfaction you must cultivate it, just as you should cultivate

☐ Resident of Germany.

everything that gives you some joy in being alive. The idea of suicide, understandable as it is, does not seem commendable to me. We live in order to attain the greatest possible amount of spiritual development and self-awareness. As long as life is possible, even if only in a minimal degree, you should hang on to it, in order to scoop it up for the purpose of conscious development. To interrupt life before its time is to bring to a standstill an experiment which we have not set up. We have found ourselves in the midst of it and must carry it through to the end. That it is extraordinarily difficult for you, with your blood pressure at 80, is quite understandable, but I believe you will not regret it if you cling on even to such a life to the very last. If, aside from your work, you read a good book, as one reads the Bible, it can become a bridge for you leading inwards, along which good things may flow to you such as you perhaps cannot now imagine.

You have no need to worry about the question of a fee. With best wishes,

Yours sincerely, C. G. JUNG

To Eleanor Bertine

[ORIGINAL IN ENGLISH]

Dear Dr. Bertine, 25 July 1946

. . .

I'm just spending a most agreeable time of rest in my tower and enjoy sailing as the only sport which is still available to me. I have just finished two lectures for the Eranos meeting of this summer.[1] It is about the general problem of the psychology of the unconscious and its philosophical implications.

And now I have finally rest and peace enough to be able to read your former letters and to answer them. I should have thanked you for your careful reports about Kristine Mann's illness and death long ago,[2] but I never found time enough to do so. There have been so many urgent things to be done that all my time was eaten up and I cannot work so quickly any longer as I used to do.

It is really a question whether a person affected by such a terrible

---

[1] Combined as "Der Geist der Psychologie," Eranos Jahrbuch 1946; published in revised form as "Theoretische Ueberlegungen zum Wesen des Psychischen," Von den Wurzeln des Bewusstseins (1954); now "On the Nature of the Psyche," CW 8.
[2] Cf. Kristine Mann, 1 Feb. 45. M. had died on 12 Nov. 45.

illness should or may end her life. It is my attitude in such cases not to interfere. I would let things happen if they were so, because I'm convinced that if anybody has it in himself to commit suicide, then practically the whole of his being is going that way. I have seen cases where it would have been something short of criminal to hinder the people because according to all rules it was in accordance with the tendency of their unconscious and thus the basic thing. So I think nothing is really gained by interfering with such an issue. It is presumably to be left to the free choice of the individual. Anything that seems to be wrong to us can be right under certain circumstances over which we have no control and the end of which we do not understand. If Kristine Mann had committed suicide under the stress of unbearable pain, I should have thought that this was the right thing. As it was not the case, I think it was in her stars to undergo such a cruel agony for reasons that escape our understanding. Our life is not made entirely by ourselves. The main bulk of it is brought into existence out of sources that are hidden to us. Even complexes can start a century or more before a man is born. There is something like karma.

Kristine's experience[3] you mention is truly of a transcendent nature. If it were the effect of morphine it would occur regularly, but it doesn't. On the other hand it bears all the characteristics of an *ekstasis*. Such a thing is possible only when there is a detachment of the soul from the body. When that takes place and the patient lives on, one can almost with certainty expect a certain deterioration of the character inasmuch as the superior and most essential part of the soul has already left. Such an experience denotes a partial death. It is of course a most aggravating experience for the environment, as a person whose personality is so well known seems to lose it completely and shows nothing more than demoralization or the disagreeable symptoms of a drug-addict. But it is the lower man that keeps on living with the body and who is nothing else but the life of the body. With old people or persons seriously ill, it often happens that they have peculiar states of withdrawal or absent-mindedness, which they them-

---

[3] About 3 or 4 months before her death, while in hospital with a good deal of pain, depressed and unhappy, Dr. Mann saw one morning an ineffable light glowing in her room. It lasted for about an hour and a half and left her with a deep sense of peace and joy. The recollection of it remained indelible, although after that experience her state of health worsened steadily and her mind deteriorated. Jung felt that at the time of the experience her spirit had left her body.

selves cannot explain, but which are presumably conditions in which the detachment takes place. It is sometimes a process that lasts very long. What is happening in such conditions one rarely has a chance to explore, but it seems to me that it is as if such conditions had an inner consciousness which is so remote from our matter-of-fact consciousness that it is almost impossible to retranslate its contents into the terms of our actual consciousness. I must say that I have had some experiences along that line. They have given me a very different idea about what death means.

I hope you will forgive me that I'm so late in answering your previous letters. As I said, there has been so much in between that I needed a peaceful time when I could risk entering into the contents of your letter.

My best wishes!

Yours sincerely, c. g. j u n g

To Father Victor White

[ORIGINAL IN ENGLISH]

Dear Father White,   18 December 1946

Thank you for your dear letter. It is a great consolation to know that one's included in the prayers of fellow beings. The *aspectus mortis*[1] is a mighty lonely thing, when you are so stripped of everything in the presence of God. One's wholeness is tested mercilessly. An accumulation of drugs however necessary has made a complete rag of myself. I had to climb out of that mess and I am now whole again. Yesterday I had a marvellous dream: One bluish diamond, like a star high in heaven, reflected in a round quiet pool—heaven

☐ (Handwritten in pencil.)

[1] Over a month earlier Jung had had a very serious heart embolism. His letter is written by hand, apparently lying down. It is the first of a long series of hand-written letters, often of many pages, showing his great personal interest in the correspondence with W., who seemed able to give Jung what he felt he needed most: a man with whom he could discuss on equal terms matters of vital importance to him. It is significant that with the growing estrangement over the problem of the *privatio boni* (cf. White, 31 Dec. 49, n. 11) the handwritten letters are replaced by dictated, typed ones, except for the very last two (25 Mar. 60, 30 Apr. 60), written during W.'s fatal illness. About three-quarters of Jung's letters to him, comprising all the important discussions of psychological and religious problems, are published in this selection, but some of a too private nature are omitted.

69

above, heaven below.[2] The *imago Dei* in the darkness of the earth, this is myself. The dream meant a great consolation. I am no more a black and endless sea of misery and suffering but a certain amount thereof contained in a divine vessel. I am very weak. The situation dubious. Death does not seem imminent, although an embolism can occur anytime again. I confess I am afraid of a long drawn-out suffering. It seems to me as if I am ready to die, although as it looks to me some powerful thoughts are still flickering like lightnings in a summer night. Yet they are not mine, they belong to God, as everything else which bears mentioning.

Please write again to me. You have a purity of purpose which is beneficial. Thank you for the records, quite interesting!

I don't know whether I can answer your next letter again. But let us hope. Gratefully,

Yours, c. g. jung

[2] From the alchemical saying:

Heaven above	All that is above
Heaven below	Also is below
Stars above	Grasp this
Stars below	And rejoice.

Cf. "The Psychology of the Transference," CW 16, par. 384.

To Philip Wylie

[ORIGINAL IN ENGLISH]

Dear Mr. Wylie: 19 February 1947

I have owed you a letter for a long time. Unfortunately your *Generation of Vipers*[1] has been hidden from my sight for quite a time, and when I began to read it last fall I fell seriously ill—your book was not the cause of it!—and now I'm just slowly recovering. No sooner could I open my eyes again that I continued reading your book and have read it from cover to cover with the most intense interest. You can shock people sky-high, and apparently they need it.

I have enjoyed your book thoroughly, although I must confess I

☐ (1902–1971), American author. Jung had met him in the U.S.A. in 1936 and had visited him at the time of his Terry Lectures on "Psychology and Religion" at Yale U. in 1937. — This letter and Wylie 27 June 47 are published by courtesy of Princeton University Library and Mrs. Philip Wylie.
[1] Pub. 1942. Cf. White, 19 Dec. 47, for further comment.

felt critical at certain passages. For instance: 'The affair of the ecclesiastical Jesus is not so damn simple as your critique seems to suggest. Half of the picture you paint is absolutely true and I can subscribe to every word of it. All that dogmatic stuff heaped around the figure of the Redeemer can be brushed aside easily if you swing your rationalistic broom, but you overlook entirely the fact that out of that philosophic and speculative scholasticism something has grown which you cannot wipe off the slate, and that is science and the scientific attitude, which is characterized by sincerity, devotion, and honesty. As William James rightly said: "Our scientific temper is devout."[2]

Although your book is modest enough not to claim to be more than a *Kulturkritik* of America, it is valid also for our European civilization, if one is still allowed to speak of such a thing. With some slight variations your book is applicable to almost any cultured nation. I'm now busy spreading its fame over here in Switzerland, and I try to get it known as much as possible.

At the moment when I had finished reading the *Generation of Vipers* your book *On Morals*[3] arrived, which I'm going to read at once.

In a further edition of your *Generation of Vipers* you should add an illustration of Grant Wood's wonderful painting: Daughters of Revolution.[4]

I hear complaints from all sides that my books are not getatable in the U. S. I can tell you now that an English firm is going to publish all my books in a decent form as a complete edition.[5] But that will take its time, particularly under the present economic conditions prevailing in England.

There is a real need of books like yours, because somebody ought to wake up, since mankind has now reached the straight road to hell.

Thank you for your honesty and courage!

Yours sincerely, C. G. JUNG

---

[2] *Pragmatism* (1907), p. 15.

[3] *An Essay on Morals* (1947); see Wylie, 27 June 47, par. 2.

[4] Wood (1891–1942) was known for his paintings of the American scene. *Daughters of Revolution* satirizes bigoted mother-types.

[5] Routledge & Kegan Paul Ltd., London, and the Bollingen Foundation, through Pantheon Books Inc., New York, collaborated in publishing the Collected Works.

71

To Julia Schmid-Lohner

Dear Frau Schmid-Lohner, 20 May 1947

I think I can set your mind at rest in regard to your question whether the days of the gospel are numbered. People will read the gospel again and again and I myself read it again and again. But they will read it with much more profit if they have some insight into their own psyches. Blind are the eyes of anyone who does not know his own heart, and I always recommend the application of a little psychology so that he can understand things like the gospel still better.

Yours sincerely, C. G. JUNG

☐ Biel, Switzerland.

To Erich Neumann

Dear Colleague, 1 July 1947

The only disturbing term that struck me as I read your first volume[1] was the so-called "castration complex." I regard this term not only as an aesthetic mistake but also as an erroneous overvaluation of sexual symbolisms. This complex actually has to do with the archetype of sacrifice, a far more comprehensive term and one which takes account of the fact that for primitives sex does not have anything like the significance it has for us. In primitive psychology one must always bear in mind that the search for food, or hunger, often plays a decisive role. Thus the symbols of sacrifice are not just castrations or derivates of the same, as is especially obvious when you consider the taboos, all of which have a sacrificial meaning. The tabooing of words or syllables, for instance, can only be derived from castration by sheer force. Rather we must look at actual or alleged castration in the light of the archetype of sacrifice, which would make all these manifold forms far easier to understand in an unobjectionable way. The term "castration complex" is much too concretistic for my taste and too one-sided, although there are plenty of phenomena to which it proves perfectly applicable. But I would have avoided everything that gives the appearance of deriving psychic events from a specific instinct. We must put the essence of the psyche at the beginning as a

[1] First part of the MS of *The Origins and History of Consciousness*.

72

phenomenon *sui generis* and understand the instincts as being in a special relationship to it. If we don't do this, all psychic differentiation is at bottom "nothing but." And then what does one do with a castrated Origen?[2]

This is the only point I must take exception to. For the rest I must say that I deeply admire your lucid exposition, crammed full of ideas. I have spoken with Rascher and he says he is ready to take on the book, but not until next year because of business reasons. An unavoidable lowering of prices is expected, and this makes all publishers hesitant. If I should come across anything else I will let you know. I shall now scrutinize your smaller writings[3] more closely, as there is a chance that Rascher will eventually bring out a collection of them. But this question has not been clarified yet. So you see that since things are going better with me I am busying myself with your affairs and doing my best to facilitate publication. But it's not all that simple in view of the scope of your work. Meanwhile with best regards,

Ever sincerely yours, C . G . J U N G

[2] Origen castrated himself in literal interpretation of Matthew 19:12: ". . . there be eunuchs, which have made themselves eunuchs for the kingdom of heaven's sake." Cf. *Psychological Types*, pars. 21ff.

[3] Not identifiable in detail. Among them was the first draft of *Depth Psychology and a New Ethic* (1969; orig. 1949).

To Erich Neumann

Dear Colleague,   Bollingen, 19 July 1947

What I can do for your extremely valuable works I will do with pleasure. Unfortunately everything has been greatly delayed by my illness, which cost me a tidy ½ year. In old age time presses and the years become ever fewer, i.e., it is plain to behold: *Utendum est aetate, cito pede labitur aetas / Nec bona tam sequitur quam bona prima fuit!*[1]

I cannot deny the justification for the term "castration complex" and still less its symbolism, but I must dispute that "sacrifice" is not a symbol. In the Christian sense it is actually one of the most im-

□ (Handwritten.)

[1] "Hurry with the time, for time rushes with fleet foot, and that which follows is not as good as the one that was." Ovid, *Ars amatoria*, 3, 65.

portant symbols. The etymology² is obscure: there is as much to be said for *offerre* [to offer] as for *operari* [to effect, to be active]. "Sacrifice" is both active and passive: one *offers* a sacrifice and one *is* a sacrifice. (Both together in the sacrifice symbolism in the Mass!) It is the same with *incest,* for which reason I had to supplement it with the concept of the *hierosgamos.* Just as the pair of concepts "incest/hierosgamos" describes the whole situation, so does "castration/sacrifice." Couldn't one, to proceed cautiously, say instead of castration complex castration *symbol,* or castration *motif* (like incest motif)?

You have still to go through the experience of being misunderstood. The possibilities are beyond conception. Perhaps you had better insert in your text a short explanation of the negative and positive aspects of the symbol, right at the beginning where you speak of the castration complex.

I very much hope it will be possible for you to come to Switzerland. At the moment I am enjoying my urgently needed holiday in my tower on the Upper Lake. Our Club wants to found a "C.G. Jung Institute for Complex Psychology." Preparations are already in progress. Frau Jaffé will be secretary. She has written a magnificent essay on E.T.A. Hoffmann which I shall publish in my *Psychologische Abhandlungen.*³

I am doing pretty well, but feel the burden of my 73 years. With best regards,

Your devoted C. G. JUNG

² The German word for "sacrifice" is *Opfer,* offering. Cf. *Psychology and Alchemy,* par. 417.
³ The essay was published in *Gestaltungen des Unbewussten = Psychologische Abhandlungen,* VII.

To Aniela Jaffé

Dear Aniela,   Bollingen, 10 August 1947

I thank you with all my heart for your response to my "Trinity": I couldn't imagine a more beautiful one. It is a "total" reaction, and it had a "total" effect on me too. You have perfectly imaged what I imagined into my work. It again became clear to me from your letter how much one misses when one receives no response or a mere frag-

□ (Handwritten.)

ment, and what a joy it is to experience the opposite—a creative resonance which is at the same time like a revelation of the feminine being. It is as though a wine, which by dint of toil and sweat, worry and care has finally become mature and good, were being poured into a precious beaker. Without this receptacle and acceptance a man's work remains a delicate child, followed with doubting eyes and released into the world with inner anxiety. But when a soul opens to the work, it is as though a seed were lodged in good earth, or the gates of a city were closed in the evening, so that it can enjoy surer repose.

I thank you.

Cordially, C.G.J.

To Gualthernus H. Mees

[ORIGINAL IN ENGLISH]

Dear Dr. Mees,   15 September 1947

I'm very sorry indeed that I had no chance to answer your three letters[1] which I have received in the last years. First I couldn't because we were surrounded on all sides by the Nazis and later on I had two serious illnesses which have prevented me from coping with my enormous mail. Thus I'm also late in answering your last letter which somehow got snowed under.

I often thought of you and I'm very sorry to hear that you had a bad time. I hope that by now you have recovered completely from your ailments.

I was very much interested in your news about the Maharshi.[2] I'm well aware of the fact that my very Western criticism of such a phenomenon as the Maharshi was rather upsetting to you. I consider a man's life lived for 65 years in perfect balance as most unfortunate. I'm glad that I haven't chosen to live such a miracle. It is so utterly inhuman that I can't see for the life of me any fun in it. It is surely very wonderful but think of being wonderful year in year out! More-

---

□ Dutch sociologist whom Jung had met in India, and pupil of Shri Ramana Maharshi. He founded his own ashram in Travancore.

[1] One letter is from 1944, another from 1945, and the last from Feb. 1947.

[2] Jung edited Zimmer's book on the Maharshi, *Der Weg zum Selbst: Lehre und Leben des indischen Heiligen Shri Ramana Maharshi aus Tiruvannamalai* (1944) (Zimmer died in 1943) and wrote an introduction to it: "The Holy Men of India," CW 11.

over I think it is generally much more advisable not to identify with the self. I quite appreciate the fact that such a model is of high paedagogical value to India. Right now such a wonderful example of balance would be most needed in the Punjab or in Calcutta or in the respective governments of Hindustan and Pakistan.[3]

Concerning Zimmer's book I must say that I had no hand in its publication except that I took it in hand to be published by my Swiss publisher. Thus I was fully unaware of how the text came into existence or what its defects are. I had to leave the entire responsibility to my friend Zimmer who was a great admirer of the Maharshi.

I'm sorry that I was under the impression when we met in Trivandrum[4] that you introduced your friend Raman Pillai[5] as a remote pupil of Shri Ramana. This however doesn't matter very much, since the basic coincidence of most of the Indian teaching is so overwhelmingly great that it means little whether the author is called Ramakrishna[6] or Vivekananda[7] or Shri Aurobindo,[8] etc.

I only hope that you didn't endanger your health too much! It must be awful to live in a continuous sweat-bath for 6 months of the year. I should much appreciate it if you could once enlighten me about the Maharshi's daily activities. I wonder wherein his self-realization consists and what he actually did do. We know this running away business from parents etc. with our saints too![9] But some of them have done something tangible—if it was only a crusade or something like a book or the *Canto di Sole*.[10] I had a chance, when I was in Madras, to see the Maharshi, but by that time I was so imbued with the overwhelming Indian atmosphere of irrelevant wisdom and with the obvious Maya of this world that I didn't care any more if there had been twelve Maharshis on top of each other. I was pro-

[3] The partition of British India into the two Dominions of India and Pakistan in July 1947 was followed by the mutual massacre of Indians and Moslems.
[4] During his stay in India, in 1938, Jung was invited to give two lectures at the U. of Trivandrum, capital of Travancore.
[5] Jung refers to Raman Pillai, without mentioning his name, in "The Holy Men of India," par. 578: "In Trivandrum . . . I ran across a disciple of the Maharshi. He was an unassuming little man . . . modest, kindly, devout, and childlike . . . a man who had absorbed the wisdom of the Maharshi with utter devotion . . . I acknowledge with deep gratitude this meeting with him."
[6] Indian holy man and ascetic (1834–1886). Cf. ibid., pars. 958, 962.
[7] Indian religious reformer, pupil of Ramakrishna (1862–1902).
[8] Shri Aurobindo Ghose (1870–1950), religious reformer.
[9] For instance, Niklaus von der Flüe. Cf. Blanke, 2 May 45, n. 9.
[10] The *Canto di Sole* of St. Francis of Assisi.

foundly overawed and the black pagoda of Bhuvaneshvara[11] took all the air out of me. India is marvellous, unique, and I wish I could stand once more on Cape Comorin[12] and know once more that this world is an incurable illusion. This is a very helpful and salutary insight, when you must not live daily in this damn machinery and these undeniable realities which behave exactly as if they were real.

I'm sending this to the address you gave me in Holland, hoping that it will be forwarded to you if you have left.

Yours sincerely, c. g. j u n g

[11] Presumably the ruined sun temple at Konarak, to which a road leads from Bhuvaneshvara. The "Black Pagoda," Surya Deul, is famous for its erotic sculptures. Cf *Memories*, pp. 277f./259f., and "What India Can Teach Us," CW 10, par. 1013. Cf. also *Aion*, par. 339, n. 1.
[12] Cape Comorin is the southernmost point of India.

Anonymous

From a letter of condolence, 1947

. . . I was grieved for him. Now he has vanished and stepped outside time, as all of us will do after him. Life, so-called, is a short episode between two great mysteries, which yet are one. I cannot mourn the dead. They endure, but we pass over. . .

To Father Victor White

[ORIGINAL IN ENGLISH]

Dear Victor,   30 January 1948

Many thanks for your personal willingness to contribute to our endeavours![1] I have not yet heard from Rome.

Many thanks also for the other contents of your letters! It took me a while to digest everything properly. I am particularly glad that you have sent me your dream you had at a time (1945) when you did not yet know me personally. It is very helpful to me. Your interpretation is quite correct as far as it goes. Of course the dream leads up to our personal discussion; it paves the way to it. Thus I am still left some-

☐ (Handwritten.)
[1] Cf. White, 27 Dec. 47, n. 7. W.'s letter has not been preserved, but from Jung's next sentence it appears that W. had tried to interest the higher Catholic authorities in Rome in the C. G. Jung Institute.

what as the representative of the argument pro S. Spiritu.[2] But the argument started in yourself. It is quite clear that the unconscious insists rather vehemently upon the problem of the S. Spir., which I can confirm from many of my own dreams, including the one I have sent to you, i.e., the one about the *senex venerabilis*.[3] In your dream you are separated from me and connected with me by an anima-figure,[4] as by the *platform*,[5] by which you are either separated from the sea or enabled to reach it. Further on in Zurich you must celebrate Mass *among the women*.[6] The female factor, i.e., the anima, is the bridge and the *conditio sine qua non*. The unknowable *Veritas Prima*[7] solved the problem for the time being.

The emphasis on the anima means of course the totality of man: male plus female = conscious plus unconscious. Whatever the unconscious and whatever the S. Spir. is, the unconscious realm of the psyche is the place where the living Spirit that is more than man manifests itself. I should not hesitate to call your dream a manifestation of the S. Spir. that leads you on to deeper understanding, away from the narrowness of formulas and concepts to the living truth.

Something similar happened in my dream,[8] of which, unfortunately, I have given you the mere outlines. While I stood before the bed of the Old Man, I thought and felt: *Indignus sum Domine*.[9] I know Him very well: He was my "guru" more than 30 years ago,[10] a real ghostly guru—but that is a long and—I am afraid—exceedingly strange story. It has been since confirmed to me by an old Hindu.[11] You see, something has taken me out of Europe and the Occident and has opened for me the gates of the East as well, so that I should understand something of the *human* mind.

Soon after this particular dream, I had another one continuing a

---

[2] In W.'s dream Jung was talking about the Holy Ghost as manifested in the unconscious.

[3] The dream mentioned in White, 19 Dec. 47, par. 3.

[4] Jung's wife was sitting between them.

[5] He was outside a house by the seashore, but separated from the sea by a raised platform.

[6] He had to celebrate Mass in a nuns' chapel.

[7] The dream ends with W. explaining to Jung "St. Thomas Aquinas' teaching about Faith in the Unknown and Unseen Veritas Prima."

[8] See n. 3 above.

[9] "I am not worthy, Lord."

[10] The fantasy of Philemon who represented "superior insight." Cf. *Memories*, p. 183/176.

[11] Ibid., p. 184/177.

subject alluded to in the former dream, viz. the figure of the priest, the head of the library. His carriage and the fact that he unexpectedly had a short grey beard reminded me strongly of my own father. The second dream[12] is very long and has many scenes, of which I can only relate the last one. In all parts of the dream I was concerned with my father. In the last scene I was in *his house* on the ground floor, very much preoccupied by a peculiar question which had been raised at the beginning of the dream: "How is it possible that my mother celebrates her 70th birthday in this year 1948 while I am reaching my 74th year?" My father is going to answer it and he takes me up with him to the first floor by way of a narrow winding staircase in the wall. Coming out on the 1st floor, we find ourselves in a (circular) gallery, from which a small bridge leads to an isolated cuplike platform in the centre of the room. (The room has otherwise no floor, it is open down to the ground floor.) From the platform a narrow staircase, almost a ladder, leads up to a small door high up in the wall. I know this is *his* room. The moment we enter the bridge, I fall on my knees, completely overcome by the sudden understanding that my father is going to lead me into the "supreme presence." By sympathy he kneels at my side and I try to touch the ground with my forehead. I almost reach it and there I woke up.

The peculiar 1st floor is exactly like the famous *diwan-i-khas* (hall of audience) of Akbar the Great[13] in Fatehpur-Sikri, where he used to discuss philosophy and religion with the representatives of all philosophies and all creeds.

Oh yes, it is my way all right. I don't despise the fish.[14] I am glad you share it with me. I can eat fish on Fridays. I have brethren and sisters in the spirit and where once I felt godforsaken and really lonely, there was my guru. Surely there is something the matter with the solitary man;[15] if he is not a beast, he is conscious of St. Paul's words: τοῦ γὰρ καὶ γένος ἐσμέν.[16] The Divine Presence is more than

---

[12] Ibid., pp. 218f./207f.

[13] Ibid. Akbar the Great, Jalal ud-Din Mohammed (1542–1605), the greatest of the Mogul emperors of India. Fatehpur-Sikri was one of his capitals.

[14] In a letter of 3 Jan. 48 W. reported a dream in which he and Jung were having a meal together on a Friday. W. was surprised when Jung asked him to pass the fish to him, since he, as a non-Catholic, was under no obligation to abstain from meat.

[15] In the same letter W. quoted Aristotle's words: "The solitary man is either a beast or a god."

[16] Acts 17:28: "For we also are his offspring." Quotation from the Stoic Aratus of Soli, *Phaenomena*.

anything else. There is more than one way to the rediscovery of the *genus divinum* in us. This is the only thing that really matters. Was there ever a more solitary man than St. Paul? Even his "evangelium" came to him immediately and he was up against the men in Jerusalem as well as the whole Roman Empire. I wanted the proof of a living Spirit and I got it. Don't ask me at what a price.

When I said that the Protestant has to digest his sins alone, I really meant: he must carry them, because how can God take him with his sins if he does not carry them? if he has been relieved from the weight of his burden?

Concerning "barracks"[17] you are quite right; they mean submission and discipline, of which I could tell you a very long story indeed. Whoever has clearly understood what it means: *Qui fidelis est in minimo*,[18] is overwhelmed with the dire necessity of submission and discipline of a subtler kind than the *regula S. Benedicti*. I don't want to prescribe a way to other people, because I know that my way has been prescribed to me by a hand far above my reach.

I know it all sounds so damned grand. I am sorry that it does, but I don't mean it. *It* is grand, and I am only trying to be a decent tool and don't feel grand at all.

Happily the cloud of sleeplessness has lifted recently. My brain had been too active. My paper about the Ἰχθύς[19] has disturbed the tranquillity of my mind in its deepest layers, as you can imagine.

In a Catholic Journal (published by Routledge and Sons)[20] a somebody "condemns" my Essays on Cont. Hist.[21] because my attitude to religion and to rational philosophy is, as he says, "ambiguous." *O sancta simplicitas*!

I hope that your writing is progressing and that you enjoy your interesting holiday in U.S. I have just read Kravchenko's book on Russia.[22] Worth reading! You get an idea of the *princeps hujus mundi* and his remarkable works.

Cordially yours, C. G.

---

[17] Cf. White, 19 Dec. 47, par. 3.

[18] Luke 16:10: "He that is faithful in that which is least."

[19] Cf. White, 19 Dec. 47, n. 6.

[20] According to a communication from Routledge & Kegan Paul, London, they never published a Catholic journal.

[21] *Essays on Contemporary Events* (1947). The essays are republished in CW 10 and 16.

[22] Victor Kravchenko, *I Chose Freedom* (1947). He was a former Soviet spy whose revelations about conditions in Russia and Russian espionage created a sensation.

P.S. My mother = anima is younger than myself.[23] When I was 3 years old I had my first anima-experience,[24] the woman that was *not* my mother. It means a lot that escapes me for the time being.

[23] Cf. the statement in Jung's second dream that his mother was 70 when he was reaching 74.
[24] *Memories*, p. 8/22f.

To C. R. Birnie

[ORIGINAL IN ENGLISH]

Dear Dr. Birnie, 14 May 1948

. . .

I have never come across a case where a woman actually had a child by her own father, but I've seen a number of cases where such consequences might easily have happened, i.e., incest with father and mother. The actual event of incest means nearly always a terrific blow to the psychic structure, except in cases of very primitive minds. The incest has the importance of a real trauma. Its effect is a fixation to the time and the circumstances of the incest as well as to the person of the perpetrator. This is the meaning of the dream that repeats itself in your case.[1] She is still her father's prisoner. A dream that repeats itself always refers to one and the same psychological situation that lasts as long as the dream repeats itself. The unconscious brings up the fact as a sort of compensatory act with the intention that it should be remembered and introduced into consciousness. As it [incest] is a trauma it is always held at bay and is partially repressed. It cannot be assimilated and so the dream brings it back in the more or less vain hope that consciousness will be able to assimilate it. It can be assimilated provided that consciousness understands the symbolic meaning of the event. Consciousness, of course, is exclusively fascinated by the external moral and factual aspect of the act. But that is not enough: the main point is that incest arouses an archaic level of mind (which I call the collective unconscious) in which one finds a highly archaic meaning of paternal incest.

☐ London.
[1] B. reported the recurrent dream of a woman of 35 who "at the age of 23 had a child by her supposed father." In the dream "she was locked in a dark room with a window" and "a door outside which her father stood." It was the actual room in which her father had locked her "from early childhood in order to coerce her into sexual acts."

When one has to treat such a condition, one ought to get the patient to reproduce the (unconscious) fantasies round the incest, applying the method of active imagination if the dreams don't produce the necessary stuff.

. . .

There is an interesting difference between maternal and paternal incest as the former is more archaic and affects the feeling life of the son. Paternal incest on the other hand is of a more recent nature and affects the mind of the daughter, because the father has to do with everything that is mental and spiritual. In such a case a thorough explanation of the mental and spiritual implications of the incestuous act is unavoidable, since its nature is highly symbolical and as a rule refers to the sacred mysteries of the faith, namely to the myth of Mary who gives rebirth to her father in producing his son ("qui de sa fille fit sa mère").[2] In the mediaeval representations of the Antichrist you always find a careful description of how the father (the devil) has sexual intercourse with his daughter and thereby produces the Antichrist. This is one of the classic representations of the archetype of paternal incest. I'm afraid it is a pretty complicated business.

. . .

Sincerely yours, C. G. JUNG

[2] "[God] who made his daughter into his mother." Quotation from Chrétien de Troyes, 12th cent. poet, author of *Le Conte du Graal*. For the reverse of this process cf. Dante, *Paradiso*, XXXIII, 1: "O Virgin Mother, daughter of thy son."

To Father Victor White

[ORIGINAL IN ENGLISH]

Dear Victor! 21 May 1948

Finally I am able to write to you. I thank you very much for your excellent lecture on Gnosticism.[1] I much admire your balanced judgment and your just evaluation of a subject that has been so often represented in a wrong light and misunderstood by all sorts of comprehensible and incomprehensible prejudices. Your presentation of

☐ (Handwritten.)
[1] The lecture was read to the Analytical Psychology Club of New York, 20 Feb. 48, and to the Guild of Pastoral Psychology, London, 10 Dec. 48; published Apr. 49 as Lecture No. 59.

the Pistis Sophia[2] is excellent. Among the patristic writers about Gnosticism I missed Hippolytos,[3] the most thorough and the most intelligent of all. Epiphanius,[4] who shares the former's lot, does not deserve much praise. Your paper has made me think: *Have I faith or a faith or not?* I have always been unable to produce faith and I have tried so hard that I finally did not know any more what faith is or means. I owe it to your paper that I have now apparently an answer: faith or the equivalent of faith with me is what I would call *respect*. I have respect for the Christian Truth. Thus it seems to come down to an involuntary assumption in me that there is something to the dogmatic truth, something *indefinable* to begin with. Yet I feel respect for it, although I don't really understand it. But I can say my life-work is essentially an attempt to understand what others apparently can believe. There must be—so I conclude—a rather strong motive-power connected with the Christian Truth, otherwise it would not be explicable why it influences me to such an extent. My respect is—mind you—involuntary; it is a "datum" of irrational nature. This *is* the nearest I can get to what appears to me as "faith." There is however nothing specific in it, since I feel the same kind of respect for the basic teachings of Buddhism and the fundamental Taoist ideas. In the case of the Christian Truth one would be inclined to explain this *a priori* respect through my Christian education. Yet the same cannot be said in the case of Buddhism, Taoism and certain aspects of Islam. Hindu theology curiously enough never had the same appeal, although it has gripped my intellect at times quite powerfully.

Gnosticism has renewed its vitality with me recently, as I was deeply concerned with the question of how the figure of Christ was received into Hellenistic nature-philosophy and hence into alchemy. A little book[5] has grown out of such studies within the last months.

---

[2] = Trustful Wisdom, title of a Gnostic work in Coptic; tr. Mead, *Pistis Sophia* (1921).

[3] Bishop of Portus Romanus (d. ca. 230), Greek writer of the Early Church. His writings, rediscovered only in the 19th cent. and at first attributed to Origen, are an indispensable source for the teachings of Gnosticism. His *Philosophumena; or, The Refutation of All Heresies* (tr. 1921) is copiously quoted in Jung's later works, under the title *Elenchos*.

[4] Epiphanius, bishop of Constantia (ca. 315–402), Church Father who in his youth was greatly influenced by Gnostic teachings. His main work is *Panarion*, a treatise on heresies.

[5] *Aion*.

It will be, I am afraid, a shocking and difficult book. It has reduced me to a most curious attempt to formulate the progress of symbolism within the last two thousand years through the figure of 4 quaternities[6] based upon 2 quaterniones of the Naassenes[7] as mentioned by Hippolytos. The first one is the so-called Moses-quaternio.[8]

. . .

Well, it is a mad thing, which I cannot explain here but it seems *hellishly important* in so far as it winds up with the physical time-space quaternio.[9] The whole seems to be logically watertight.

I feel reasonably well and hope you do the same. You must have had an interesting time. A Jesuit professor of theology at Louvain[10] is coming to see me next week. They begin to sit up. Looking forward to the summer, when I hope to see you again at Bollingen,

Yours cordially, c. g.

[6] Ibid., ch. XIV. The quaternios are on pp. 227, 231, 236, 238.

[7] A Gnostic sect in which the serpent (*naas* from Hebrew *nachasch*) occupied a central place of worship. Cf. *Psychology and Alchemy*, par. 527.

[8] Here follows a sketch, with short commentary, of the quaternio in *Aion*, p. 227.

[9] Ibid., p. 252.

[10] Probably Father Raymond Hostie. At that time, however, he was not a professor of theology but still a seminarist at Louvain. Later he became professor of the Faculty of the Society of Jesus in Louvain and wrote a book, *Du mythe à la réligion*, 1955 (tr., *Religion and the Psychology of Jung*, 1957), of which Jung disapproved strongly (cf. Hostie, 25 Apr. 55).

To Jürg Fierz

Dear Dr. Fierz,   13 January 1949

Above all you must realize that I am not in the habit of interfering with my pupils. I have neither the right nor the might to do that. They can draw such conclusions as seem right to them and must accept full responsibility for it. There have been so many pupils of mine who have fabricated every sort of rubbish from what they took over from me. I have never said that I stand "uncompromisingly" behind Neumann.[1] There is naturally no question of that. It should be obvious that I have my reservations.

[1] Neumann's *Depth Psychology and a New Ethic* had aroused considerable controversy (cf. Neumann, Dec. 1948).

84

If you want to understand Neumann properly you must realize that he is writing in the spiritual vacuum of Tel-Aviv. Nothing can come out of that place for the moment except a monologue. He writes as he fancies. No doubt this is provocative, but I have found that provocative books are by no means the worst. They get people's goat only because such people cannot be reached in any other way.

If people want to know what I think about these things they have my books, and everyone is free to listen to my views. They could just as well read my books instead of getting worked up about Neumann. If I recommend his book it is chiefly because it shows the sort of conclusions you come to when you ruthlessly think out ethical problems to the end. One must also remember that Neumann is a Jew and consequently knows Christianity only from the outside; and further, that it has been drastically demonstrated to the Jews that evil is continually projected. For the rest—where confession is concerned—it is indeed the case that if a person does not regard something as a sin he has no need to confess it. If Neumann recommends the "inner voice" as the criterion of ethical behaviour instead of the Christian conscience, this is in complete agreement with the Eastern view that in everybody's heart there dwells a judge who knows all his evil thoughts. In this respect Neumann also stands on the best footing with very many Christian mystics. If the mentally insane assert the same thing, that has always been so, only one should know that the voices of the insane are somewhat different from what Neumann calls the inner voice. Many insane people play themselves up as ethicists *par excellence* with no encouragement from Neumann. There is of course no external justification for the inner voice, for the simple reason that nobody knows what is good and what evil. It would all be terribly simple if we could go by the decalogue or the penal code or any other moral codex, since all the sins catalogued there are obviously so pointless or morbid that no reasonable person could fail to see how fatuous they are. Ethical decision is concerned with very much more complicated things, namely conflicts of duty, the most diabolical things ever invented and at the same time the loneliest ever dreamt of by the loneliest of all, the Creator of the world. In conflicts of duty one codex says Whoa there! and the other says Gee up! and you are none the wiser for it. It is an actual fact that what is good to one appears evil to the other. You have only to think of the careworn mother who meddles in all her son's doings—from the most selfless solicitude of course—but in reality with murderous

85

effect. For the mother it is naturally a good thing if the son does not do this and does not do that, and for the son it is simply moral and physical ruin—so scarcely a good thing.

You are quite right when you say that Neumann's individual ethic makes far heavier demands on us than the Christian ethic does. The only mistake Neumann commits here is a tactical one: he says out loud, imprudently, what was always true. As soon as an ethic is set up as an absolute it is a catastrophe. It can only be taken relatively, just as Neumann can only be understood relatively, that is, as a religious Jew of German extraction living in Tel-Aviv. If one imagines one can simply make a clean sweep of all views of the world, one is deceiving oneself: views of the world are grounded in archetypes, which cannot be tackled so easily. What Neumann offers us is the outcome of an intellectual operation which he had to accomplish for himself in order to gain a new basis for his ethic. As a doctor he is profoundly impressed by the moral chaos and feels himself in the highest degree responsible. Because of this responsibility he is trying to set the ethical problem to rights, not in order to give out a legal ukase but to clarify his ethical reflections, naturally in the expectation of doing this also for the world around him.

In reading such a book you must also consider what sort of a world we are living in. You know, perhaps, that today Christianity is relativized by the splitting of the Church into so-and-so many million Catholics and so-and-so many million Protestants and that Bolshevism reigns supreme from Thüringen to Vladivostok—and on top of this there is an East with several billion non-Christians who have their views of the world too. Since this world is one world we are faced with the question: How do we come to grips with it? We cannot simply restrict ourselves to *our* view of the world, but must perforce find a standpoint from which a view will be possible that goes a little step beyond the Christian as well as the Buddhist, etc. As a Christian you must exert yourself and make it your daily pre-occupation to bridge the woeful conflict in the Church by finding a mediating position. One cannot be simply Protestant or Catholic. That is much too facile, for in the end the one is the other's brother and this cannot be got rid of simply by declaring one of them invalid. Neumann postulates a position which in the deepest sense is valid for everyone. If there is an inner deciding factor it must be valid for all men. The question is only: Is there an inner voice, i.e., a vocation? Undoubtedly there isn't for 99% of humanity, just as a whole lot of

86

things don't exist for this vast majority for the simple reason that they don't know about them. There isn't even a quite ordinary hygiene which would be valid for more than about 90% of humanity, let alone a corresponding moral code. If ethical decision is not in the last resort somehow inherent in human nature, then the case is completely hopeless, for no book of laws has lasted in the long run. Subjectively I am absolutely convinced of the inner deciding factor and my practical work with patients aims exclusively at bringing it to consciousness. What you can learn from moral codes and manuals of morality and penal codes are practicalities which no intelligent person will overlook. But no book of laws has ever been written for conflicts of duty and there alone does the real ethical problem begin. There alone will you learn ethical responsibility. Everything else is settled by adaptation and plain horse sense. I do not regard it for a moment as particularly meritorious morally for a person to avoid everything that is customarily considered a sin. Ethical value attaches only to those decisions which are reached in situations of supreme doubt. That is the question that burns Neumann's soul and in this he has my support, no matter whether my position is relativized or not. I am no opportunist, but I observe in this respect certain fundamental ethical principles and not utilitarian ones.

If I were to write about ethics[2] I would naturally not express myself like Neumann. But neither am I the Neumann who has been pushed by an atrocious fate into a militant counterposition. If he has confronted the world with a difficulty which so-and-so many people have to torment themselves with, it does not surprise me in the least and I shall not fault him for that. Nor can I regret it if these so-called Christians are tormented a bit. They have richly deserved it. They are always gabbling about Christian morality and I would just like to see someone for once who really follows it. They can't muster even the slightest understanding for Neumann, let alone brotherly love. I only wish the Christians of today could see for once that what they stand for is not Christianity at all but a god-awful legalistic religion from which the founder himself tried to free them by following his voice and his vocation to the bitter end. Had he not done so there would never have been a Christianity. It is quite certain that the "community" will be outraged by this problem of an individual ethic, but that must be so for the question nowadays is: Community

---

[2] Cf. "A Psychological View of Conscience," CW 10.

of whom or with whom? Not community as such, for we have always had that and what was the result? The "people's community" in Germany and suchlike. It is high time people reflected how they are constituted or what is the constitution of the thing they want to introduce into a community. A bad cause is not made better by multiplying it by 10,000 and 100 rapscallions do not add up to a single decent man.

As a first rule for book-reading I would recommend you always to consider *who* the author is. We should have learnt by now that thoughts expressed by words never represent anything absolute, and that only the clueless make themselves new garments out of the rags of thought. With best regards,

Yours sincerely, C. G. JUNG

To Henri Flournoy

Dear Colleague,   29 March 1949

I have just read your sympathetic report of my work with particular pleasure. Thank you for the interest you have been good enough to take in the objective exposition of my ideas.

It interested me very much, however, to find in your epilogue a few references to the archetypes which seem to me to contain some misunderstandings. I do not deny the existence of facts whose existence Freud has proved. I do not believe in theories and have no intention at all of replacing his theory with another. What I intend is to demonstrate new facts—the existence of archetypes, for example —whose existence, moreover, has already been accepted by other sciences: in ethnology as *représentations collectives* (Lévy-Bruhl); in biology (Alverdes[1]); in history (Toynbee); in comparative mythology

□ (Translated from French.) Henri Flournoy, son of the Swiss psychiatrist Théodore Flournoy (1854–1920). T. Flournoy's translation of the "Miller Fantasies," i.e., "Quelques Faits d'imagination créatrice subconsciente" in *Archives de psychologie* (Geneva), V (1906), formed the starting point for Jung's *Symbols of Transformation.* Jung describes the role he played in his development in *Erinnerungen, Träume, Gedanken,* pp. 378f. (this section is omitted in the English and American ed.). In *Memories,* p. 162/158 he refers to him as his "revered and fatherly friend."

[1] Friedrich Alverdes, German zoologist. Cf. Jung, "Instinct and the Unconscious," CW 8, par. 282, n. 12, citing Alverdes, "Die Wirksamkeit von Archetypen in den Instinkthandlungen der Tiere," *Zoologischer Anzeiger* (Leipzig), CXIX, 9/10 (1937).

(Kerényi, Tucci,[2] Wilhelm, and Zimmer, representing ancient Greece, Tibet, China, and India); and in folklore as "motifs." The well known idea of the "behaviour pattern" in biology is synonymous with that of the archetype in psychology. As the term "archetypus" clearly shows, the idea is not even original; this notion is found with the same significance as early as in Philo Judaeus, in the *Corpus Hermeticum*, and in Dionysius the Areopagite. My inventiveness consists in nothing but the fact that I believe I have proved that archetypes do not appear only in the "migration of symbols"[3] but in the individual unconscious fantasies of everyone without exception. I have furnished proof of this in several large volumes which unfortunately have not yet been published in French. As I see it, the idea of a psychic "pattern of behaviour" is not at all astonishing, since the similarity of autochthonous psychic products was admitted to be a fact even by Freud. His is the honour of having discovered the first archetype, the Oedipus complex. That is a mythological and a psychological motif simultaneously. But obviously it is no more than a single archetype, the one representing the son's relationship to his parents. So there must be others, since there is still the daughter's relationship to the parents, the parents' relationship to the children, the relationships between man and woman, brother and sister, etc. Very probably there are also "patterns" representing the different ages of man, birth, death, etc. There are any number of typical situations, each represented by a certain innate form that forces the individual to function in a specifically human way. These are the same as the forms that force the birds to build their nests in a certain way. Instinct takes a specific form, even in man. That form is the archetype, so named because unconscious thought expresses itself mythologically (*vide* Oedipus). I am only continuing what Freud began, and I often regret that the Freudian school have not known how to develop their master's fortunate discovery.

In reading your epilogue, I asked myself whether you mistrust my qualifications or my scientific competence as the Freudians generally

---

[2] Giuseppe Tucci, Italian Orientalist, professor of the religion and philosophy of India and the Far East at the U. of Rome. Lectured at Eranos 1953 on "Earth as Conceived of in Indian and Tibetan Religion, with Special Regard to the Tantras."

[3] One of the theories for explaining the concordance of myths and symbols among different civilizations is that they were transmitted by migration and tradition. Cf. "Constitution and Heredity in Psychology," CW 8, par. 228.

do. There is undoubtedly a basis for your criticism, but unfortunately I do not know the reasons for it, and it would be most useful to me to know them. No one has yet been able to prove my hypothesis false. Freud himself certainly did not think it necessary to know Greek mythology in order to have an Oedipus complex (and neither do I, for that matter). Obviously the existence of an archetype—that is to say, the possibility of developing an Oedipus complex—does not depend on historical mythologems. What is the logical error in this reasoning?

I have never been able to discover the slightest difference between incestuous Greek fantasy and modern fantasy. Undoubtedly incestuous fantasy is pretty universal and obviously it is not unique in being able to express itself through a mythologem. What more natural conclusion can we draw than that we are dealing here with a generally human disposition, which is instinctive and innate, as instinct is with all animals? How else can we explain identical or analogous products among tribes and individuals who could not have known of the existence of parallel creations? Do you really believe that every chick invents its own way of breaking out of the egg? Or that every eel makes an individual decision to start for the Bermudas, as though the idea were entirely novel? Why don't people take into account the thoroughly documented facts that I present in my alchemical studies? But they don't read those books, and they are satisfied with quite puerile prejudices, like the one that I mean inherited ideas, and other nonsensical things!

So—while I admire the conscientious way you presented my essays —I admit that I cannot help being somewhat sorry that you could not avoid making such a derogatory reference without the slightest proof or explanation. After your fine attempt to be strictly objective, a confession of your Freudian faith would perhaps have been enough to ease your conscience. But it seems to me you could have done that without disqualifying the heretic.

I do not habitually write letters of this sort. But I thought I should make this exception in view of the personal esteem which has always characterized my relations with both your father and yourself. I am, dear colleague,

Yours with best regards, C. G. JUNG

To Aniela Jaffé

Dear Aniela,   Bollingen, 12 April 1949

Your letter dropped in on me at a time of difficult reflection. I'm sorry I can't tell you anything more. It would be too much. Also, I haven't yet reached the end of my thorny path. Hard and burdensome insights[1] have come to me. After long wanderings in the darkness, glaring lights have gone up which mean I don't know what. At any rate I know why I need the seclusion of Bollingen. It is more necessary than ever. . . .

I congratulate you on the completion of "Séraphita."[2] Though it didn't help Balzac to turn aside from the self, one would like to be able to. But I know one would have to pay for it even more dearly. I wish I had a Jahwe Sabaoth as a κύριος τῶν δαιμόνων.[3] I understand more and more why I nearly died and I can't help wishing I had. The draught is bitter. With cordial greetings,

Yours ever, c. g.

□ (Handwritten.)
[1] Jung was at that time working on *Aion*, which contains the seeds of many ideas eventually formulated in "Answer to Job" and "Synchronicity."
[2] J. gave two (unpublished) lectures at the Psychological Club, Zurich, on the life of Balzac and his novel *Séraphita*.
[3] = Lord of the Daemons.

To Virginia Payne

[ORIGINAL IN ENGLISH]
Dear Miss Payne,   23 July 1949

I do remember the Clark Conference of 1909.[1] It was my first visit to the United States and for this reason my recollections are particularly vivid, although I must say that the details of the Conference itself have largely disappeared. But I do remember some incidents.

I travelled on the same boat with Professor Freud who was also invited and I remember vividly our discussion of his theories. We chiefly analysed our dreams during the trip and also during our stay

[1] P. asked Jung for his recollections of this Conference (cf. Forel, 12 Oct. 09, n. 1), on which she was writing her doctoral thesis at the U. of Wisconsin.

in America and on the way back. Professor William Stern[2] from Breslau was on the same boat, but Freud didn't feel particularly enthusiastic about the presence of an academic psychologist. No wonder, because his position of pioneer in Europe was not particularly enviable. I still sympathize entirely with his negative feelings, since I enjoyed the same fate for over 30 years.

Two personalities I met at the Clark Conference made a profound and lasting impression on me. One was Stanley Hall,[3] the President, and the other was William James whom I met for the first time then. I remember particularly an evening at President Hall's house. After dinner William James appeared and I was particularly interested in the personal relation between Stanley Hall and William James, since I gathered from some remarks of President Hall that William James was not taken quite seriously on account of his interest in Mrs. Piper[4] and her extra-sensory perceptions. Stanley Hall had prepared us that he had asked James to discuss some of his results with Mrs. Piper and to bring some of his material. So when James came (there was Stanley Hall, Professor Freud, one or two other men and myself) he said to Hall: "I've brought you some papers in which you might be interested." And he put his hand to his breastpocket and drew out a parcel which to our delight proved to be a wad of dollar bills. Considering Stanley Hall's great services for the increase and the welfare of Clark University and his rather critical remarks as to James' pursuits, it looked to us a particularly happy rejoinder. James excused himself profusely. Then he produced the real papers from the other pocket.

I spent two delightful evenings with William James alone and I was tremendously impressed by the clearness of his mind and the complete absence of intellectual prejudices. Stanley Hall was an equally clear-headed man, but decidedly of an academic brand.

The Conference was noteworthy on account of the fact that it was the first time that Professor Freud had an immediate contact with America. It was the first official recognition of the existence of psychoanalysis and it meant a great deal to him, because recognition in Europe for him was regrettably scarce. I was a young man then. I

[2] (1871–1938), German psychologist, professor of psychology at the Universities of Breslau and Hamburg; from 1933 in U.S.A.
[3] American psychologist (1844–1924), professor of psychology and President of Clark University. Cf. *Memories*, p. 366/337. (See pl. II.)
[4] Cf. Künkel, 10 July 46, n. 3.

92

lectured about association tests and a case of child psychology.[5] I was also interested in parapsychology and my discussions with William James were chiefly about this subject and about the psychology of religious experience.

As far as I remember we didn't make many contacts with psychologists or psychiatrists with the exception of old Dr. Putnam,[6] who curiously enough was an adept of Hegel's philosophy. Apart from that he was an unprejudiced, very human personality whom I liked and admired.

Since it was our first stay in America we thought it all very strange and we felt we didn't speak the same mental language as our American surroundings. I had many discussions with Professor Freud about the peculiar American psychology which, to myself at least, was more or less enigmatical. I only got the gist of it when I came back in 1912.[7] Then only did I begin to understand the main and distinctive features of American compared with European psychology.[8]

We spent a very interesting week in Dr. Putnam's camp in the Adirondacks and continued to be bewildered by the peculiar ways and ideas of the many native guests at that camp. It was a large party of about 40 people.

I cannot remember much of the papers presented at the Conference, nor of other discussions that took place, but we felt very much that our point of view was very different and that there hardly existed a bridge between the then prevailing American views and our peculiar European standpoint.

It is not for me to judge the effect on psychiatry in general, since this is a specifically American development which I haven't followed up. The influence of psychology on psychiatry is still very small for obvious reasons. In any great institution there is no time at all for individual investigation—at least it is so in Europe, and the number of alienists I have taught is quite small.

---

[5] "The Association Method" and "The Family Constellation" (CW 2), and "Psychic Conflicts in a Child" (CW 17).

[6] James Jackson Putnam (1846–1915), American physician, professor of neurology at Harvard; a founder of the American Psychoanalytical Association.

[7] In Sept. 1912 Jung gave a series of lectures on "The Theory of Psychoanalysis" (CW 4), at Fordham U., New York.

[8] Cf. "The Complications of American Psychology," CW 10.

Hoping I have been able to give you at least an idea of my recollections of the Clark Conference, I remain,

Yours sincerely, c. g. j u n g

To Emanuel Maier

[ORIGINAL IN ENGLISH]

Dear Professor Maier,   24 March 1950

I must apologize for the long delay in answering your letter of January 16th. I'm a very busy man and suffer from an overwhelming correspondence which I'm hardly able to cope with.

I know Hesse's work and I know him personally. I knew the psychiatrist who treated him. He died several years ago. Through him Hesse received some influences originating in my work (which show for instance in *Demian, Siddhartha,* and *Steppenwolf*).[1] It was about that time (1916) that I made Hesse's personal acquaintance. The psychiatrist was Dr. J. B. Lang.[2] He was a very curious, though extremely learned man, who had studied oriental languages (Hebrew, Arabic, and Syrian) and was particularly interested in Gnostic speculation. He got from me a considerable amount of knowledge concerning Gnosticism which he also transmitted to Hesse. From this material he wrote his *Demian.* The origin of *Siddhartha* and *Steppenwolf* is of a more hidden nature. They are—to a certain extent— the direct or indirect results of certain talks I had with Hesse. I'm unfortunately unable to say how much he was conscious of the hints and implications which I let him have. I'm not in a position to give you full information, since my knowledge is strictly professional.

I have never done any systematic work on any of Hesse's novels.

☐ M., Professor of German at the U. of Miami (Florida), was working on a dissertation (N.Y.U., 1953) "The Psychology of C. G. Jung in the Works of Hermann Hesse." It was never published and the MS is now in the Hesse Archiv, Marbach, Württemberg. — Jung's letter was published in an essay by Benjamin Nelson, "Hesse and Jung. Two Newly Recovered Letters," *The Psychoanalytic Review* (New York), vol. 50 (1963), 11–16. See also below, Addenda (2).

[1] *Demian* (orig. 1919), *Siddhartha* (orig. 1922), *Steppenwolf* (orig. 1927).
[2] Josef B. Lang, M.D., (1881–1945), psychotherapist in Lugano, an early pupil of Jung's who later separated from him. Cf. his "Zur Bestimmung des psychoanalytischen Widerstandes" and "Eine Hypothese zur psychologischen Bedeutung der Verfolgungsidee," both in Jung (ed.), *Psychologische Abhandlungen,* I (1914). — In his *Demian,* Hesse modelled the figure of Pistorius on Dr. Lang, then about 35. See Hesse, 3 Dec. 19, n. 2, in Addenda (1).

It would be, I admit, an interesting psychological study, particularly from the standpoint of my theoretical conceptions. It is possible for anyone sufficiently aware of my work to make the necessary applications. Unfortunately my time doesn't allow me to go into detail, because this would amount to a new dissertation which would demand an extra amount of work which I'm not able to produce.

I should be very much interested to know about the results of your researches.

Yours sincerely, c. g. j u n g

To Joseph Goldbrunner

Dear Herr Goldbrunner,   14 May 1950

Permit me, as one who is, in a manner of speaking, both known and unknown to you, to express my best thanks for your objective and sympathetic exposition of my psychology.[1] There are indeed few authors, as you yourself have probably observed, who could wring from themselves an objective evaluation of my work. So much the more reason for me to be sincerely grateful to you for your achievement. I would gladly content myself with an unqualified appreciation of your book but for a few points which seem to me to require clarification.

You rightly emphasize that man in my view is enclosed in *the* psyche (not in *his* psyche). Could you name me any idea that is *not* psychic? Can man adopt any standpoint outside the psyche? He may assert that he can, but the assertion does not create a point outside, and were he there he would have no psyche. Everything that touches us and that we touch is a reflection, therefore psychic.

That my psychology is wholly imprisoned in the psyche is a fact that cannot be otherwise. You would not, presumably, object that geology treats of nothing but the earth, or that astronomy only circles round the starry sky?

Psychology is, strictly speaking, the science of conscious contents. Its object therefore is not metaphysical, otherwise it would be metaphysics. Does one hold it against physics that it is not metaphysics? It is self-evident that all objects of physics are physical phenomena. Why should psychology be the only exception to this rule?

[1] *Individuation; A Study of the Depth Psychology of Carl Gustav Jung* (1955; orig. 1949).

95

Everything that man conceives as God is a psychic image, and it is no less an image even if he asseverates a thousand times that it is not an image. If it were not, he would be unable to conceive anything at all. That is why Meister Eckhart says, quite rightly, "God is pure nothing."

As an empirical science, psychology can only establish that the unconscious spontaneously produces images which have always been spoken of as "God-images." But as the nature of the psyche is wholly unknown to us, science cannot establish *what* the image is a reflection of. We come here to the "frontier of the human," of which G. von Le Fort[2] says that it is the "portcullis of God." In my private capacity as a man I can only concur with this view, but with the best will in the world I cannot maintain that this is a verifiable assertion, which is what science is all about in the end. It is a subjective confession which has no place in science.

It is equally out of place to say that individuation is *self redemption*. This is precisely what it is not. As you yourself have described so beautifully, man exposes himself to all the powers of the non-ego, of heaven and hell, of grace and destruction, in order to reach that point where he has become simple enough to accept those influences, or whatever it is we call "God's will," which come from the Unfathomable and whose source lies behind those same psychic images which both reveal and conceal. How one could see through this "hoarding" is, frankly, beyond my comprehension. How can one see, think, or conceive that which is non-psychic? Even if I aver that it is not psychic, it is still my conception standing before the unknowable fact; and if it is non-psychic then it cannot be conceived at all.

We take it for granted that images are reflections of *something*. In so far as this something is supposed not to be psychic, it is necessarily inconceivable—even the spectacular blue of the sky does not exist in physics but is expressed by the mathematical concept of wave-lengths. Am I, then, to declare that because I see blue, blue exists in itself and is not psychic? That would be against my better knowledge and therefore immoral.

I am deeply impressed by man's proneness to error and self-deception. I therefore deem it a moral command not to make assertions about things we can neither see nor prove, and I deem it an epistemological transgression if one nevertheless does so. These rules hold good for empirical science; metaphysics holds to others. I recognize

[2] Gertrud von le Fort (1876–1971), German Catholic writer.

the rules of empirical science as binding upon myself. Hence no metaphysical assertions will be found in my writings, and, n.b., *no denials of metaphysical assertions.*

Hoping that these explanations may perhaps be of service to you, I remain,

Yours very sincerely, C. G. JUNG

Anonymous

Dear Dr. N.,   10 June 1950

You get nowhere with theories. Try to be simple and always take the next step. You needn't see it in advance, but you can look back at it afterwards. There is no "how" of life, one just does it as you wrote your letter, for instance. It seems, however, to be terribly difficult for you *not* to be complicated and to do what is simple and closest to hand. You barricade yourself from the world with exaggerated saviour fantasies. So climb down from the mountain of your humility and follow your nose. That is *your* way and the straightest. With kind regards,

Yours sincerely, C. G. JUNG

☐ (Handwritten.) To a woman.

To Chang Chung-yuan

[ORIGINAL IN ENGLISH]

Dear Sir,   26 June 1950

I have read your pamphlet[1] with great interest and I can tell you that I fundamentally agree with your views. I see Taoism in the same light as you do. I'm a great admirer of Ch'uang-tze's philosophy. I was again immersed in the study of his writings when your letter arrived in the midst of it.

You are aware, of course, that Taoism formulates psychological principles which are of a very universal nature. As a matter of fact,

☐ Ph.D., 1947–53 professor of Chinese classics at the Asia Institute, New York; lectured at the Eranos meetings 1955, 1956, 1958. Now professor of philosophy, U. of Hawaii.
[1] "An Interpretation of Taoism in the Light of Modern Philosophy," unpublished; expanded as *Creativity and Taoism* (1963).

they are so all-embracing that they are, as far as they go, applicable to any part of humanity. But on the other hand just because Taoist views are so universal, they need a re-translation and specification when it comes to the practical application of their principles. Of course it is undeniable that general principles are of the highest importance, but it is equally important to know in every detail the way that leads to real understanding. The danger for the Western mind consists in the mere application of words instead of facts. What the Western mind needs is the actual experience of the facts that cannot be substituted by words. Thus I'm chiefly concerned with the ways and methods by which one can make the Western mind aware of the psychological facts underlying the concept of Tao, if the latter can be called a concept at all. The way you put it is in danger of remaining a mere idealism or an ideology to the Western mind. If one could arrive at the truth by learning the words of wisdom, then the world would have been saved already in the remote times of Lao tse. The trouble is, as Ch'uang-tze rightly says, that the old masters failed to enlighten the world, since there weren't minds enough that could be enlightened. There is little use in teaching wisdom. At all events wisdom cannot be taught by words. It is only possible by personal contact and by immediate experience.

The great and almost insurmountable difficulty consists in the question of the ways and means to induce people to make the indispensable psychological experiences that open their eyes to the underlying truth. The truth is one and the same everywhere and I must say that Taoism is one of the most perfect formulations of it I ever became acquainted with.

Sincerely yours, C. G. JUNG

To Manfred Bleuler

Dear Colleague,   19 August 1950

Your kind letter with wishes for my birthday came as a surprise and joy. I was very touched to receive such a cordial message from my old place of work, where everything that happened afterwards had its beginning. All the more so as I have never had the pleasure

☐ Professor of psychiatry at the U. of Zurich; 1942–70 director of the Burghölzli Clinic; son of Eugen Bleuler.

98

of meeting you in your later years. I remember you only as a small boy at a time which for me lies in the far-off past.

All the more vivid in my memory are the impressions and the encouragement I received from your father, to whom I shall always be grateful. Not only am I deeply indebted to psychiatry, but I have always remained close to it inwardly, since from the very beginning one general problem engrossed me: From what psychic stratum do the immensely impressive ideas found in schizophrenia originate? The questions that resulted have seemingly removed me far from clinical psychiatry and have led me to wander all through the world. On these adventurous journeys I discovered many things I never yet dreamt of in Burghölzli, but the rigorous mode of observation I learnt there has accompanied me everywhere and helped me to grasp the alien psyche objectively.

While thanking you for your cordial message I would also like to ask you to convey my gratitude to all those who were kind enough to sign your letter. With collegial regards,

Yours sincerely, c. g. j u n g

To Hermann Hesse

Dear Herr Hesse, 19 August 1950

Among the many messages and signs my 75th birthday brought me, it was your greeting that surprised and delighted me most. I am especially grateful for your *Morgenlandfahrt*,[1] which I have set aside to read at a quiet moment. Since my birthday, however, this quiet moment still hasn't arrived, for I am swamped with a flood of letters and visitors beyond my control. At my age it means going "slow and with care," nor is my working capacity what it was, especially when you have all sorts of things on your programme which you want to bring to the light of day. I have made a late start with them, which may well be due to the difficulty of the themes that have dropped into my head.

Allow me to reciprocate your gift with a specimen of my latest publications[2] bordering on the domain of literature. Meanwhile you

[1] *The Journey to the East* (orig. 1932).
[2] Probably *Gestaltungen des Unbewussten* (1950), which contains "Psychology and Literature," CW 15.

too have moved up into the higher age bracket and so will be in a position to empathize with my preoccupations. With best thanks,

Yours sincerely, C. G. JUNG

To Hanna Oeri

Dear Dr. Oeri,   23 December 1950

The great tiredness I saw and felt in my friend on my visit to Basel has now run speedily to its end. The dead are surely not to be pitied—they have so infinitely much more before them than we do— but rather the living who are left behind, who must contemplate the fleetingness of existence and suffer parting, sorrow, and loneliness in time.

I know what Albert's death must mean to you, for with him my last living friend has also departed. We are but a remnant of the past, more and more so with each coming year. Our eyes turn away from the future of the human world in which our children, but not ourselves, will live. Enviable the lot of those who have crossed the threshold, yet my compassion goes out to those who, in the darkness of the world, hemmed in by a narrow horizon and the blindness of ignorance, must follow the river of their days, fulfilling life's task, only to see their whole existence, which once was the present brimming with power and vitality, crumbling bit by bit and crashing into the abyss. This spectacle of old age would be unendurable did we not know that our psyche reaches into a region held captive neither by change in time nor by limitation of place. In that form of being our birth is a death and our death a birth. The scales of the whole hang balanced. With heartfelt sympathy,

Yours sincerely, C. G. JUNG

□ The wife of Albert Oeri.

To Heinrich Boltze

Dear Herr Boltze,   13 February 1951

For your orientation: I am a psychiatrist and not a philosopher, merely an empiricist who ponders on certain experiences. *Psyche* for me is an inclusive term for the totality of all so-called psychic proc-

100

esses. *Spirit* is a qualitative designation for certain psychic contents (rather like "material" or "physical"). *Atlantis*: a mythical phantasm. L. *Frobenius*: an imaginative and somewhat credulous original. Great collector of material. Less good as a thinker.

God: an inner experience, not discussable as such but impressive. Psychic experience has two sources: the outer world and the unconscious. *All immediate experience is psychic.* There is physically transmitted (outer world) experience and inner (spiritual) experience. The one is as valid as the other. God is not a *statistical* truth, hence it is just as stupid to try to prove the existence of God as to deny him. If a person feels happy, he needs neither proof nor counterproof. Also, there is no reason to suppose that "happiness" or "sadness" cannot be experienced. God is a universal experience which is obfuscated only by silly rationalism and an equally silly theology. (Cf. my little book *Psychologie und Religion*, Rascher-Verlag, Zurich 1940, where you will find something on this theme.)

What mankind has called "God" from time immemorial you experience every day. You only give him another, so-called "rational" name—for instance, you call him "affect." Time out of mind he has been the psychically stronger, capable of throwing your conscious purposes off the rails, fatally thwarting them and occasionally making mincemeat of them. Hence there are not a few who are afraid "of themselves." God is then called "I myself," and so on. *Outer world and God are the two primordial experiences* and the one is as great as the other, and both have a thousand names, which one and all do not alter the facts. The roots of both are unknown. The psyche mirrors both. It is perhaps the point where they touch. Why do we ask about God at all? God effervesces in you and sets you to the most wondrous speculations.

People speak of *belief* when they have lost *knowledge*. Belief and disbelief in God are mere surrogates. The naïve primitive *doesn't believe, he knows*, because the inner experience rightly means as much to him as the outer. He still has no theology and hasn't yet let himself be befuddled by boobytrap concepts. He adjusts his life—of necessity—to outer and inner *facts*, which he does not—as we do—feel to be discontinuous. He lives in *one* world, whereas we live only in one half and merely believe in the other or not at all. We have blotted it out with so-called "spiritual development," which means that we live by self-fabricated electric light and—to heighten the comedy—believe or don't believe in the sun.

101

Stalin in Paris[1] would have become *une espèce d'existentialiste* like Sartre, a ruthless doctrinaire. What generates a cloud of twaddle in Paris causes the ground to tremble in Asia. There a potentate can still set himself up as the incarnation of reason instead of the sun.

Yours very truly, c. g. j u n g

☐ Western Germany.
[1] B. expressed his regret that Stalin had not been born in Paris.

To Adolf L. Vischer

Dear Colleague,   21 March 1951

I am sorry I am thanking you only now for your very kind letter of 26.XII.50. Your sympathy over the death of my last close friend, Albert Oeri,[1] was veritable balm. One can indeed feel the pain of such a loss without making oneself guilty of undue sentimentality. One notices on all such occasions how age gradually pushes one out of time and the world into wider and uninhabited spaces where one feels at first rather lonely and strange. You have written so sympathetically and perceptively in your book[2] of the peculiarities of old age that you will have an understanding heart for this mood. The imminence of death and the vision of the world *in conspectu mortis* is in truth a curious experience: the sense of the present stretches out beyond today, looking back into centuries gone by, and forward into futures yet unborn. With heartfelt thanks,

Affectionately yours, c. g. j u n g

☐ See Vischer, 10 Oct. 44 (in vol. 1).
[1] Cf. Oeri, 12 Feb. 20, n. ☐.
[2] *Das Alter als Schicksal und Erfüllung* (1942).

To Aniela Jaffé

Dear Aniela,   Bollingen, 29 May 1951

So it goes all the time: memories rise up and disappear again, as it suits them. In this way I have landed the great whale; I mean "Answer to Job." I can't say I have fully digested this *tour de force* of the unconscious. It still goes on rumbling a bit, rather like an earth-

☐ (Handwritten.) See Jaffé, 22 Dec. 42 (in vol. 1).

quake. I notice it when I am chiselling away at my inscription (which has made good progress). Then thoughts come to me, as for instance that consciousness is only an organ for perceiving the fourth dimension, i.e., the all-pervasive meaning, and itself produces no real ideas. I am getting much better. Only my sleep is still rather delicate. I oughtn't to talk much, or intensely. Luckily occasions for this are rare.

How are you? I hope you are not overstraining yourself at the Institute. I won't make any false promises about a visit from you, but I am thinking of it. Meanwhile with cordial greetings,

C. G.

Anonymous

Dear Herr N.,   1 November 1951

I am sorry to be late with my answer. I was away on holiday and your letter was lying around for some time.

You have experienced in your marriage what is an almost universal fact—that individuals are different from one another. Basically, each remains for the other an unfathomable enigma. There is never complete concord. If you have committed a mistake at all, it consisted in your having striven too hard to understand your wife completely and not reckoning with the fact that in the end people don't want to know what secrets are slumbering in their souls. If you struggle too much to penetrate into another person, you find that you have thrust him into a defensive position, and resistances develop because, through your efforts to penetrate and understand, he feels forced to examine those things in himself which he doesn't want to examine. Everybody has his dark side which—so long as all goes well—he had better not know about. That is no fault of yours. It is a universal human truth which is nevertheless true, even though there are plenty of people who will assure you that they'd be only too glad to know everything about themselves. It is as good as certain that your wife had many thoughts and feelings which made her uneasy and which she wanted to hide even from herself. That is simply human. It is also the reason why so many elderly people withdraw into their own solitude where they won't be disturbed. And it is always about things

□ Germany.

103

they would rather not be too clearly conscious of. Certainly *you* are not responsible for the existence of these psychic contents. If nevertheless you are still tormented by guilt feelings, then consider for once what sins you have not committed which you would have liked to commit. This might perhaps cure you of your guilt feelings towards your wife. With kind regards,

Yours sincerely, C. G. JUNG

To Hans Schär

Dear Dr. Schär,   16 November 1951

Best thanks for your friendly letter. I am glad you have not damned me. What offends you bothered me too. I would have liked to avoid sarcasm and mockery but couldn't, for that is the way I felt and if I had not said so it would have been all the worse, but hidden. I realized only afterwards that they have their place as expressing resistance to God's nature, which sets us at odds with ourselves. I had to wrench myself free of God, so to speak, in order to find that unity in myself which God seeks through man. It is rather like that vision of Symeon the Theologian,[1] who sought God in vain everywhere in the world, until God rose like a little sun in his own heart. Where else, after all, could God's antinomy attain to unity save in the vessel God has prepared for himself for this purpose? It seems to me that only the man who seeks to realize his own humanity does God's will, but not those who take to flight before the bad fact "man," and precipitately turn back to the Father or have never left the Father's house. To become man is evidently God's desire in us.

Sarcasm is certainly not a pretty quality, but I am forced to use even means I find reprehensible in order to deliver myself from the Father. God himself uses very different means to jolt these human beings of his into consciousness. It has not yet been forgotten, I hope, what happened in Germany and what is happening day after day in Russia. Job's suffering never ceases and multiplies a millionfold. I cannot avert my eyes from that. By remaining with the Father, I

☐ (1910–68), Swiss Protestant theologian, late professor of theology at the U. of Bern. (Cf. Neumann, 5 Aug. 46, n. 2.) He officiated at the funerals of Mrs. Jung and Prof. Jung, and also at that of Toni Wolff. (Part of this letter is published in Ges. Werke, XI, pp. 685f.)

[1] Symeon Metaphrastes, 10th cent., Byzantine hagiographer.

104

deny him the human being in whom he could unify himself and become One, and how can I help him better than by becoming One myself? (*Nunquam unum facies, nisi prius ex te ipso fiat unum.*)[2] God has quite obviously not chosen for sons those who hang on to him as the Father, but those who found the courage to stand on their own feet.

Sarcasm is the means by which we hide our hurt feelings from ourselves, and from this you can see how very much the knowledge of God has wounded me, and how very much I would have preferred to remain a child in the Father's protection and shun the problem of opposites. It is probably even more difficult to deliver oneself from good than from evil. But without sin there is no breaking away from the good Father; sarcasm plays the corresponding role in this case. As I hinted in the motto, *Doleo super te*,[3] I am sincerely sorry to wound praiseworthy feelings. In this regard I had to overcome misgivings aplenty. I shall have to suffer anyway for being one against an overwhelming majority. Every development, every change for the better, is full of suffering. It is just the Reformers who should know this best. But what if they themselves are in need of reform? One way or another certain questions have to be openly asked and answered. I felt it my duty to stimulate this. Again with best thanks,

Yours sincerely, C. G. JUNG

[2] "Thou wilt never make (from others) the One (that thou seekest), except there first be made one thing of thyself." A much-quoted saying from Gerhard Dorn, "Philosophia meditativa," *Theatrum chemicum*, I (1602). Cf. *Psychology and Alchemy*, CW 12, par. 358.
[3] II Samuel 1:26: "I am distressed for thee, my brother," forms the motto to "Answer to Job."

To J. Wesley Neal

[ORIGINAL IN ENGLISH]

Dear Sir, 9 February 1952

It is not so easy to answer your question about the "Island of Peace."[1] I seem to have quite a number of them, a sort of peaceful archipelago. Some of the main islands are: my garden, the view of distant mountains, my country place where I withdraw from the noise

☐ Long Beach, California.
[1] N. asked if Jung had an "island of peace" which offered him a "refuge in the stream of daily living."

105

of city life, my library. Also small things like books, pictures, and stones.

When I was in Africa the headman of my safari, a Mohammedan Somali, told me what his Sheik had taught him about Chadir.[2] He said: "He can appear to thee like light without flame and smoke, or like a man in the street, or like a blade of grass."

I hope this will answer your question.

Yours sincerely, C. G. JUNG

[2] Cf. Irminger, 22 Sept. 44, n. 3. For the quotation cf. "Concerning Rebirth," CW 9, i, par. 250.

To Father Victor White

[ORIGINAL IN ENGLISH]

Dear Victor,   Park Hotel, Locarno, 9 April 1952 until 14th

Thank you for your human letter.[1] It gives me some idea of what is happening inside of you.

The *privatio boni* does not seem to me such a particular puzzle, but I understand that it is of the greatest importance. It is perhaps best if I set forth my point of view, so that you can see how I look at it. At the same time I shall try to consider your standpoint too.

I think you agree with me that within our empirical world good and evil represent the indispensable parts of a logical judgment, like white and black, right-left, above-below, etc. These are equivalent opposites and it is understood that they are always relative to the situation of the one that makes the statement, a person or a law. Empirically we are unable to confirm the existence of anything absolute, i.e., there are no logical means to establish an absolute truth, except a tautology.

Yet we are moved (by archetypal motifs) *to make such statements,* viz. religious or metaphysical assertions such as the Trinity, the Virgin Birth and other exceedingly improbable and physically impossible things. One of these assertions is the *Summum Bonum*[2] and its con-

□ (Handwritten.)

[1] Cf. preceding letter, n. 6. In the same letter of April 5 W. expressed his desire to find some common ground on the problem of the *privatio boni*, "which must affect one's value-*judgments* on almost everything (alchemy, gnosticism, Christ and anti-Christ, the Second Coming, the whole orientation of psychotherapy), without there being any dispute about the *facts*."

[2] God as the Summum Bonum, the Ultimate Good, is "the effective source of the concept of the *privatio boni*" (*Aion*, CW 9, ii, par. 80).

106

sequence, the *privatio boni*. The latter is logically as impossible as the Trinity. It is therefore a truly religious statement: *prorsus credibile quia ineptum*.[3] Divine favour and daemonic evil or danger are archetypal. Even if you know that your judgment is entirely subjective and relative you are nevertheless forced to make such statements more than a dozen times every day. And when you are religious you talk in terms of impossibilities. I have no arguments against these facts. I only deny that the *privatio boni* is a logical statement, but I admit the obvious truth that it is a "metaphysical" truth based upon an archetypal "motif."

The way in which opposites are reconciled or united in God we just don't know. Nor do we understand how they are united in the self. The self is transcendental and is only partially conscious. Empirically it is good and evil. The same as the "acts of God" have decidedly contradictory aspects. This fact however does not justify the theological judgment that God is either good or evil. He is transcendental, just as much as the self and therefore not subject to human logic.

The supreme powers are assumed to be either indifferent or more often good than evil. There is an archetypal accent upon the good aspect, but only slightly so. This is understandable, because there must be some sort of equilibrium, otherwise the world could not exist.

The great difficulty seems to consist in the fact that on the one hand we must defend the sanity and logic of the human mind, and on the other hand we have to accept and to welcome the existence of illogical and irrational factors transcending our comprehension. We must deal with them as rationally as we can, even if there is no hope of ever getting on top of them. As we can't deal with them rationally we have to formulate them symbolically. A symbol when taken literally is nearly always impossible. Thus I should say that the *privatio boni* is a *symbolic truth*, based on archetypal motivation, not to be defended rationally any more than the Virgin Birth.

Excuse my bad writing. I am in the garden and there is no table but my knee. Answer not expected. I will try to help you as much as possible.

Yours, c. g.

---

[3] = "immediately credible because absurd." Cf. Wegmann, 20 Nov. 45, n. 2.

To R. J. Zwi Werblowsky

Dear Dr. Werblowsky,   17 June 1952

Many thanks for kindly sending me your critical reflections.[1] For me they are valuable and interesting as the reactions of an (almost) non-participant. From touching lightly on psychology you have already acquired a "golden finger"[2] and must now give forthright answers before the world. This happens even with people who have said "good day" to me only once.

I don't know whether I ought to be glad that my desperate attempts to do justice to the reality of the psyche are accounted "ingenious ambiguity."[3] At least it acknowledges my efforts to reflect, as best I can, the "ingenious ambiguity" of the psyche.

For me the psyche is an almost infinite phenomenon. I absolutely don't know what it is in itself and know only very vaguely what it is not. Also, I know only to a limited degree what is individual about the psyche and what is universal. It seems to me a sort of all-encompassing system of relationships, in which "material" and "spiritual" are primarily designations for potentialities that transcend consciousness. I can say of nothing that it is "only psychic," for everything in my immediate experience is psychic in the first place. I live in a "perceptual world" but not in a self-subsistent one. The latter is real enough but we have only indirect information about it. This is as true of outer objects as of "inner" ones, of material existents and the archetypal factors we could also call $εἴδη$.[4] No matter what I speak about, the two worlds interpenetrate in it more or less. This is unavoidable, for our language is a faithful reflection of the psychic phenomenon with its dual aspect "perceptual" and "imaginary." When I say "God" the dual aspect of the *ens absolutum* and the hydrogen atom (or particle + wave) is already implicit in it. I try to speak "neutrally." (Prof. Pauli would say: the "neutral language"[5] between "physical" and "archetypal.")

The language I speak must be ambiguous, must have two mean-

---

[1] On the controversy between Buber and Jung.
[2] A fairytale motif: a child looks into a forbidden room and is given away by a finger turning golden. Cf. "Our Lady's Child" and "Iron Hans," *Grimm's Fairy Tales* (Pantheon edn., 1944), pp. 23ff. and 612–15.
[3] A remark of Buber's in his reply to Jung. Cf. Neumann, 28 Feb. 52, n. 9.
[4] = forms, species. Cf. "Synchronicity," CW 8, par. 942.
[5] Ibid., par. 960.

ings, in order to do justice to the dual aspect of our psychic nature. I strive quite consciously and deliberately for ambiguity of expression, because it is superior to unequivocalness and reflects the nature of life. My whole temperament inclines me to be very unequivocal indeed. That is not difficult, but it would be at the cost of truth. I purposely allow all the overtones and undertones to be heard, partly because they are there anyway, and partly because they give a fuller picture of reality. Unequivocalness makes sense only in establishing facts but not in interpreting them; for "meaning" is not a tautology but always includes more in itself than the concrete object of which it is predicated.

I define myself as an empiricist, for after all I have to be something respectable. You yourself admit that I am a poor philosopher, and naturally I don't like being something inferior. As an empiricist I have at least accomplished something. If a man is a good shoemaker and knows he is one, people will not inscribe on his tombstone that he was a bad hatmaker because he once made an unsatisfactory hat.

I am, more specifically, simply a psychiatrist, for my essential problem, to which all my efforts are directed, is psychic disturbance: its phenomenology, aetiology, and teleology. Everything else is secondary for me. I do not feel called upon to found a religion, nor to proclaim my belief in one. I am not engaged in philosophy, but merely in thinking within the framework of the special task that is laid upon me: to be a proper psychiatrist, a healer of the soul. This is what I have discovered myself to be, and this is how I function as a member of society. Nothing would seem more nonsensical and fruitless for me than to speculate about things I cannot prove, let alone know. I am quite prepared to grant that others may know more about them than I. I do not know, for example, how God could ever be experienced apart from human experience. If I do not experience him, how can I say that he exists? But my experience is extremely small and narrow, and so, in spite of oppressive intimations of the infinite, what I experience is also small and in the likeness of man—a fact which emerges clearly when one tries to express it. In our experience everything gets tainted with the ambiguity of the psyche. The greatest experience is also the smallest and narrowest, and for that reason one hesitates to boast about it, let alone philosophize about it. One is after all too small and too incompetent to be able to afford any such arrogance. That is why I prefer ambiguous language, since it does equal justice to the subjectivity of the archetypal idea and to the autonomy of the archetype. "God," for example, is on the one hand

109

an inexpressible *ens potentissimum*, and on the other hand an exceedingly inadequate token and expression of human impotence and perplexity—an experience, therefore, of the most paradoxical nature. The realm of the psyche is immeasurably great and filled with living reality. At its brink lies the secret of matter and of spirit. I do not know whether this schema means anything to you or not. For me it is the frame within which I can express my experience. With best regards,

Yours sincerely, c. g. j u n g

To Upton Sinclair

[ORIGINAL IN ENGLISH]

Dear Mr. Sinclair, 3 November 1952

I have read your book A *Personal Jesus*[1] carefully and with great interest. It is certainly of great merit and will help your public to appreciate a religious figure from a new angle. I was curious to see in which way you would tackle such a difficult task as the reconstruction of a Jesus biography. Being the son of a parson, and having grown up in an atmosphere steeped in theology, I learnt about a number of attempts such as those of Strauss,[2] Renan,[3] Moore,[4] etc., and in later years I was an ardent reader of A. Schweitzer's work.[5] I have repeatedly, i.e., at different phases of my life, tried to realize what kind of personality—explaining the *whole effect* of its existence—could be reconstructed from the scanty historical evidence offered by

☐ (1878–1968), American writer. — This letter, with minor changes (some incorporated here), was published in *The New Republic* (Washington), vol. 128, no. 17, issue 2004, 27 Apr. 1953.
[1] New York, 1952.
[2] David Friedrich Strauss (1808–74), German theologian and philosopher. His *Das Leben Jesu, kritisch bearbeitet*, 1835–36 (tr. George Eliot, *The Life of Jesus*, 1846), produced a sensation by interpreting most of the history of Jesus as mythological and attempting to establish a life of Jesus free from all supernatural elements.
[3] Ernest Renan (1823–92), French philosopher. In his *Vie de Jésus* (1863), the first volume of his *Histoire des origines du Christianisme* (1863–81), he tried to combine positivistic science and Christianity and to explain the life of Jesus in purely human terms. (Tr. *Life of Jesus*, Everyman's Library, no. 805, 1927.)
[4] Presumably George Foot Moore (1851–1931), American Biblical scholar, author of a *History of Religions* (1913–19).
[5] *The Quest of the Historical Jesus* (1906; tr. 1910), in which he expounds the eschatological, messianic view of the life of Jesus.

110

the New Testament. Having had a good deal of psychological experience, I should have been sufficiently equipped for such a task, but in the end I came to the conclusion that, owing on the one hand to the paucity of historical data, and on the other to the abundance of mythological admixtures, I was unable to reconstruct a personal character free from rather fatal contradictions.

You have certainly succeeded in presenting an acceptable picture of a certain Jesus. I should venture to say that it is even a likely portrait of such a presumably unique character. It may even be convincing to a modern American mind, but seen from the standpoint of a European scientist, your *modus procedendi* seems to be a bit too selective; that is, you exclude too many authentic statements for no other reason than that they do not fit in with your premises, for instance, predestination and esoterism, which cannot be excluded for textual reasons. They cannot be dismissed as mere interpolations. There is also incontestable textual evidence for the fact that Jesus foresaw his tragic end. Moreover, you exclude practically the whole overwhelming amount of eschatology, the authenticity of which is undeniable whether it offends our reason or not.

Then you paint a portrait; though of the highest literary quality, it is subject to the same critique you apply to John the Evangelist (p. 155 seq.): "We are going to learn what this Hellenized intellectual thinks about Jesus." We learn from your book what a modern American writer "thinks about Jesus." This is not meant to be derogatory; on the contrary, it merely shows my perplexity. Surely we can draw a portrait of Jesus that does not offend our rationalism, but it is done at the expense of our *loyalty* to the textual authority. As a matter of fact, *we can omit nothing* from the authentic text. We cannot create a true picture of Hermetic philosophy in the IVth century if we dismiss half of the *libelli* contained in the *Corpus Hermeticum.* The New Testament as it stands is the "Corpus Christianum," which is to be accepted as a whole or not at all. We can dismiss nothing that stands up to a reasonable philological critique. We cannot suppress any single contradiction because we have no anterior or better or more reliable evidence. We have to take the whole and make the best of it.

The "Corpus Christianum" tells the story of a God-Man and of the various ways in which His life and teaching were understood. If Jesus was, as you portray Him, a rationally understandable teacher of fine morals and a devout believer in a good Father-God, why should the Gospels be stuffed with miracle stories and He Himself saddled with

111

esoteric and eschatological statements, showing Him in the role of a Son-God and cosmological saviour?

If Jesus had indeed been nothing but a great teacher hopelessly mistaken in His messianic expectations,[6] we should be at a complete loss in understanding His historical effect, which is so clearly visible in the New Testament. If, on the other hand, we cannot understand by rational means what a God-Man is, then we don't know what the New Testament is all about. But it would be just our task to understand what they meant by a "God-Man."

You give an excellent picture of a possible religious teacher, but you give us no understanding of what the New Testament tries to tell, namely the life, fate, and effect of a God-Man, whom we are asked to believe to be a divine revelation.

These are the reasons why I should propose to deal with the Christian *Urphänomen* in a somewhat different way. I think we ought to admit that we don't understand the riddle of the New Testament. With our present means we cannot unravel a rational story from it unless we interfere with the texts. If we take this risk we can read various stories into the texts and we can even give them a certain amount of probability:

1. Jesus is an idealistic, religious teacher of great wisdom, who knows that His teaching would make the necessary impression only if He were willing to sacrifice His life for it. Thus He forces the issue in complete foreknowledge of the facts which He intends to happen.

2. Jesus is a highly strung, forceful personality, forever at variance with His surroundings, and possessed of a terrific will to power. Yet being of superior intelligence, He perceives that it would not do to assert it on the worldly plane of political sedition as so many similar zealots in His days had done. He rather prefers the role of the old prophet and reformer of His people, and He institutes a spiritual kingdom instead of an unsuccessful political rebellion. For this purpose He adopts not only the messianic Old Testament expectations, but also the then popular "Son of Man" figure in the Book of Enoch. But meddling with the political whirlpool in Jerusalem, He gets Himself caught in its intrigues and meets a tragic end with a full recognition of His failure.

3. Jesus is an incarnation of the Father-God. As a God-Man He

---

[6] Cf. Matthew 16:27f.

walks the earth drawing to Himself the ἐκλεκτοί[7] of His Father, announcing the message of universal salvation and being mostly misunderstood. As the crowning of His short career, He performs the supreme sacrifice in offering Himself up as the perfect host, and thus redeems mankind from eternal perdition.

You can make out a pretty good case from the texts for each of these three highly different variants, with the necessary omissions and violations of scriptural authority. The first and second variants are "rational," i.e., they happen to be within the frame of our contemporary understanding, while the third is definitely outside it; although up to about 200 years ago nobody thought so.

If we avoid violations of the authentic texts, we have to take into consideration the three possibilities, and perhaps some more, and then we must try to find out which theory would fit the complete picture. Since the Gospels do not give, and do not even intend to give, a biography of the Lord, the mere reconstruction of a life of Jesus could never explain the picture given by the texts. The little we know of His biography must needs be supplemented by a very careful study of the peculiar mental and spiritual atmosphere of the time and place of the gospel writers. People at that time were highly Hellenized. Jesus Himself was under the influence of eschatological literature, as υἱὸς ἀνθρώπου[8] bears out. (Cf. also the synagogue of the Dura Europos,[9] which throws a new light on Jewish syncretism.)

What we call "Jesus Christ" is—I am afraid—much less a biographical problem than a social, i.e., collective, phenomenon, created by the coincidence of an ill-defined yet remarkable personality with a highly peculiar *Zeitgeist* that has its own no less remarkable psychology.

I must, dear Sir, apologize for the length of my letter. Having myself given a great deal of thought to the problem of Jesus, and

---

[7] = chosen (Matthew 22:14).

[8] = Son of Man.

[9] Dura Europos, ancient city on the Euphrates, founded under Seleukos I (312–280 B.C.), rediscovered 1921, excavated 1928–37. Among the extremely valuable objects discovered is a synagogue dating back to the 3rd cent. A.D. It contains frescoes with scenes from the OT, thus infringing the orthodox Jewish law against the making of images and showing the influence of the local Oriental civilization. For details cf. E. R. Goodenough, *Jewish Symbols in the Greco-Roman Period* (13 vols., 1953–68), vols. 9–11.

having also done some spadework in this field, I felt I had to give you an account of how and where I slipped up in trying to cope with the challenge of the Christian enigma.

Sure enough, we must believe in Reason. But it should not prevent us from recognizing a mystery when we meet one. It seems to me that no rational biography could explain one of the most "irrational" effects ever observed in the history of man. I believe that this problem can only be approached through his history and comparative psychology of symbols. Attempts in this direction have already yielded some interesting results. (Unfortunately there are no English publications yet to which I could refer.)

I am deeply obliged to you for your kind attention and I remain,

Yours sincerely, C. G. JUNG

To James Kirsch

[ORIGINAL IN ENGLISH]

Dear Kirsch,   18 November 1952

I am sending you an English letter this time as I am still unable to write longhand letters myself. I had another attack of arrhythmia and tachycardia due to overwork. I am now slowly recovering and my pulse is normal again for almost a week, but I am still tired and have to go slowly.

Your question[1] is a very important one and I think I can understand its full import. I would not be able to give you a satisfactory answer, yet having studied the question as far as is possible, I can call your attention to the extraordinary development in the Kabbalah. I am rather certain that the *sefiroth* tree[2] contains the whole symbolism of Jewish development parallel to the Christian idea. The characteristic difference is that God's incarnation is understood to be a historical fact in the Christian belief, while in the

---

□ See Kirsch, 26 May 34 (in vol. 1). — Published in *Psychological Perspectives* (Los Angeles), III:1 (spring 1972).

[1] Regarding the role which Christ and the Christian mystery play in the Jewish psyche.

[2] Cf. Fischer, 21 Dec. 44, n. 5. The ten *sefiroth* are usually arranged in the shape of a tree.

Jewish Gnosis it is an entirely pleromatic process symbolized by the concentration of the supreme triad of Kether, Hokhmah, and Binah in the figure of Tifereth.[3] Being the equivalent of the Son and the Holy Ghost, he is the *sponsus* bringing about the great solution through his union with Malkhuth. This union is equivalent to the *assumptio beatae virginis*, but definitely more comprehensive than the latter as it seems to include even the extraneous world of the Kelipoth.[4] X. is certainly all wet when he thinks that the Jewish Gnosis contains nothing of the Christian mystery. It contains practically the whole of it, but in its unrevealed pleromatic state.

There is a very interesting little Latin mediaeval book written either by Knorr von Rosenroth or at least under his direct influence. It is called *Adumbratio Kabbalae Christianae, Id est Syncatabasis Hebraizans, Sive Brevis Applicatio Doctrinae Hebraeorum Cabbalisticae Ad Dogmata Novi Foederis*. Francofurti, 1684. This little book is highly worth while; it contains a very useful parallel to the Christian and the Kabbalistic mystery and might give you much help as it has helped me in understanding this all-important problem of the Jewish religious development. It would be highly commendable to translate the book. I am pretty certain that the extraordinary and venomous response of the orthodox rabbis against the Kabbalah is based upon the undeniable fact of this most remarkable Judeo-Christian parallelism. This is hot stuff, and since the 17th century, as far as my knowledge goes, nobody has dared to touch it, but we are interested in the soul of man and therefore we are not blindfolded by foolish confessional prejudices.

.   .   .

Sincerely yours, c. g. j u n g

---

[3] Cf. ibid., also Neumann, 5 Jan. 52, n. 7. Hokhmah ("wisdom" of God) is the second *sefirah*; Binah ("intelligence" of God) the third. Malkhuth ("kingdom" of God) is the tenth, the mystical archetype of Israel's community, the Shekhinah. Cf. G. Scholem, *Major Trends in Jewish Mysticism* (1941), p. 209.

[4] The *kelipoth*, "shards" or "shells," are the daemonic forces of evil. According to the Kabbalist Isaac Luria (1534–72), they originated in the "breaking of the vessels" of the *sefiroth* which could not contain the power of God. The world of the *kelipoth* is the counterpole to the world of the *sefiroth*. Cf. "Answer to Job," CW 11, par. 595, n. 8, and Jaffé, *The Myth of Meaning*, pp. 122ff.

To Carl Seelig

Dear Dr. Seelig,   25 February 1953

I got to know Albert Einstein[1] through one of his pupils, a Dr. Hopf[2] if I remember correctly. Professor Einstein was my guest on several occasions at dinner, when, as you have heard, Adolf Keller[3] was present on one of them and on others Professor Eugen Bleuler, a psychiatrist and my former chief. These were very early days when Einstein was developing his first theory of relativity.[4] He tried to instil into us the elements of it, more or less successfully. As non-mathematicians we psychiatrists had difficulty in following his argument. Even so, I understood enough to form a powerful impression of him. It was above all the simplicity and directness of his genius as a thinker that impressed me mightily and exerted a lasting influence on my own intellectual work. It was Einstein who first started me off thinking about a possible relativity of time as well as space, and their psychic conditionality. More than thirty years later this stimulus led to my relation with the physicist Professor W. Pauli and to my thesis of psychic synchronicity. With Einstein's departure from Zurich my relation with him ceased, and I hardly think he has any recollection of me. One can scarcely imagine a greater contrast than that between the mathematical and the psychological mentality. The one is extremely quantitative and the other just as extremely qualitative.

With kind regards,

Yours sincerely, C. G. JUNG

□ (1894–1962), Swiss author, journalist, and theatre critic. Cf. his *Albert Einstein. Eine dokumentarische Biographie* (1952); *Albert Einstein, Leben und Werk eines Genies unserer Zeit* (1954). He asked Jung for his impressions of Einstein. — The letter was published in *Spring*, 1971.

[1] Einstein (1879–1955) had been living in Bern until 1909 as an examiner of patents at the Patent Office, during which period he took his Ph.D. at the U. of Zurich. After publishing several papers on physical subjects, he was appointed extraordinary professor of theoretical physics at the U. in 1909, and in 1912 professor at the Federal Polytechnic (E.T.H.). Cf. *The Freud/Jung Letters*, 230J, par. 1.

[2] Ludwig Hopf, theoretical physicist.

[3] Cf. Keller, 26 Mar. 51.

[4] In 1905 Einstein published his famous *On the Electrodynamics of Moving Bodies*, in which the principle of relativity is mentioned for the first time.

116

To Josef Rudin

Dear Dr. Rudin,   14 March 1953

I owe you many thanks for kindly sending me your essay[1] about *Job*. Psychologically, the divine polarity is a question of *oppositio* and not *contradictio*,[2] hence Nicolaus Cusanus speaks of *opposita*. The non-reciprocity of the God-man relationship[3] is a hard doctrine. Creatures would then be things but not free individuals, and what in the world would be the motive for the Incarnation if man's fate didn't affect God? Also, no one has ever heard of a bridge that leads only to the *other* bank of the river. Isn't the original idea that man can exercise no *compulsion* on God? But that man's prayers can reach God? And that the Incarnation makes God still more reachable?

Please excuse these naïve questions. They don't need answering.

Yours sincerely, C. G. JUNG

☐ S.J., psychotherapist, since 1967 professor at the U. of Innsbruck. Cf. his *Psychotherapie und Religion* (1964); *Fanatismus* (1965).
[1] "Antwort auf Hiob. Zum gleichnamigen Buch von C. G. Jung," *Orientierung* (Zurich), 28 Feb. 1953.
[2] R. suggested that the problem of the dual aspect of God might be solved by introducing the scholastic distinction between "opposition" and "contradiction," in the sense that an inner opposition of divers attributes could be ascribed to God but no contradiction.
[3] The Catholic teaching admitting the relation of man to God as necessary but not of God to man.

To Henry Corbin

Dear M. Corbin,   4 May 1953

A few days ago I received an offprint of your essay "La Sophie Éternelle."[1] Unfortunately it is impossible for me to express all the thoughts and feelings I had upon reading your admirable presentation of your subject. My French is so rusty that I cannot use it to formulate exactly what I want to say to you. Yet I must tell you how de-

☐ (Translated from French.) Henry Corbin, professor of Islamic religion at the École des Hautes Études, Sorbonne; directeur de département d'Iranologie de l'Institut Franco-Iranien, Teheran. Frequent lecturer at the Eranos meetings.
[1] *La Revue de culture européenne* (Paris), III:5 (1953).

117

lighted I was by your work. It was an extraordinary joy to me, and not only the rarest of experiences but even a unique experience, to be fully understood. I am accustomed to living in a more or less complete intellectual vacuum, and my *Answer to Job* has done nothing to diminish it. On the contrary, it has released an avalanche of prejudice, misunderstanding, and, above all, atrocious stupidity. I have received hundreds of critical reviews, but not a single one that comes anywhere near yours in its lucid and penetrating understanding. Your intuition is astounding: Schleiermacher[2] really is one of my spiritual ancestors. He even baptized my grandfather—born a Catholic—who by then was a doctor.[3] This grandfather became a great friend of the theologian de Wette,[4] who had connections of his own with Schleiermacher. The vast, esoteric, and individual spirit of Schleiermacher was a part of the intellectual atmosphere of my father's family. I never studied him, but unconsciously he was for me a *spiritus rector*.

You say you read my book as an "oratorio." The book "came to me" during the fever of an illness. It was as if accompanied by the great music of a Bach or a Handel. I don't belong to the auditory type. So I did not hear anything, I just had the feeling of listening to a great composition, or rather of being at a concert.

I should mention that de Wette had a tendency, as he said, to "mythize" the "marvellous" Bible stories (that is, the shocking ones). Thus he preserved their symbolic value. This is exactly what I have been forced to do not only for the Bible but also for the misdeeds in our dreams.

I don't know how to express my gratitude but, once again, I must

[2] Friedrich Schleiermacher (1768–1834), German Protestant theologian and philosopher. His writings excel by their combination of deep religiosity, clear intellect, and vivid sense of reality. Cf. Jung, 30 Dec. 59.

[3] Cf. ibid. Jung's grandfather Carl Gustav Jung (1794–1864), a convert to Protestantism, had to leave Germany for Switzerland in 1820 on account of his liberal political activities, after spending over a year in prison. In 1822 he became professor of medicine at the U. of Basel. Cf. Jung and Jaffé, *Erinnerungen, Träume, Gedanken*, pp. 400ff. (This section on the Jung family by Jaffé is omitted in the American/English edns. of *Memories*.) For his portrait, see *Memories*, facing p. 110/64.

[4] Wilhelm de Wette (1780–1849), German theologian. He was dismissed as professor of theology at Berlin U. on account of his progressive political sympathies in 1819, but three years later was appointed professor of theology at the U. of Basel. He has been described (by Julius Wellhausen, the German biblical scholar and Orientalist, 1844–1918, famous for his critical investigations into OT history) as "the epoch-making opener of the historical criticism of the Pentateuch."

tell you how much I appreciate your goodwill and your unique understanding.

My compliments to Madame Corbin. The caviar is not forgotten. With grateful regards,

Sincerely yours, c. g. j u n g

To Aniela Jaffé

Dear Aniela,   29 May 1953

. . .

The spectacle of eternal Nature gives me a painful sense of my weakness and perishability, and I find no joy in imagining an equanimity *in conspectu mortis*. As I once dreamt, my will to live is a glowing daimon, who makes the consciousness of my mortality hellish difficult for me at times. One can, at most, save face like the unjust steward, and then not always, so that my Lord wouldn't find even that much to commend. But the daimon recks nothing of that, for life, at the core, is steel on stone.

Cordially, c. g.

☐ (Handwritten.)

Anonymous

Dear N.,   Bollingen, 3 August 1953

Hearty thanks for your kind birthday wishes! Unfortunately I can't remember here in Bollingen what you sent me. There was such a flood of letters, flowers, and things pouring in on me that I can remember absolutely nothing except your letter with its main point, the question of *prayer*. This was and still is a problem for me. Some years ago I felt that all demands which go beyond what *is* are unjustified and infantile, so that we shouldn't ask for anything that is not granted. We can't remind God of anything or prescribe anything for him, except when he tries to force something on us that our human limitation cannot endure. The question is, of course, whether such things happen. I think the answer is yes, for if God needs us as regulators of his incarnation and his coming to consciousness, it is because in his

☐ (A woman in Switzerland.) (Handwritten.)

119

boundlessness he exceeds all the bounds that are necessary for becoming conscious. Becoming conscious means continual renunciation because it is an ever-deepening concentration.

If this is right, then it may be that God has to be "reminded." The innermost self of every man and animal, of plants and crystals, is God, but infinitely diminished and approximated to his ultimate individual form. In approximating to man he is also "personal," like an antique god, and hence "in the likeness of a man" (as Yahweh appeared to Ezekiel).

An old alchemist formulated the relation to God thus: "Help me, that I may help you!"[1]

With cordial greetings, c. g. j u n g

[1] Cf. *Psychology and Alchemy*, CW 12, par. 155, where Jung quotes a passage from the *Rosarium philosophorum* (Frankfurt a. M., 1150) in which the *lapis* says, "Protege me, protegam te" (Protect me, I will protect you).

To Aniela Jaffé

Dear Aniela,   Bollingen, 16 September 1953

Forgive me for answering your last letter only now. I was swamped with proof-reading and correspondence. On top of that the English proofs of "Synchronicity" with a lot of questions about terminology. I have at least 3 hours of writing to do 4 days a week. That is the maximum I can accomplish without having to pay for the excess with disturbed sleep and heart symptoms.

. . .

I have about 5 MSS to read here and besides that a lot of little jobs to do in and about the house. Everything goes slow, and I have to spare myself as my heartbeat is still arrhythmical. In general I'm getting better, as I can sleep properly again. Luckily the weather in the last weeks has been wonderfully kind to me.

Nothing doing with the mountains. It's all too complicated. I can walk only for ¼ hour at most and you get nowhere with that.

I see to my horror that I talk only of myself. Please excuse this senile egoism. The 79th year is 80 – 1, and that is a *terminus a quo* which you can't help taking seriously. The provisionalness of life is indescribable. Everything you do, whether watching a cloud or cooking soup, is done on the edge of eternity and is followed by the suffix

☐ (Handwritten.)

of infinity. It is meaningful and futile at once. And so is oneself, a wondrously living centre and at the same time an instant already sped. One is and is not. This frame of mind encompasses me and hems me in. Only with an effort can I look beyond into a semi-self-subsistent world I can barely reach, or which leaves me behind. Everything is right, for I lack the power to alter it. This is the débâcle of old age: "Je sais bien qu'à la fin vous me mettrez à bas."

Cordially, c . g .

To Pastor L. Memper

Dear Pastor Memper,   29 September 1953

Please excuse the lateness of my answer. Your letter was a great joy and brought back memories of old, long vanished times. It is now 59 years since I left the vicarage in Klein-Hüningen.[1] I thank you kindly for your invitation.[2] Formerly I would have accepted it without a qualm, because I feel a bond with all the stations of my way, but now I am too old and for reasons of health can no longer take on the responsibility of giving a difficult public address. It is a difficult art to speak to a simple public about a complicated matter. Anyway I would not have mounted the pulpit. This happened to me only once, at a teachers' congress in Bern, which without my previous knowledge was held in a church. To my terror I was forced into a pulpit, which gave me such a shock that I have never spoken in a church again. I hadn't realized how much a sacred and hallowed precinct meant to me. The profane use Protestants make of their churches I regard as a grave error. God may be everywhere, but this in no way absolves believers from the duty of offering him a place that is declared holy, otherwise one could just as well get together for religious purposes in the 3rd class waiting-room of a railway station. The Protestant is not even granted a quiet, pious place where he can withdraw from the turmoil of the world. And nowhere does there exist for God a sanctified *temenos*[3] which serves only one and a sacred purpose. No wonder so few people attend church.

[1] In 1879 Jung's father moved to Klein-Hüningen, near Basel, now M.'s parish. Cf. *Memories*, pp. 15ff./28ff.
[2] To address his congregation from the very pulpit from which Jung's father had preached.
[3] In Homer's usage, a king or a god's domain; in later times the sanctuary or

121

Formerly, in spite of my willingness to oblige, I would also have had to stipulate that the meeting should not in God's name be held in a church, as I am a practising anti-profanist. I hope you will forgive me for taking your kind invitation as a pretext for voicing my subjective protest. But I know from my many years of psychological practice how painful the rationalistic profanation of our churches is for very many educated people.

I have heard that my father's tombstone was set up near the church. Unfortunately I did not know at the time when the stone was made that my father was described as Dr. theol. instead of Dr. phil. He graduated as an Orientalist, in Arabic.

I was very glad to hear once again of my old home where I spent at least 16 years of my youth. I hope you won't mind my scruples. I found a magnificent temple in India,[4] now standing derelict in the desert. It was desecrated by the Moslems 400 years ago, which resulted in permanent desacralization. It gave me some idea of the strength of this feeling for a sacred precinct, and for the emptiness which arises when the profane breaks in. With kindest regards,

Yours sincerely, c. g. jung

---

precinct surrounding the altar. Jung makes frequent use of this term to describe a numinous area (cf. *Psychology and Alchemy*, CW 12, index). Mandalas often appear in this form.
[4] Apparently the ruined temple at Konarak. Cf. Mees, 15 Sept. 47, n. 10.

To John Weir Perry

[ORIGINAL IN ENGLISH]

Dear Perry,   8 February 1954

I am sorry that you had to wait so long until you got my answer to your question.[1] All sorts of things have intervened in the meantime, and my health also has misbehaved. I will try to answer your question as simply as possible; it is a difficult problem as you probably realize.

First of all, the regression that occurs in the rebirth or integration process is in itself a normal phenomenon inasmuch as you observe it also with people that don't suffer from any kind of psychopathic ailment. When it is matter of a schizoid condition, you observe very much the same, but with the difference that there is a marked ten-

---

[1] "Has it been your experience that in regression and rebirth, as the divine child emerges, the personal infantile complexes and needs tend to coincide and merge with it?"

dency of the patient to get stuck in the archetypal material. In this case, the rebirth process is repeated time and again. This is the reason why the classical schizophrenia develops stereotype conditions. Up to a certain point, you have the same experience with neurotic individuals. This is so because the archetypal material has a curious fascinating influence which tries to assimilate the individuals altogether. They are tempted to identify with any of the archetypal figures characteristic of the rebirth process. For this reason schizophrenic cases retain nearly always a certain markedly childish behaviour. You can observe approximately the same with neurotic patients; either they develop inflations on account of identification with the archetypal figures, or they develop a childish behaviour on account of the identity with the divine child. In all these cases the real difficulty is to free the patients from the fascination. Schizoid cases as well as neurotic ones very often repeat their personal infancy story. This is a favourable sign in so far as it is an attempt to grow up into the world again as they had done before, viz. in their infancy. They are children again after rebirth exactly as you say happened in the *Taurobolia*.[2]

As a rule, you haven't to take care of making patients revive their infantile reminiscences; generally they produce it all by themselves, because it is an unavoidable mechanism, and, as I said, a teleological attempt to grow up again. If you go quietly along with the material the patients produce, you will see that they can't help getting into their infantile reminiscences and habits and ways, and that they project particularly the parental images. Wherever there is a transference, you get unavoidably involved and integrated into the patient's family atmosphere. The insistence of the Freudians upon making people revive their past simply shows that in the Freudian analysis people don't naturally take to living their past again, simply because they have resistance against the analyst. If you let the unconscious have its natural way, then you may be sure everything the patient needs to know will be brought up, and you may be equally sure that everything you bring out from the patient by insistence on theoretical grounds will not be integrated into the patient's personality, at least not as a positive value, but maybe as a lasting resistance. Did it never occur to you that in my analysis we talked very little of "resistance," while in the Freudian analysis it is the term that most frequently occurs?

[2] Ritual baths of initiation in the blood of a sacrificial bull. They were taken over from the cult of Kybele into that of the Indo-Iranian god Mithras. Cf. Perry, *The Self in Psychotic Process*, p. 118.

When it comes to schizoid patients, there of course the difficulty of liberating them from the grip of the unconscious is much greater than in ordinary neurotic cases. Often they can't find their way back from their archetypal world to the equivalent personal infantile world where there would be a chance for liberation. Not in vain Christ insists upon "becoming like unto children," which means a conscious resolution to accept the attitude of the child as long as such an attitude is demanded by the circumstances. Since it is always the problem of accepting the shadow, it needs the simplicity of a child to submit to such a seemingly impossible task. So when you find that the rebirth process shows a tendency to repeat itself, you must realize that the fascination of the archetypal material has still to be overcome, perhaps because your help has been insufficient or the patient's attitude was unfavourable to it. But this aetiological question matters little. You simply must try again to convert the archetypal fascination into a child-like simplicity. There are of course many cases where our help is insufficient or comes too late, but that is so in all branches of medicine. I always try to follow the path of nature and I avoid as much as possible the application of theoretical viewpoints, and I have never regretted this principle.

I include a *charming example*[3] of a particularly enlightened American doctor just for your amusement or as a sort of consolation in case you don't get the desired understanding from your contemporaries.

Hoping you are in good health, I remain,

Yours cordially, c. g. j u n g

P.S. I think we underrate in Europe the difficulties you have to put up with in America as soon as you try to communicate something to your audience that demands a certain humanistic education. I am afraid that your educational system produces the same technological and scientific one-sidedness and the same social welfare idealism as Russia. Most of your psychologists, as it looks to me, are still in the XVIIIth century inasmuch as they believe that the human psyche is *tabula rasa*[4] at birth, while all somewhat differentiated animals are born with

---

[3] According to a communication from P., this is "a scurrilous and irresistibly witty diatribe called 'Jung Revisited' by Hiram Johnson, in a New Jersey psychiatric journal, of late '53 or early '54." It could not be traced.

[4] Jung repeatedly rejected the idea that the child is born with an "empty" psyche (*tabula rasa*, "erased tablet," is the wax writing tablet of the Romans on which the writing was erased after use). He held that "the child is born with a differentiated brain that is predetermined by heredity" ("Concerning the Archetypes, with Special Reference to the Anima Concept," CW 9, i, par. 136).

specific instincts. Man's psyche seems to be less [differentiated] than a weaver bird's or a bee's.

To James Kirsch

Dear Kirsch,   16 February 1954

. . .

I scarcely think that the Jews have to accept the Christ symbol. They need only understand its meaning. Christ wanted to change Yahweh into a moral God of goodness, but in so doing he tore apart the opposites (Satan falling from heaven, Luke 10:18) that were united in him (God) though in an inharmonious and unconscious way; hence the suspension between the opposites at the crucifixion. The purpose of the Christian reformation through Jesus was to eliminate the evil moral consequences that were caused by the amoral divine prototype. One cannot "strain at a gnat and swallow a camel" (Matt. 23:24) or "serve two masters" (Matt. 6:24) at the same time.

This moral differentiation is a necessary step on the way of individuation. Without thorough knowledge of "good and evil," ego and shadow, there is no recognition of the self, but at most an involuntary and therefore dangerous identification with it.

The Jew has roughly the same moral development behind him as the Christian European, consequently he has the same problem. A Jew can recognize the *self* in that hostile pair of brothers, Christ and Satan, as well as I can or perhaps even better, and with it the incarnation or Yahweh's assimilation to man. Naturally the status of man is profoundly altered because of this.

The Jew has the advantage of having long since anticipated the development of consciousness in his own spiritual history. By this I mean the Lurianic stage of the Kabbalah, the breaking of the vessels and man's help in restoring them.[1] Here the thought emerges for the first time that man must help God to repair the damage wrought by the Creation. For the first time man's cosmic responsibility is acknowledged. Naturally it is a question of the self and not the ego, although the latter will be deeply affected.

That is the answer I would give a Jew. With best regards,

Yours sincerely, C. G. JUNG

☐ (Handwritten.) Published (in K.'s tr.) in *Psychological Perspectives*, III:2 (fall 1972).
[1] Cf. Kirsch, 18 Nov. 52, n. 4.

To the Rev. Erastus Evans

[ORIGINAL IN ENGLISH]

Dear Mr. Evans,   17 February 1954

Allow me to tell you that I am profoundly grateful to you for your most remarkably objective review[1] of my uncouth attempt to disturb the obnoxious somnolence of the guardians. That is the way in which this damnable little book looks to me. *Habent sua fata libelli!* I would not have written this thing. I had kept away from it studiously. I had published before the volume *Aion* in polite language and as much man-made as possible. It was not sufficient apparently, because I got ill and when I was in the fever it caught me and brought me down to writing despite my fever, my age, and my heart that is none too good. I can assure you I am a moral coward as long as possible. As a good little bourgeois citizen, I am lying low and concealed as deeply as possible, still shocked by the amount of the indiscretions I have committed, swearing to myself that there would be no more of it because I want peace and friendly neighbourhood and a good conscience and the sleep of the just. Why should I be the unspeakable fool to jump into the cauldron?

Well, I don't want to be melodramatic. This is just for your personal information. I have no merit and no proper guilt since I got to it "like a dog to a kick," as we say. And the little moral coward I am goes on whining: why should I be always the one that collects all available kicks?

I tell you these things because you have been nice, just, and lenient with me. The attribute "coarse" is mild in comparison to what you feel when God dislocates your hip or when he slays the firstborn. I bet Jacob's punches he handed to the angel were not just caresses or polite gestures.[2] They were of the good hard kind; as you rightly say, "with the gloves off."

That is *one side* of my experiences with what is called "God." "Coarse" is too weak a word for it. "Crude," "violent," "cruel," "bloody," "hellish," "demonic" would be better. That I was not downright blasphemous I owe to my domestication and polite cowardice.

□ London.

[1] *An Assessment of Jung's "Answer to Job"* (Guild of Pastoral Psychology, Lecture No. 78; London, 1954).

[2] Cf. *Memories*, p. 344/317, where the situation of the individual who is compelled by dire necessity to act with "savage fatefulness"—as Jung was when writing "Job"—is illustrated by the story of Jacob's fight with the angel (Gen. 32:24ff.).

And at each step I felt hindered by a beatific vision of which I'd better say nothing.

You have interpreted my thoughts most admirably. There is only one point where it seems to me you slipped up, viz. in attributing the traditional, dogmatic, and "colloquial" picture of Christ to me. This is not my personal idea of Christ at all, as I am quite in sympathy with a much darker and harsher image of the man Jesus. The dogmatic and traditional conception of Christ however must be and is made as bright as possible—*lumen de lumine*[3]—and the black substance all in the other corner.

You have probably been shocked by the idea of the "hostile brethren"[4] and the incomplete incarnation.[5] If it had been complete, the logical consequence, the *parousia*, would have taken place. But Christ was in error about it.

Practically, it makes no difference whether the Christ of the gospels is undergoing an enantiodromia[6] into the relentless judge of the Revelations, or the God of love becoming the Destroyer.

Christ has an opposite—the Antichrist or (and) the Devil. If you see a bit too much darkness in his picture, you make him too much into the likeness of his father, and then it becomes difficult to understand why he taught a God so very different from the one of the OT. Or you disown the whole Christian tradition of the better part of 1900 years.

Christ is most decidedly not the whole Godhead as God is ἓν τὸ πᾶν.[7] Christ is the Anthropos that seems to be a prefiguration of what the Holy Ghost is going to bring forth in the human being. (I wish you would read my volume *Aion*, where you find most of the material behind *Answer to Job*.) In a tract of the *Lurianic Kabbalah*, the remark-

---

[3] Cf. White, 24 Nov. 53, n. 16.

[4] In "Answer to Job," CW 11, pars. 628f., it is argued that Satan and Christ, following the pattern of Cain and Abel, correspond to the archetype of the hostile brothers. The parallel is quite explicit in "Dogma of the Trinity," CW 11, par. 254, n. 19.

[5] "Answer to Job," pars. 657f.: "God's Incarnation in Christ requires continuation and completion because Christ, owing to his virgin birth and his sinlessness, was not an empirical being at all. . . . Christ is the first-born who is succeeded by an ever-increasing number of younger brothers and sisters." Cf. Matt. 16:27f.

[6] Literally, "running counter to," a philosophical term coined by Heraclitus, who conceived the universe as a conflict of opposites ruled by eternal justice. Jung used the term to describe "the emergence of the unconscious opposite in the course of time." Cf. *Psychological Types*, CW 6, Def. 18.

[7] = the One, the All.

127

able idea is developed that man is destined to become God's helper in the attempt to restore the vessels[8] which were broken when God thought to create a world. Only a few weeks ago, I came across this impressive doctrine which gives meaning to man's status exalted by the incarnation. I am glad that I can quote at least one voice in favour of my rather involuntary manifesto. Or don't you think that mankind should produce some adequate reflections before it blows itself up into eternity? I realized something when fire was raining upon German cities and Hiroshima was flashed out of existence. I thought it is a rather drastic world in which we live. There is a proverb that says: a coarse block wants a coarse wedge. No time for niceties! This is one of the troubles of our Christianity. I remain, dear Mr. Evans,

Yours gratefully, C. G. JUNG

[8] Cf. Kirsch, 18 Nov. 52, n. 4.

Anonymous

[ORIGINAL IN ENGLISH]

Dear Mr. N.,   2 October 1954

Not knowing the case of Mrs. N., I am quite unable to give you any advice how to treat her. At all events, at that age a psychosis is always a serious thing which transcends all human efforts. It all depends whether one can establish a mental and moral rapport with the patients. The shock treatment, as a rule, dulls their mental perception, so that there is usually little hope of gaining an influence on them. I certainly wouldn't know how you could set about giving her a religious outlook, since you yourself have a merely intellectual conception of the deity. I wouldn't go so far as to suggest that people with a religious outlook would be immune to psychosis. Such statement would only be true in borderline cases. The question of religion is not so simple as you see it: it is not at all a matter of intellectual conviction or philosophy or even belief, but rather a matter of inner experience. I admit that this is a conception which seems to be completely ignored by the theologians in spite of the fact that they talk a lot of it. St. Paul for instance was not converted to Christianity by intellectual or philosophical endeavour or by a belief, but by the force of his immediate inner experience. His belief was based upon it, but our modern theology turns the thing round and holds that we first ought to

☐ U.S.A.

128

believe and then we would have an inner experience, but this reversal forces people directly into a wrong rationalism that excludes even the possibility of an inner experience. It is quite natural that they identify the deity with cosmic energy, which is evidently impersonal and almost physical, and to which nobody can pray, but the inner experience is utterly different: it shows the existence of personal forces with which an intimate contact of a very personal nature is thoroughly possible. Nobody who is not really aware of an inner experience is able to transmit such a conviction to somebody else; mere talk—no matter how good its intention is—will never convey conviction. I have treated a great number of people without religious education and without a religious attitude, but in the course of the treatment, which as a rule is a long and a difficult undertaking, they inevitably had some inner experiences that gave them just the right attitude.

It is of course quite impossible to give you a short account of the way in which you attain that inner experience. It is particularly not true that anyone could say: it is so and so; it is not transmitted by words. I don't know whether you know something of my writings; there I say a lot about ways and means, but the danger is that when you read such things you get quite confused. You might have a talk with one of my pupils, e.g. Mrs. Frances G. Wickes,[1] 101 East 74th Street, New York. She could explain things to you better than I can do it in a letter.

Sincerely yours, C. G. JUNG

[1] Cf. Wickes, 9 Aug. 46.

To Aniela Jaffé

Dear Aniela,   22 October 1954

At last I have succeeded in assimilating coherently your 16 pages on *Der Tod des Vergil*.[1] It made a very powerful impression on me and I admired your careful hand, feeling its way along Broch's secret guidelines and from time to time bringing a treasure to light. You're quite right: *it's all there.*

I have wondered all the more about my reluctance which on all

☐ (Handwritten.)
[1] MS of an essay on Hermann Broch's novel *The Death of Vergil* (1945; tr. 1946). An expanded version of the essay was published in *Studien zur analytischen Psychologie C. G. Jungs*, II (1955).

sorts of pretexts has hitherto held me back from letting this *Tod des Vergil* approach me too closely. This morning the insight came to me: I was *jealous* of Broch because he has succeeded in doing what I had to forbid myself on pain of death. Whirling in the same netherworld maelstrom and wafted to ecstasy by the vision of unfathomable images I heard a voice whispering to me that I could make it "aesthetic," all the while knowing that the artist in words within me was the merest embryo, incapable of real artistry.[2] I would have produced nothing but a heap of shards which could never have been turned into a pot. In spite of this ever-present realization the artist homunculus in me has nourished all sorts of resentments and has obviously taken it very badly that I didn't press the poet's wreath on his head.

I had to tell you quickly about this psychological intermezzo. Next week I shall try to go on holiday. You can imagine my letter chaos—with no secretary!

Cordial greetings,

Very sincerely, C. G. JUNG

P.S. Anyway why did it have to be *the death of the poet?*

[2] Cf. *Memories*, pp. 185ff./178f.

To Upton Sinclair

[ORIGINAL IN ENGLISH]

Dear Mr. Sinclair,   7 January 1955

Having read your novel *Our Lady*[1] and having enjoyed every page of it, I cannot refrain from bothering you again with a letter. This is

□ This letter was published, with minor changes and some omissions, in *New Republic*, vol. 132, no. 8, issue 2100 (21 Feb. 1955). — As some of Jung's comments will hardly be intelligible to readers unfamiliar with *Our Lady*, a brief summary is given: The heroine of the story is Marya, a widow and grandmother, a peasant woman of ancient Nazareth speaking only Aramaic. Her son Jeshu, who is depicted as a religious and social revolutionary, has gone away on a mission, and in an agony of fear as to his future she consults a sorceress. Under a spell, she awakens in a great city (Los Angeles), moving with the crowd into a stadium where she witnesses what she takes to be a battle: the football game between Notre Dame U., Indiana, and the U. of California. Sitting next to her is a professor of Semitic languages at Notre Dame; on addressing the utterly bewildered woman he learns to his astonishment that she speaks ancient Aramaic. He hears her story and takes her to the bishop, who exorcises the demons and sends her back to Nazareth with no enlightenment whatever. There she rebukes the sorceress, saying: "I asked to see the future of myself and my son: and nothing I saw has anything to do with us."

[1] Emmaus, Pennsylvania, 1938.

the trouble you risk when giving your books to a psychologist who has made it his profession to receive impressions and to have reactions. On the day after I had read the story, I happened to come across the beautiful text of the "Exultet" in the Easter night liturgy:

> O inaestimabilis dilectio caritatis
> Ut servum redimeres, Filium tradidisti!
> O certe necessarium Adae peccatum,
> Quod Christi morte deletum est!
> O felix culpa
> Quae talem ac tantum meruit habere Redemptorem![2]

Although I am peculiarly sensitive to the beauty of the liturgical language and of the feeling expressed therein, something was amiss, as if a corner had been knocked off or a precious stone fallen from its setting. When trying to understand, I instantly remembered the bewildered Marya confronted with the incongruities of the exorcism, her beautiful and simple humanity caught in the coils of a vast historical process which had supplanted her concrete and immediate life by the almost inhuman superstructure of a dogmatic and ritual nature, so strange that, in spite of the identity of names and biographical items, she was not even able to recognize the story of herself and of her beloved son. By the way, a masterful touch! I also remembered your previous novel[3] about the idealistic youth who had almost become a saviour through one of those angelic tricks well known since the time of Enoch (the earthly adventure of Samiasaz[4] and his angelic host). And moreover, I recalled your Jesus biography.[5] Then I knew what it was that caused my peculiarly divided feeling: it was your common sense and realism, reducing the Holy Legend to human

---

[2] The Missale Romanum (liturgy of the Roman Catholic Mass), has the following text for Holy Saturday: "Oh unspeakable tenderness of charity! In order to redeem the servant, Thou hast given the son. Oh truly necessary sin of Adam which has been redeemed through the death of Christ. Oh happy guilt which has found so great a Redeemer!" — The term "felix culpa" (happy fault) goes back to St. Augustine.

[3] What Didymus Did (London, 1954), the story of a young gardener in a suburb of Los Angeles who is visited by an angel and receives the power to perform miracles. (Didymus, "twin," is the name of the apostle Thomas. Cf. John 11:16.)

[4] In the Book of Enoch, Samiasaz is the leader of the angels who took human wives (Gen. 6:2). Cf. "Answer to Job," CW 11, par. 689.

[5] Cf. Sinclair, 3 Nov. 52: A Personal Jesus.

131

proportions and to probable possibilities, that never fails in knocking off a piece of the spiritual architecture or in causing a slight tremor of the Church's mighty structure. The anxiety of the priests to suppress the supposedly satanic attempt at verisimilitude is therefore most convincing, as the devil is particularly dangerous when he tells the truth, as he often does (*vide* the biography of St. Anthony of Egypt by St. Athanasius[6]).

It is obviously your *laudabilis intentio* to extract a quintessence of truth from the incomprehensible chaos of historical distortions and dogmatic constructions, a truth of human size and acceptable to common sense. Such an attempt is hopeful and promises success, as the "truth" represented by the Church is so remote from ordinary understanding as to be well-nigh inacceptable. At all events, it conveys nothing any more to the modern mind that wants to understand since it is incapable of blind belief. In this respect, you continue the Strauss-Renan tradition in liberal theology.

I admit it is exceedingly probable that there is a human story at the bottom of it all. But under these conditions I must ask: Why the devil had this simple and therefore satisfactory story to be embellished and distorted beyond recognition? Or why had Jesus taken on unmistakably mythological traits already with the Gospel writers? And why is this process continued even in our enlightened days when the original picture has been obscured beyond all reasonable expectation? Why the Assumptio of 1950 and the Encyclical *Ad caeli Reginam*[7] of Oct. 11, 1954?

The impossibility of a concrete saviour, as styled by the Gospel writers, is and has always been to me obvious and indubitable. Yet I know my contemporaries too well to forget that to them it is news hearing the simple fundamental story. Liberal theology and incidentally your *laudabilis intentio* have definitely their place where they make sense. To me the human story is the inevitable *point de*

[6] St. Athanasius (*ca.* 293–373), archbishop of Alexandria, wrote a biography of St. Anthony (*ca.* 250–350), the first Christian monk. St. Anthony is noted for his fights with the devil, who appeared to him under manifold disguises. In one story the devil admits defeat by the saint, hoping to seduce him into the sin of pride. A long excerpt from the biography, "Life of St. Anthony," in *The Paradise or Garden of the Holy Fathers* (1904), is in *Psychological Types*, CW 6, par. 82.
[7] After having promulgated the dogma of the bodily assumption of Mary into heaven in *Munificentissimus Deus*, Nov. 1950, Pius XII confirmed it in his Encyclical *Ad Caeli Reginam*, 11 Oct. 1954, which established a yearly feast in honour of Mary's "royal dignity" as Queen of Heaven and Earth.

départ, the self-evident basis of historical Christianity. It is the "small beginnings" of an amazing development. But the human story—I beg your pardon—is just ordinary, well within the confines of everyday life, not exciting and unique and thus not particularly interesting. We have heard it a thousand times and we ourselves have lived it at least in parts. It is the well-known psychological *ensemble* of Mother and beloved Son, and how the legend begins with mother's anxieties and hopes and son's heroic fantasies and helpful friends and foes joining in, magnifying and augmenting little deviations from the truth and thus slowly creating the web called the *reputation of a personality*.

Here you have me—the psychologist—with what the French call his *déformation professionnelle*. He is *blasé*, overfed with the "simple" human story, which does not touch his interest and particularly not his religious feeling. The human story is even the thing to get away from, as the small story is neither exciting nor edifying. On the contrary, one wants to hear the great story of gods and heroes and how the world was created and so on. The small stories can be heard where the women wash in the river, or in the kitchen or at the village well, and above all everybody lives them at home. That has been so since the dawn of consciousness. But there was a time in antiquity, about the fourth century B.C. (I am not quite certain about the date. Being actually away on vacation, I miss my library!), when a man Euhemeros[8] made himself a name through a then new theory: The divine and heroic myth is founded upon the small story of an ordinary human chief or petty king of local fame, magnified by a minstrel's fantasy. All-Father Zeus, the mighty "gatherer of clouds," was originally a little tyrant, ruling some villages from his *maison forte* upon a hill, and "nocturnis ululatibus horrenda Proserpina"[9] was presumably his awe-inspiring mother-in-law. That was certainly a time sick of the old gods and their ridiculous fairy stories, curiously similar to the "enlightenment" of our epoch equally fed up with its "myth" and welcoming any kind of iconoclasm, from the *Encyclopédie*[10] of the XVIIIth century to the Freudian theory reducing the religious "illusion" to the basic "family romance" with its incestuous innuendos

[8] Euhemeros, Greek philosopher (*fl.* 4th–3rd cent. B.C.). He taught that the Olympians were originally great kings and war heroes.
[9] "Proserpine striking terror with midnight ululations." — Apuleius, *The Golden Ass*, XI, 2.
[10] *Encyclopédie ou Dictionnaire raisonée des sciences, des arts et des métiers*, edited by Diderot (1713–84), became one of the most important influences in the French Enlightenment.

in the early XXth century. Unlike your predecessor, you do not insist upon the *chronique scandaleuse* of the Olympians and other ideals, but with a loving hand and with decency like a benevolent pedagogue, you take your reader by the hand: "I am going to tell you a better story, something nice and reasonable, that anybody can accept. I don't repeat these ancient absurdities, these god-awful theologoumena[11] like the Virgin Birth, blood and flesh mysteries, and other wholly superfluous miracle gossip. I show you the touching and simple humanity behind these gruesome inventions of benighted ecclesiastical brains."

This is a kind-hearted iconoclasm far more deadly than the frankly murderous arrows from M. de Voltaire's quiver: all these mythological assertions are so obviously impossible that their refutation is not even needed. These relics of the dark ages vanish like morning mist before the rising sun, when the idealistic and charming gardener's boy experiments with miracles of the good old kind, or when your authentic Galilean grandmother "Marya" does not even recognize herself or her beloved son in the picture produced by the magic mirror of Christian tradition.

Yet, why should a more or less ordinary story of a good mother and her well-meaning idealistic boy give rise to one of the most amazing mental or spiritual developments of all times? Who or what is its *agens*? Why could the facts not remain as they were originally? The answer is obvious: The story is so ordinary that there would not have been any reason for its tradition, quite certainly not for its world-wide expansion. The fact that the original situation has developed into one of the most extraordinary myths about a divine *heros*, a God-man and his cosmic fate, is not due to its underlying human story, but to the powerful action of pre-existing mythological motifs attributed to the biographically almost unknown Jesus, a wandering miracle Rabbi in the style of the ancient Hebrew prophets, or of the contemporary teacher John the Baptizer, or of the much later Zaddiks of the Chassidim.[12] The immediate source and origin of the myth projected upon the teacher Jesus is to be found in the then popular Book of Enoch and its central figure of the "Son of Man" and his messianic mission.

[11] Teachings not part of Church dogma but supported by theologians; more generally, theological formulations of the nature of God.
[12] The Chassidim (or Hasidim) were a mystical sect of Judaism, founded shortly before the middle of the 18th cent. by the mystic Israel Baal Shem ("Master of the Holy Name"; 1700–1760). The leaders were called Zaddiks (righteous men).

From the Gospel texts it is even manifest that Jesus identified himself with this "Son of Man." Thus it is the spirit of his time, the collective hope and expectation, which caused this astounding transformation and not at all the more or less insignificant story of the man Jesus. The true *agens* is the archetypal image of the God-man, appearing in Ezekiel's vision[13] for the first time in Jewish history, but in itself a considerably older figure in Egyptian theology, viz., Osiris and Horus.

The transformation of Jesus, i.e., the integration of his human self into a super- or inhuman figure of a deity, accounts for the amazing "distortion" of his ordinary personal biography. In other words: the essence of Christian tradition is by no means the simple man Jesus whom we seek in vain in the Gospels, but the lore of the God-man and his cosmic drama. Even the Gospels themselves make it their special job to prove that their Jesus is the incarnated God equipped with all the magic powers of a κύριος τῶν πνευμάτων.[14] That is why they are so liberal with miracle gossip which they naïvely assume proves their point. It is only natural that the subsequent post-apostolic developments even went several points better in this respect, and in our days the process of mythological integration is still expanding and spreading itself even to Jesus' mother, formerly carefully kept down to the human rank and file for at least 500 years of early church history. Boldly breaking through the sacrosanct rule about the definability of a new dogmatic truth, viz., that the said truth is only *definibilis* inasmuch as it was believed and taught in apostolic times, *explicite* or *implicite*, the pope has declared the *Assumptio Mariae* a dogma of the Christian creed. The justification he relies on is the pious belief of the masses for more than 1000 years, which he considers sufficient proof of the work of the Holy Ghost. Obviously the "pious belief" of the masses continues the process of projection, i.e., of transformation of human situations into myth.

But why should there be myth at all? My letter is already too long so that I can't answer this last question any more, but I have written several books about it. I only wanted to explain to you my idea that in trying to extract the quintessence of Christian tradition, you have removed it like Prof. Bultmann in his attempt at "demythologizing" the Gospels. One cannot help admitting that the human story is so very much more probable, but it has little or nothing to do with the problem of the myth containing the essence of Christian religion. You

13 Ezekiel 1:26.
14 = Lord of the spirits.

catch your priests most cleverly in the disadvantageous position which they have created for themselves by their preaching a concrete historicity of clearly mythological facts. Nobody reading your admirable novel can deny being deeply impressed by the very dramatic confrontation of the original with the mythological picture, and very probably he will prefer the human story to its mythological "distortion."

But what about the εὐαγγέλιον, the "message" of the God-man and Redeemer and his divine fate, the very foundation of everything that is holy to the Church? There is the spiritual heritage and harvest of 1900 years still to account for, and I am very doubtful whether the reduction to common sense is the correct answer or not. As a matter of fact, I attribute an incomparably greater importance to the dogmatic truth than to the probable human story. The religious need gets nothing out of the latter, and at all events less than from a mere belief in Jesus Christ or any other dogma. Inasmuch as the belief is real and living, it works. But inasmuch as it is mere imagination and an effort of the will without understanding, I see little merit in it. Unfortunately, this unsatisfactory condition prevails in modern times, and in so far as there is nothing beyond belief without understanding but doubt and scepticism, the whole Christian tradition goes by the board as a mere fantasy. I consider this event a tremendous loss for which we are to pay a terrific price. The effect becomes visible in the dissolution of ethical values and a complete disorientation of our *Weltanschauung*. The "truths" of natural science or "existential philosophy" are poor surrogates. Natural "laws" are in the main mere abstractions (being statistical averages) instead of reality, and they abolish individual existence as being merely exceptional. But the individual as the only carrier of life and existence is of paramount importance. He cannot be substituted by a group or by a mass. Yet we are rapidly approaching a state in which nobody will accept individual responsibility any more. We prefer to leave it as an odious business to groups and organizations, blissfully unconscious of the fact that the group or mass psyche is that of an animal and wholly inhuman.

What we need is the development of the inner spiritual man, the unique individual whose treasure is hidden on the one hand in the symbols of our mythological tradition, and on the other hand in man's unconscious psyche. It is tragic that science and its philosophy discourage the individual and that theology resists every reasonable

136

attempt to understand its symbols. Theologians call their creed a *symbolum*,[15] but they refuse to call their truth "symbolic." Yet, if it is anything, it is anthropomorphic symbolism and therefore capable of re-interpretation.

Hoping you don't mind my frank discussion of your very inspiring writings,

I remain, with my best wishes for the New Year,

Yours sincerely, c. g. j u n g

P.S. Thank you very much for your kind letter that has reached me just now. I am amazed at the fact that you should have difficulties in finding a publisher.[16] What is America coming to, when her most capable authors cannot reach their public any more? What a time!

[15] A *symbolum*, in the theological sense, is the formulation of a basic tenet of Christian faith; the creeds were *symbola*. Cf. "Dogma of the Trinity," CW 11, pars. 210ff.
[16] In his letter S. spoke of his difficulties in finding a publisher for *What Didymus Did*. It was never published in America but only in England. — This postscript was added in handwriting.

To Pater Lucas Menz, O.S.B.

Dear Pater Lucas,   22 February 1955

I have read your draft with great interest. Considering the terrible time in which we are living, I am bound to agree. It reminds me of the beneficent work of the O.S.B.[1] in those dark centuries when the culture of antiquity was gradually falling into decay. Now once again we are in a time of decay and transition, as around 2000 b.c., when the Old Kingdom of Egypt collapsed, and at the beginning of the Christian era, when the New Kingdom finally came to an end and with it classical Greece. The vernal equinox is moving out of the sign of Pisces into the sign of Aquarius, just as it did out of Taurus (the old bull gods) into Aries (the ram-horned gods) and then out of Aries (the sacrificed lamb) into Pisces ('Ιχθύς). It is to be hoped that the O.S.B. will succeed in launching another salvaging operation this time too. 1500 years ago St. Benedict could pour the new wine into new

☐ Ettal Abbey, Bavaria.
[1] Monastic Order of St. Benedict of Nursia, the Benedictines, or Black Monks.

bottles; or rather, the seeds of a new culture germinating in the decay were bedded in the new spirit of Christianity. Our apocalyptic epoch likewise contains the seeds of a different, unprecedented, and still inconceivable future which could be bedded in the Christian spirit if only this would renew itself, as happened with the seeds that sprouted from the decay of classical culture.

But here, it seems to me, lies the great difficulty. The coming new age will be as vastly different from ours as the world of the 19th century was from that of the 20th with its atomic physics and its psychology of the unconscious. Never before has mankind been torn into two halves, and never before was the power of absolute destruction given into the hand of man himself. It is a "godlike" power that has fallen into human hands. The *dignitas humani generis* has swollen into a truly diabolical grandeur.

What answer will the genius of mankind give? Or what will God do about it? You answer with the historical spirit in which St. Benedict answered, but he spoke and acted with a new spirit that was a match for the anti-spirit of his age. Is that answer also equal to the present problem? And does it comprehend the terrible grandeur that has revealed itself in man?

It seems to me we haven't yet noticed that such a question has been posed at all. We are still stuck in the fearful murk and confusion of unconsciousness. Christianity brought the world a new light, the *lux moderna*[2] (as the alchemists called their *lumen naturae*). Today this light flickers and wavers alarmingly, and the wheel of history cannot be turned back. Even the Emperor Augustus with all his power could not push through his attempts at repristination.

You have rightly guessed that I am as worried as you are and have every sympathy with your aspirations. But why do you turn to me, a dyed-in-the-wool Protestant? Presumably you are thinking of my psychology which, though born of the Christian spirit, seeks to give adequate answers to the spirit of this age: the voice of a doctor struggling to heal the psychic confusion of his time and thus compelled to use a language very different from yours. In all too many cases the old language is no longer understood, or is understood in the wrong way. If I have to make the meaning of the Christian message intel-

---

[2] The term *lux moderna*, the new light, occurs for instance in an alchemical compilation by Johann Daniel Mylius, *Philosophia reformata* (1622), p. 244. Cf. *Mysterium Coniunctionis*, CW 14, par. 718 & n. 143.

ligible to a patient, I must *translate* it with a commentary. In fact this is one practical aim of my psychology, or rather psychotherapy. The theologian could hardly go along with this, although St. Paul himself spoke Greek to the Greeks and probably wouldn't have been deterred even if the head of the community at Jerusalem had forbidden it.

I am taking the liberty of sending you my book *Aion*, from which you will see that you are dealing with a heretic and could get your fingers burned. I would like to spare you this, for you can help many people even without modern psychology. I can only wish your endeavour every success, since I understand it perfectly although outsiders can't see that. For most people my Christian standpoint remains hidden, and because of the strangeness of my language and the incomprehensibility of my interests I am given a wide berth. With kind regards,

Yours sincerely, C. G. JUNG

To Pater Lucas Menz

Dear Pater Lucas,   28 March 1955

Many thanks for your kind and illuminating letter. It affords me an invaluable glimpse into the process of becoming whole and holy. On the way back through the history of mankind[1] we integrate much that belongs to us and, deep down, also something of brother animal, who is actually holier than us since he cannot deviate from the divine will implanted in him because his dark consciousness shows him no other paths. On this way back—no matter where it is begun if only it is trodden in earnest—we fall into the fire or, as the logion says, come near to it: "He that is near me is near the fire. He that is far from me is far from the kingdom."[2]

The "taming of the beast," as you call it, is indeed a long process and coincides with the dissolution of *egohood*. What you call "deselving" I call "becoming a self": what previously seemed to be "ego" is taken up into a greater dimension which dwarfs and surrounds me on all sides, and which I cannot grasp in its totality. In this connec-

---

[1] M. wrote that for him the process of becoming holy was a journey through the entire history of mankind, back to Adam.
[2] James, *The Apocryphal New Testament*, p. 35.

tion you, like me, rightly quote Paul,[3] who formulates the same experience.

This experience is a charisma on the one hand, for it is not vouchsafed to us *nisi Deo concedente*. On the other hand it is vouchsafed only if we give up the ego as the supreme authority and put ourselves wholly under the will of God.

You yourself feel the need for a definition of "perfection." You define it as the "complete unfolding of nature on the level of holiness, brought about by surrendering to God." In so far as God is wholeness himself, himself whole and holy, man attains his wholeness only in God, that is, in self-completeness, which in turn he attains only by submitting to God's will. Since man in the state of wholeness and holiness is far from any kind of "perfection," the New Testament τέλειος[4] must surely be translated as "complete." For me the state of human wholeness is one of "completeness" and not of "perfection," an expression which, like "holiness," I tend to avoid.

You describe the ego (after the "taming of the beast") as being "in complete possession of itself." Here I would say that the resistance coming from the psychic depths ceases if we can give up our egohood, and the self (consciousness + unconscious) receives us into its greater dimension, where we are then "whole," and because of our relative wholeness we are near to that which is truly whole, namely God. (This is discussed in chs. IV and V of *Aion*.) Hence I would say that God is then "in complete possession of the ego and of myself" rather than stress the power of the ego.

I don't know whether it is permissible, in our incompetence, to think on things divine. I find that all my thoughts circle round God like the planets round the sun, and are as irresistibly attracted by him. I would feel it the most heinous sin were I to offer any resistance to this compelling force. I feel it is God's will that I should exercise the gift of thinking that has been vouchsafed me. Therefore I put my thinking at his service and so come into conflict with the traditional doctrine, above all with the doctrine of the *privatio boni*. Again, I have asked various theologians in vain what exactly is the relation-

---

[3] "For in him we live, and move, and have our being" (Acts 17:28).

[4] Cf. Matthew 5:48: "Be ye therefore perfect, even as your Father which is in heaven is perfect." The distinction between perfection and completeness plays an important role in Jung's psychology. *Psychology and Alchemy*, CW 12, par. 208: ". . . life calls not for perfection but for completeness." Cf. also *Aion*, CW 9, ii. pars. 123, 333.

ship of Yahweh to the God of the Christians, since Yahweh, though a guardian of justice and morality, is himself unjust (hence Job 16:19ff.). And how is this paradoxical being related to the Summum Bonum? According to Isaiah 48:10–11 Yahweh torments mankind for his own sake: "Propter me, propter me faciam!"[5] This is understandable in terms of his paradoxical nature, but not in terms of the Summum Bonum, which by definition already has everything it needs for perfection. Hence it has no need of man, unlike Yahweh. I must question the doctrine of the Summum Bonum because the non-existence of evil deprives evil of all substance and leaves over only the good or else nothing at all, which, since it is nothing, also effects nothing, i.e., cannot cause even the tiniest evil impulse. And since it is nothing, it cannot come from man either. Moreover the devil was there *before* man and was certainly not good. But the devil is not *nothing*. The opposite of the good is therefore not nothing but an equally real evil.

The depth of the psyche, the unconscious, is not made by man but is divinely created nature, which should on no account be reviled by man even though it causes him the greatest difficulties. Its fire, which "refines" us "in the furnace of affliction," is according to Isaiah 48:10 the divine will itself, i.e., the will of Yahweh, who *needs* man. Man's understanding and will are challenged and can help, but they can never pretend to have plumbed the depths of the spirit and to have quenched the fire raging within it. We can only hope that God, in his grace, will not compel us to go deeper and let ourselves be consumed by his fire.[6]

You have evidently offered him sacrifice enough by withstanding his fire until your egohood was sufficiently subdued. In reality your ego is by no means in complete possession of itself but has been practically reduced to ashes, so that you have become capable of a measure of selfless love. You could indeed rejoice over this did not your "joyfulness" crassly conflict with the suffering of the world and your fellow man. Even the Redeemer on the Cross uttered no joyful cry despite his having been credited with completely overcoming the world and himself. An "object" (as you put it), i.e., a *human being* who does not know that he has enkindled love in you does not feel loved but humiliated because he is simply subjected or exposed to your own psychic state in which he himself has no part. Being loved

---

[5] Isaiah 48:11: "For my own sake, even for my own sake will I do it."
[6] Most of this paragraph is quoted in Jaffé, *The Myth of Meaning* (orig. 1969; tr. 1971), p. 120.

141

in that way would leave me cold. But you yourself say that inasmuch as one is oneself one is also the *other*. Then *his* suffering will also affect *you* and detract from your joyfulness. But when you go on to say that you "don't need Creation any more" you give your fellow man (who is also part of Creation) to understand that he is superfluous for you, even though you "joyfully acclaim God through him."

It falls to the lot of anyone who has overcome something or detached himself from something to bear in the same measure the burdens of others. Generally they are so heavy that any shouts of joy die on one's lips. One is glad if only one can draw breath from time to time.

Much as I can go along with you in the process of "becoming whole and holy," or individuation, I cannot subscribe to your statements about the "ego in complete possession of itself" and unrelated universal love, although they bring you perilously close to the ideal of Yoga: *nirdvandva* (free from the opposites). I know these moments of liberation come flashing out of the process, but I shun them because I always feel at such a moment that I have thrown off the burden of being human and that it will fall back on me with redoubled weight.

You don't need to change your standpoint in any way in order to gain a knowledge of the archetypes. You are in the thick of it, even if you should take the view of the father confessor who told a student who came to him for advice on the study of psychology: "Don't study anything that upsets you."

As we have not yet reached the state of eternal bliss, we are still suspended on the Cross between ascent and descent, not only for our own but for God's sake and mankind's. With kind regards,

Yours sincerely, C. G. JUNG

To Pastor Jakob Amstutz

Dear Pastor Amstutz,   Mammern, 23 May 1955

Meanwhile I have read your typescript, "Zum Verständnis der Lehre vom werdenden Gotte." It seems to me one more proof of the overweening gnostic tendency in philosophical thinking to ascribe to God qualities which are the product of our own anthropomorphic

□ Mammern (Cant. Thurgau) is a village on Lake Constance.

142

formulations. Every metaphysical judgment is *necessarily antinomian*, since it transcends experience and must therefore be complemented by its counterposition. If we describe God as "evolving," we must bear in mind at the same time that perhaps he is so vast that the process of cognition only moves along his contours, as it were, so that the attribute "evolving" applies more to it than to him. Moreover, "evolving" as a quality of human cognition is far more probable empirically than the presumptuous projection of this quality on to a Being whose nature and scope transcend by definition our human stature in every respect. Such projective statements are pure gnosticism.

I hold the contrary view that there are certain experiences (of the most varied kinds) which we characterize by the attribute "divine" without being able to offer the slightest proof that they are caused by a Being with any definite qualities. Were such a proof possible, the Being that caused them could only have a finite nature and so, by definition, could not be God. For me "God" is on the one hand a mystery that cannot be unveiled, and to which I must attribute only *one* quality: that it exists in the form of a particular psychic event which I feel to be numinous and cannot trace back to any sufficient cause lying within my field of experience.

On the other hand "God" is a verbal image, a predicate or mythologem founded on archetypal premises which underlie the structure of the psyche as images of the instincts ("instinctual patterns"). Like the instincts, these images possess a certain autonomy which enables them to break through, sometimes against the rational expectations of consciousness (thus accounting in part for their numinosity). "God" in this sense is a biological, instinctual and elemental "model," an archetypal "arrangement" of individual, contemporary and historical contents, which, despite its numinosity, is and must be exposed to intellectual and moral criticism, just like the image of the "evolving" God or of Yahweh or the Summum Bonum or the Trinity.

"God" as a mythologem dominates your discussion, which casts a deceptive veil over the religious reality. For the religious man it is an embarrassment to speak of the mystery which he can say nothing about anyway except paradoxes, and which he would rather conceal from profane eyes if he had anything in his hands at all that he could conceal from anybody. It is unfortunately true: he has and holds a mystery in his hands and at the same time is contained in its mystery.

What can he proclaim? Himself or God? Or neither? The truth is that he doesn't know who he is talking of, God or himself.

All talk of God is mythology, an archetypal pronouncement of archetypal causation. Mythology as a vital psychic phenomenon is as necessary as it is unavoidable. Metaphysical speculations that keep within the bounds of reason (in the wider sense) are therefore quite in place so long as one is aware of their anthropomorphism and their epistemological limitations. The relatively autonomous life of the archetypes requires symbolic statements like the "evolving God" or the encyclicals *Munificentissimus Deus* and *Ad Caeli Reginam* or God as *complexio oppositorum*, etc., because collective psychic life is strongly influenced by changes in the "Pleroma" of the *mundus archetypus* (cf. Hitler's "saviour epidemic" and the worldwide Communist delusion of a Utopia peopled by human robots).

In this discussion, it seems to me, the gnostic danger of ousting the unknowable and incomprehensible and unutterable God by philosophems and mythologems must be clearly recognized, so that nothing is shoved in between human consciousness and the primordial numinous experience. The mythologem of the Incarnation seems to serve this purpose indirectly, because it is symbolic.

I hope you won't find my criticism of your discussion officious, but will take it rather as an expression of my sympathetic interest. For us psychotherapists, at any rate for those of them who have come to see how great is the importance of the religious attitude for psychic equilibrium, theological discussions are of the utmost practical value, because questions of this kind are directed to us more often than the layman imagines.

Yours sincerely, C. G. JUNG

Anonymous

[ORIGINAL IN ENGLISH]

Dear Mrs. N.,   19 November 1955

I am glad that you do understand the difficulty of your request. How can anybody be expected to be competent enough to give such advice? I feel utterly incompetent—yet I cannot deny the justification of your wish and I have no heart to refuse it. If your case were my

☐ The letter is addressed to a sick old lady in England. — Published in *Spring*, 1971, pp. 133f.

own, I don't know what could happen to me, but I am rather certain that I would not plan a suicide ahead. I should rather hang on as long as I can stand my fate or until sheer despair forces my hand. The reason for such an "unreasonable" attitude with me is that I am not at all sure what will happen to me after death. I have good reasons to assume that things are not finished with death. Life seems to be an interlude in a long story. It has been long before I was, and it will most probably continue after the conscious interval in a three-dimensional existence. I shall therefore hang on as long as it is humanly possible and I try to avoid all foregone conclusions, considering seriously the hints I got as to the *post mortem* events.

Therefore I cannot advise you to commit suicide for so-called reasonable considerations. It is murder and a corpse is left behind, no matter who has killed whom. Rightly the English Common Law punishes the perpetrator of the deed. Be sure first, whether it is really the will of God to kill yourself or merely your reason. The latter is positively not good enough. If it should be the act of sheer despair, it will not count against you, but a willfully planned act might weigh heavily against you.

This is my incompetent opinion. I have learned caution with the "perverse." I do not underestimate your truly terrible ordeal. In deepest sympathy,

Yours cordially, C. G. JUNG

To Erich Neumann

Dear Neumann,   15 December 1955

Deepest thanks for your heartfelt letter. Let me in return express my condolences on the loss of your mother. I am sorry I can only set down these dry words, but the shock I have experienced is so great that I can neither concentrate nor recover my power of speech. I would have liked to tell the heart you have opened to me in friendship that two days before the death of my wife I had what one can only call a great illumination which, like a flash of lightning, lit up a centuries-old secret that was embodied in her and had exerted an unfathomable influence on my life. I can only suppose that the illumination came from my wife, who was then mostly in a coma, and that

□ (Handwritten.)

145

the tremendous lighting up and release of insight had a retroactive effect upon her, and was one reason why she could die such a painless and royal death.

The quick and painless end—only five days between the final diagnosis and death—and this experience have been a great comfort to me. But the stillness and the audible silence about me, the empty air and the infinite distance, are hard to bear.

With best greetings also to your wife and my warmest thanks,

Ever your devoted C. G. JUNG

To Eugen Böhler

Dear Professor Böhler,   16 May 1956

Best thanks for your friendly letter and my apologies for tearing the MS[1] away from you. All the copies have still to be corrected. I have already availed myself of your valuable suggestions, as you will see in the printed text.

Your remarks[2] obviously touch on something very essential in my style, though I wasn't aware of it at all. For decades I have been either not understood or misunderstood, despite all the care I took to begin with in the matter of "communication and logical persuasion." But because of the novelty of my subject as well as of my thoughts I ran up everywhere against an impenetrable wall. This is probably why my style changed in the course of the years, since I only said what was relevant to the business in hand and wasted no more time and energy thinking about all the things that ill-will, prejudice, stupidity and whatnot can come up with. Bachofen, for example, took infinite pains to be persuasive. All in vain. His time had not yet come. I have resigned myself to being posthumous.

It is still much too early to speak to an educated public about "symbols of self-recollection." It would all be utterly incomprehensible since the foundations for any real understanding don't yet exist.

☐ (Handwritten.)
[1] The MS of "Gegenwart und Zukunft," now "The Undiscovered Self," CW 10.
[2] B. wrote that his discussions with Jung had made him aware that he, Jung, "thanks to your sharp and extensive observation and your originality, have become accustomed to seeing things only for yourself," whereas he, Böhler, was still striving for communication and logical persuasion.

First and foremost it must be understood what the bell is tolling. Your dream tells us.[3] It begins high up in metaphysics. Already it stalks the earth. Your dream is an epilogue to my MS. With best greetings,

Yours sincerely, c . g . j u n g

[3] A figure, invisible at first, approached him from the left. When the figure uncovered its face, it was Satan.

To William Kinney

[ORIGINAL IN ENGLISH]

Dear Mr. Kinney,   26 May 1956

In answering your letter of May 7th I must tell you that there is neither an easy answer to the problem of ethics,[1] nor are there any books that would give you satisfactory guidance as far as my knowledge goes. Ethics depend upon the supreme decision of a Christian conscience, and conscience itself does not depend upon man alone, but as much upon the counterpart of man, namely God. The ethical question boils down to the relationship between man and God. Any other kind of ethical decision would be a conventional one, which means that it would depend upon a traditional and collective code of moral values. Since such values are general and not specific, they don't exactly apply to individual situations, as little as a schematic diagram expresses the variations of individual events. To follow a moral code would amount to the same as an intellectual judgment about an individual, viewed from the standpoint of anthropological statistics. Moreover, making a moral code the supreme arbiter of your ethical conduct would be a substitute for the will of a living God, since the moral code is made by man and declared to be a law given by God himself. The great difficulty of course is the "Will of God." Psychologically the "Will of God" appears in your inner experience in the form of a superior deciding power, to which you may give various names like instinct, fate, unconscious, faith, etc.

The psychological criterion of the "Will of God" is forever the

[1] K., describing himself as "a freshman at Northwestern U., Evanston, Illinois, with the conscious purpose of finding some meaning in life," asked for an answer to the problem of ethics and value judgments. Later, a graduate student of philosophy at Ohio State U.

147

dynamic superiority. It is the factor that finally decides when all is said and done. It is essentially something you cannot know beforehand. You only know it after the fact. You only learn it slowly in the course of your life. You have to live thoroughly and very consciously for many years in order to understand what your will is and what Its will is. If you learn about yourself and if eventually you discover more or less who you are, you also learn about God, and who He is. In applying a moral code (which in itself is a commendable thing), you can prevent even the divine decision, and then you go astray. So try to live as consciously, as conscientiously, and as completely as *possible* and learn who you are and who or what it is that ultimately decides.

I have discussed certain aspects of this problem in one of my books, called *Aion*.[2] As soon as the translation is ready, it will appear in my Collected Works, published by the Bollingen Press, in case you don't read German.

Sincerely yours, c. g. j u n g

[2] Pars. 48ff. Cf. also "A Psychological View of Conscience," CW 10, pars. 855f.

Anonymous

[ORIGINAL IN ENGLISH]

My dear N.,   May 1956

. . .

My conceptions are empirical and not at all speculative. If you understand them from a philosophical standpoint you go completely astray, since they are not rational but mere names of groups of irrational phenomena. The conceptions of Indian philosophy however are thoroughly philosophical and have the character of postulates and can therefore only be analogous to my terms but not identical with them at all. Take f.i. the concept of *nirdvandva*. Nobody has ever been entirely liberated from the opposites, because no living being could possibly attain to such a state, as nobody escapes pain and pleasure as long as he functions physiologically. He may have occasional ecstatic experiences when he gets the intuition of a complete liberation, f.i. in reaching the state of *sat-chit-ananda*.[1] But the

☐ A man from India, living in Europe.
[1] *Sat* = being, *chit* (or *cit*) = consciousness, *ananda* = bliss. This state denotes the attainment of Brahman, ultimate reality.

148

word *ananda* shows that he experiences pleasure, and you cannot even be conscious of something if you don't discriminate between opposites, and thus participate in them.

My psychology deals with modern man in Europe, who is practically beyond the belief in philosophical postulates. They convey nothing to him any more. Whereas you are still a believer in orthodox philosophy; thus you can be compared to a staunch Christian, still convinced that he is redeemed through his Lord Jesus Christ, etc. He believes in postulates. It is quite obvious that such a man would neither have any use for a psychology of the unconscious nor would he understand such a psychology at all. He cannot imagine himself in the role of an unbeliever, moreover if he seriously tried to, he might get into a panic as he would feel the ground subsiding under his feet. He cannot admit or imagine that the idea of redemption through Christ's self-sacrifice could be an illusion, or at least a mere postulate of religious speculation, as you yourself would not dream of disbelieving the existence of the *atman*,[2] or the reality of *jivan-mukti*,[3] *samadhi*,[4] etc. This is in contradiction to the fact that a complete liberation from the opposites cannot be attained through *jivan-mukti*, the latter being a mere postulate and—as I told you above—not to be experienced in its totality.

Modern man in Europe has lost or given up—getting tired of them —his traditional beliefs and has to find out for himself what is going to happen to him in his impoverished state. Analytical psychology tells you the story of his adventures. Only if you are able to see the relativity, i.e., the uncertainty of all human postulates, can you experience that state in which analytical psychology makes sense. But analytical psychology just makes no sense for you. Nothing of the things I describe comes to life unless you can accompany or sympathize understandingly with beings that are forced to base their life upon facts to be experienced and not upon transcendental postulates beyond human experience. Thus, inasmuch as you are a believer in postulates, you have no use for my psychology and you are not even able to understand why we shouldn't simply adopt Indian philosophy if we are dissatisfied with our religious philosophy. In other

[2] The divine Self in every man, and as such identical with Brahman. The one eternal Self is also called Atman-Brahman.
[3] The state of being liberated from obstacles to union with the eternal Self; a *jivan-mukta* is "liberated while living," the divine man on earth.
[4] State of immersion in the eternal Self.

words, why study analytical psychology at all? It cannot make sense to you as it does not make sense to a Christian or any other believer. On the contrary the believer will translate the psychological terms into his metaphysical language. The Christian f.i. will call the self Christ and will not understand why I call the central symbol "self." He will not see why we need to know about the unconscious from A to Z, exactly like the Indian way. He is like you *in possession of the Truth*, while we psychologists are merely in search of something like the truth and our only source of information is the unconscious and its mythological products like archetypes, etc. We have no traditional beliefs or philosophical postulates. (. . .) Analytical psychology is an empirical science and (. . .) individuation is an empirical process and not a way of initiation at all.

. . .

Yours sincerely, c. g. j u n g

Anonymous

Dear N.,   10 August 1956

. . .

I was very pleased to hear that you now have house and land of your own. This is important for the chthonic powers. I hope you will find time to commit your plant counterparts to the earth and tend their growth, for the earth always wants children—houses, trees, flowers—to grow out of her and celebrate the marriage of the human psyche with the Great Mother, the best counter-magic against rootless extraversion!

With best regards to you and your dear husband,

Always your faithful c. g. j u n g

□ U.S.A.

To H. J. Barrett

[O R I G I N A L   I N   E N G L I S H]

Dear Mr. Barrett,   12 October 1956

Although my time is short and my old age is a real fact, I would like to answer to your questions. They are not quite easy, f.i. the first question whether I believe in personal survival after death or not.[1] I could not say that I believe in it, since I have not the gift of belief. I only can say whether I know something or not. I do know that the psyche possesses certain qualities transcending the confinement in time and space. Or you might say, the psyche can make those categories as if elastic, i.e., 100 miles can be reduced to 1 yard and a year to a few seconds. This is a fact for which we have all the necessary proofs. There are moreover certain post-mortal phenomena which I am unable to reduce to subjective illusions. Thus I know that the psyche is capable of functioning unhampered by the categories of time and space. *Ergo* it is in itself an equally transcendental being and therefore relatively non-spatial and "eternal." This does not mean that I hold any kind of convictions as to the transcendental nature of the psyche. It may be anything.

2. There is no reason whatever to assume that all so-called psychic phenomena are illusory effects of our mental processes.

3. I don't think that all reports of so-called miraculous phenomena (such as precognition, telepathy, supranormal knowledge, etc.) are doubtful. I know plenty of cases where there is no shadow of a doubt about their veracity.

4. I do not think that so-called personal messages from the dead can be dismissed *in globo* as self-deceptions.

Immanuel Kant once said that he would doubt all stories about spooks, etc., individually, but as a whole there was something in them, which reminds me fatally of a Professor of Catholic Theology who, treating the seven arguments about the existence of God, was made to admit that every one of them was a syllogism. But in the end he said: "Oh, I admit you can prove that every one taken singly may be at fault, but there are seven of them, that must mean something!" — I carefully sift my empirical material and I must say that among many most arbitrary assumptions there are some cases that made me sit up. I have made it a rule to apply Multatuli's[2] wise statement: There is nothing quite true, and even this is not quite true.

Hoping I have answered your questions to your satisfaction, I remain,

Yours sincerely, C. G. JUNG

---

[1] Cf. *Memories*, ch. XI: "On Life after Death."
[2] Pen-name of the Dutch writer Eduard Douwes Dekker (1820–87).

To Werner Nowacki

Dear Professor Nowacki,   22 March 1957

I don't want to miss the chance of thanking you for your thoughtfulness in sending me your interesting article.[1] Your ideas go back, in modern form, to the familiar world of Plato's *Timaeus*, which was a sacrosanct authority for medieval science—and rightly so! Our modern attempts at a unitary view, to which your article makes very important contributions, do indeed lead to the question of the cosmic demiurge and the psychic aspect of whole numbers.

From the fact that matter has a mainly quantitative aspect and at the same time a qualitative one, even though this appears to be secondary, you draw the weighty conclusion, which I heartily applaud, that, besides its obviously qualitative nature, the psyche has an as yet hidden quantiative aspect. Matter and psyche are thus the terminal points of a polarity. The still largely unexplored area between them forms the *terra incognita* of future research. Here tremendous problems open out which you have approached from the physical side.

It seems to me that for the time being I have exhausted my psychological ammunition. I have got stuck, on the one hand, in the acausality (or "synchronicity") of certain phenomena of unconscious provenance and, on the other hand, in the qualitative statements of numbers, for here I set foot on territories where I cannot advance without the help and understanding of the other disciplines. In this respect your article is uncommonly valuable and stimulating. I am particularly grateful to you for your appreciation of the transcendent "arranger."

Yours sincerely, C. G. JUNG

☐ (Handwritten.) Professor of mineralogy, Bern U.
[1] "Die Idee einer Struktur der Wirklichkeit," *Mitteilungen der Naturforschenden Gesellschaft in Bern*, XIV (1957). In this paper N. interprets the elements of symmetry in crystals as spiritual entities having a formative effect. He calls them "primordial images" and regards them as "irrepresentable formal factors that arrange the planes of the crystal as the material datum in a meaningful way that conforms to law" (cf. Jaffé, *The Myth of Meaning*, pp. 29f.). He arrives at the conclusion that "the regions of matter and psyche are inseparably and unconditionally interconnected" and draws a parallel between the elements of symmetry and the archetypes.

To Edith Schröder

Dear Colleague,   April [?] 1957

In reply to your letter of the 26th inst. I must remark that many important things could be said about the theme you propose, "The Significance of Freud's Jewish Descent for the Origin, Content, and Acceptance of Psychoanalysis," if only the problem could be treated on a very high level. Racial theories and the like would be a most unsatisfactory foundation, quite apart from the futility of such speculations. For a real understanding of the Jewish component in Freud's outlook a thorough knowledge would be needed of the specifically Jewish assumptions in regard to history, culture and religion. Since Freud calls for an extremely serious assessment on all these levels, one would have to take a deep plunge into the history of the Jewish mind. This would carry us beyond Jewish orthodoxy into the subterranean workings of Hasidism (e.g., the sects of Sabbatai Zwi[1]), and then into the intricacies of the Kabbalah, which still remains unexplored psychologically. The Mediterranean man, to whom the Jews also belong, is not exclusively characterized and moulded by Christianity and the Kabbalah, but still carries within him a living heritage of paganism which could not be stamped out by the Christian Reformation.

I had the privilege of knowing Freud personally and have realized that one must take all these facts into consideration in order to gain a real understanding of psychoanalysis in its Freudian form.

I do not know how far you are acquainted with these various sources, but I can assure you that I myself could carry out such a task only in collaboration with a Jewish scholar since unfortunately I have no knowledge of Hebrew.

In view of the blood-bespattered shadow that hangs over the so-called "Aryan understanding of the Jew," any assessment that fell below the level of these—as it may seem to you—high-falutin conditions would be nothing but a regrettable misunderstanding, especially on German soil.

☐ M.D., U. Policlinic, Würzburg.

[1] Sabbatai Zwi or Zevi (1625–76), of Anatolia, claimed to be the Messiah but later was forced to convert to Islam. Nevertheless the sect of the Sabbatians played for some time a considerable role in the development of Jewish mysticism. Cf. Gershom Scholem, *Sabbatai Ṣevi, The Mystical Messiah* (tr. 1973).

Despite the blatant misjudgment I have suffered at Freud's hands, I cannot fail to recognize, even in the teeth of my resentment, his significance as a cultural critic and psychological pioneer. A true assessment of Freud's achievement would take us far afield, into dark areas of the mind which concern not only the Jew but European man in general, and which I have sought to illuminate in my writings. Without Freud's "psychoanalysis" I wouldn't have had a clue.

I am sorry that I have nothing but difficulties to offer you, but superficiality would be worse than silence. With collegial regards,

Yours sincerely, c. g. jung

To Mrs. C.

[ORIGINAL IN ENGLISH]

Dear Mrs. C.,   21 May 1957

Sorry to hear that you are having such a difficult time with X. Apparently you are not yet in such a state of simplicity that you could accept the helpful intentions of those knowing less than you. The more you know, the more you will grow out of the number of children needing parents. It seems to me as if there were something fateful about the so-called misunderstandings with X. (. . .) Such things usually occur when the time has come to give up the infantile way and to learn about the adult way, when one creates those people and those relationships one really needs. I am sure you have some amongst your [friends] to whom you might be able to talk and to explain yourself. One has no authority when one cannot risk it, and you will be quite astonished how very helpful people we might consider inferior can be. Even the Pope has a Father Confessor who is a simple priest and by no means one of the Cardinals. If you are all alone then it is because you isolate yourself; if you are humble enough you are never alone. Nothing isolates us more than power and prestige. Try to come down and be humble and you are never alone! I could easily contrive to be marvellously alone, because I never had the chance to get a superior Father Confessor. Not being able to get the necessary help from above, I need to fetch it from below, and what I was able to do you might do also. Try not to be tempted too much to draw help from me; it is so very much more

☐ England.

154

useful to get it indirectly from yourself, from those who got it originally from yourself. My best wishes,

Yours, C. G. JUNG

To Gustav Schmaltz

Dear Schmaltz,   30 May 1957

I understand your wish[1] very well, but must tell you at once that it does not fit in with my situation. I am now getting on for 82 and feel not only the weight of my years and the tiredness this brings, but, even more strongly, the need to live in harmony with the inner demands of my old age. Solitude is for me a fount of healing which makes my life worth living. Talking is often a torment for me, and I need many days of silence to recover from the futility of words. I have got my marching orders and only look back when there's nothing else to do. This journey is a great adventure in itself, but not one that can be talked about at great length. What you think of as a few days of spiritual communion would be unendurable for me with anyone, even with my closest friends. The rest is silence! This realization becomes clearer every day as the need to communicate dwindles.

Naturally I should be glad to see you one afternoon for about 2 hours, preferably in Küsnacht, my door to the world. Around August 5th would suit me best, as I shall be at home then in any case. Meanwhile with best greetings,

Yours ever, JUNG

☐ See Schmaltz, 9 Apr. 32 (in vol. 1).
[1] S., an old acquaintance of Jung's, asked if he could spend a few days with him at Bollingen for an exchange of ideas.

To Erich Neumann

Dear Neumann,   3 June 1957

I was very glad to hear from you again and to see that you have read my brochure.[1] It seems to have been a hit here for a 2nd edition is already on the way.

[1] "The Undiscovered Self," CW 10.

Basically we are in entire agreement about the so-called "New Ethic,"[2] but I would rather express this tricky problem in somewhat different terms. For it is not really a question of a "new" ethic. Evil is and remains what you know you shouldn't do. But unfortunately man overestimates himself in this respect: he thinks he is free to choose evil or good. He may imagine he can, but in reality, considering the magnitude of these opposites, he is too small and impotent to choose either the one or the other voluntarily and under all circumstances. It is rather that, for reasons stronger than himself, he does or does not do the good he would like, in exactly the same way that evil comes upon him as a misfortune.

An ethic is that which makes it impossible for him *deliberately* to do evil and urges him—often with scant success—to do good. That is to say, he can do good but cannot avoid evil even though his ethic impels him to test the strength of his will in this regard. In reality he is the victim of these powers. He is forced to admit that under no circumstances can he avoid evil absolutely, just as on the other side he may cherish the hope of being able to do good. Since evil is unavoidable, he never quite gets out of sinning and this is the fact that has to be recognized. It gives rise not to a new ethic but to differentiated ethical reflections such as the question: How do I relate to the fact that I cannot escape sin? The guidance offered by Christ's logion, "If thou knowest what thou doest . . . ,"[3] points the way to the ethical solution of the problem: I know that I do not want to do evil yet do it just the same, not by my own choice but because it overpowers me. As a man I am a weakling and fallible, so that evil can overpower me. I know that I do it and know what I have done and know that all my life long I shall stand in the torment of this contradiction. I shall avoid evil when I can but shall always fall into this hole. But I shall try to live as if it were not so; I shall make the best of a bad job, like the unjust steward[4] who

---

[2] *Depth Psychology and a New Ethic* (tr. 1969; orig. 1949). Jung's foreword is in CW 18, pars. 1408ff. Cf. Neumann, Dec. 48.

[3] An uncanonical saying of Jesus, relating to Luke 6:4, in Codex Bezae Cantabrigiensis, a Greek New Testament MS of the 5th cent. The complete passage runs: "On the same day, seeing one working on the sabbath, he said unto him: Man, if indeed thou knowest what thou doest, thou are blessed: but if thou knowest not, thou art cursed, and a transgressor of the law." Cf. James, *The Apocryphal New Testament*, p. 33.

[4] Luke 16:1–13.

knowingly presented a false account. I shall do this not because I want to deceive myself, let alone the Lord, but so that I may not give public offence on account of the weakness of my brothers, and may preserve my moral attitude and some semblance of human dignity. I am therefore like a man who feels hellishly afraid in a dangerous situation and would have run for his life had he not pulled himself together on account of others, feigning courage in his own eyes and theirs in order to save the situation. I have not made my panic unreal but have got away with it by hiding behind the mask of courage. It is an act of supreme hypocrisy, just another sin without which we would all be lost. This is not a new ethic, merely a more differentiated one, disabused of illusion, but the same as it always was.

You can tell these subtle reflections to Zeus but not to an ox.[5] They are so subtle because they presuppose quite special conditions. They are valid only for a person who is really conscious of his shadow, but for anyone who treats his shadow as a passing inconvenience or, lacking all scruple and moral responsibility, brushes it off as irrelevant, they offer dangerous opportunities for aberrations of moral judgment, such as are characteristic of people with a moral defect who consequently suffer from an intellectual inflation. Many a conflict can be eased by winking the moral eye or by stretching a point or two, but one should know that it has to be paid for, since "every sin avenges itself on earth."[6]

Just now I am engaged on a work with a quite different theme, but the discussion made it necessary for me to mention the ethical problem. I couldn't avoid repudiating the expression "new ethic," though I named no names.[7] This is yet another of those sins, a kind of disloyalty, which descends like doom the moment I have to protect the incomparably higher aspect of our psychology from the crudities of vulgar understanding, and to the general advantage at that. In this case the whole difficulty lies with the slipperiness of language. Hence one is forced to scatter sand, and occasionally it gets into the eyes of the reader.

[5] "Quod licet Jovi non licet bovi."
[6] Goethe, *Wilhelm Meisters Lehrjahre*, Book II, ch. 13.
[7] The book Jung was working on was "Flying Saucers" (cf. Harding, 30 May 57, n. 3), where the ethical problem is discussed in pars. 676f. of the CW 10 version; par. 676 also cites the uncanonical saying and the parable of the unjust steward. There is, however, no reference to a "new ethic," so one must conclude that Jung later deleted his repudiation of the term.

I am looking forward to your extension of *Origins* to child psychology.[8] Plenty of illustrative material could be found there.

I feel very uncertain about the question of pessimism and optimism[9] and must leave the solution to fate. The only one who could decide this dilemma—God—has so far withheld his answer.

I hope all goes well with you in *ce meilleur des mondes possibles. Tout cela est bien dit, mais il faut cultiver notre jardin.* With best greetings,

Ever sincerely yours, J U N G

[8] N. had planned for some time to extend certain concepts in his *The Origins and History of Consciousness* to the psychological development of the child. The plan remained uncompleted but the extant MS was posthumously edited by his widow, Julie Neumann, and appeared as *Das Kind* (1963; tr., *The Child*, 1973).

[9] N. thought that "The Undiscovered Self" might be regarded as too pessimistic, and that individuation, as a collective process, would be successful even if it took centuries (cf. esp. pars. 582–83).

To Ralf Winkler

Dear Herr Winkler,   5 June 1957

I am sorry you knocked at my door in vain, and that my secretary may not have made the true state of affairs sufficiently clear to you.[1] I understand your need for people very well, also your wish to make contact with people who really have something to say. At the age of nearly 82 perhaps I may say without being presumptuous that in my long life I have seen so many people, and also helped them, that my present seclusion seems to me well earned and ought not to be grudged. The obligation to be there for others must now be taken over by others who have more strength. This has nothing to do with "lack of humanity" on my part, rather I appeal to your humanity to understand my situation.

Perhaps you also will one day understand that it is only the man who is really capable of being alone, and without bitterness, who attracts other people. Then he doesn't need to seek them any more,

☐ Bassersdorf, Cant. Zurich.
[1] W. had appeared unannounced at Jung's door in Küsnacht in order to tell Jung his personal problems. Because Jung did not receive him, W. blamed him for want of humanity and left his address in the hope of receiving a letter.

they come all by themselves, among them the very ones whom he himself needs. With my best wishes,

Yours, c. g. j u n g

To Aniela Jaffé

Dear Aniela,   Bollingen, 9 July 1957

. . .

Unlike me, you torment yourself with the ethical problem. I am tormented *by* it. It is a problem that cannot be caught in any formula, twist and turn it as I may; for what we are dealing with here is the living will of God. Since it is always stronger than mine, I find it always confronting me; I do not hurl myself upon it, it hurls itself upon me; I put up no resistance yet am compelled to fight against it, for God's power is greater than my will. I can only be its servant, but a servant with knowledge who can make infinitesimal corrections for better or worse. I am dependent on God's verdict, not he on mine. Therefore I cannot reason about ethics. I feel it unethical because it is a presumption. God presents me with facts I have to get along with. If he doesn't reject them, I cannot. I can only modify them the tiniest bit.

    Good holidays!

Yours, c. g. j.

□ (Handwritten.)

To Betty Grover Eisner

[O R I G I N A L   I N   E N G L I S H]

Dear Mrs. Eisner,   12 August 1957

Thank you for your kind letter.[1] Experiments along the line of mescalin and related drugs are certainly most interesting, since such drugs lay bare a level of the unconscious that is otherwise accessible only under peculiar psychic conditions. It is a fact that you get certain perceptions and experiences of things appearing either in mystical states or in the analysis of unconscious phenomena, just like the

□ Clinical psychologist, Los Angeles, California.
[1] E. stated that for her LSD was "almost a religious drug."

159

primitives in their orgiastic or intoxicated conditions. I don't feel happy about these things, since you merely fall into such experiences without being able to integrate them. The result is a sort of theosophy, but it is not a moral and mental acquisition. It is the eternally primitive man having experience of his ghost-land, but it is not an achievement of your cultural development. To have so-called religious visions of this kind has more to do with physiology but nothing with religion. It is only that mental phenomena are observed which one can compare to similar images in ecstatic conditions. Religion is a way of life and a devotion and submission to certain superior facts—a state of mind which cannot be injected by a syringe or swallowed in the form of a pill. It is to my mind a helpful method to the barbarous Peyotee, but a regrettable regression for a cultivated individual, a dangerously simple "Ersatz" and substitute for a true religion.

Sincerely yours, C. G. JUNG

To Roswitha N.

Dear Miss Roswitha, 17 August 1957

Many thanks for the kind letter you sent me on my birthday. I have heard with great sorrow of your father's illness and can only hope that it will soon take a turn for the better.

I was very interested to hear of the success of your lecture. My little book on Job is naturally meant for older people, and especially for those who have some knowledge of my psychology. They must also have pondered a good deal on religious questions in order to understand it properly. Because there are very few people who meet these conditions, my book has been widely misunderstood. They should also know something about the unconscious. As an introduction to this I would recommend another little book of mine, "On the Psychology of the Unconscious," and, on the religious problem, "Psychology and Religion." *Symbolik des Geistes* and *Von den Wurzeln des Bewusstseins* probe rather more deeply into these matters.

You are undoubtedly right to tackle the problem of society first.

☐ The recipient was a young Swiss girl about 20 years old.

160

There you learn the ways of other people and are forced to find a common basis of understanding.

The question of the young architect as to what it might mean for God if he demands Christianity of us: first one must understand what Christianity means. This is obviously the psychology of the Christian and that is a complicated phenomenon which cannot be taken for granted. And what something might mean for God we cannot know at all, for we are not God. One must always remember that God is a mystery, and everything we say about it is said and believed by human beings. We make images and concepts, and when I speak of God I always mean the image man has made of him. But no one knows what he is like, or he would be a god himself. Looking at it in one way, however, we do indeed partake of divinity, as Christ himself pointed out when he said: "Ye are gods."[1] You will find a lot about this in *Answer to Job*.

Your question why it is more difficult for us to do good than to do evil is not quite rightly put, because doing good is as a rule easier than doing evil. True, it is not always easy to do good, but the consequences of doing good are so much more pleasant than those of doing evil that if only for practical reasons one eventually learns to do good and eschew evil. Of course evil thwarts our good intentions and, to our sorrow, cannot always be avoided. The task is then to understand why this is so and how it can be endured. In the end good and evil are human judgments, and what is good for one man is evil for another. But good and evil are not thereby abolished; this conflict is always going on everywhere and is bound up with the will of God. It is really a question of recognizing God's will and wanting to do it.

The other question of what meaning the Bible ascribes to society is of great importance, for the solidarity and communal life of mankind go to the roots of existence. But the question is complicated by the fact that the individual should also be able to maintain his independence, and this is possible only if society is accorded a relative value. Otherwise it swamps and eventually destroys the individual, and then there is no longer any society either. In other words: a genuine society must be composed of independent individuals, who can be social beings only up to a certain point. They alone can fulfil the divine will implanted in each of us.

[1] John 10:34.

The paths leading to a common truth are many. Therefore each of us has first to stand by his own truth, which is then gradually reduced to a common truth by mutual discussion. All this requires psychological understanding and empathy with the other's point of view. A common task for every group in quest of a common truth. With best greetings,

Yours sincerely, c. g. jung

To Karl Oftinger

Dear Professor Oftinger,   September 1957

Unfortunately I am so old and tired that I am no longer able to comply with your wish.[1] You may be assured, however, that I have every sympathy with your project and understand it only too well. I personally detest noise and flee it whenever and wherever possible, because it not only disturbs the concentration needed for my work but forces me to make the additional psychic effort of shutting it out. You may get habituated to it as to over-indulgence in alcohol, but just as you pay for this with a cirrhosis of the liver, so in the end you pay for nervous stress with a premature depletion of your vital substance. Noise is certainly only one of the evils of our time, though perhaps the most obtrusive. The others are the gramophone, the radio, and now the blight of television. I was once asked by an organization of teachers why, in spite of the better food in elementary schools, the curriculum could no longer be completed nowadays. The answer is: lack of concentration, too many distractions. Many children do their work to the accompaniment of the radio. So much is fed into them from outside that they no longer have to think of something they could do from inside themselves, which requires concentration. Their infantile dependence on the outside is thereby increased and prolonged into later life, when it becomes fixed in the well-known attitude that every inconvenience should be abolished by order of the State. *Panem et circenses*—this is the degenerative symptom of urban civilization, to which we must now add the nerve-shattering din of our technological gadgetry. The alarming pollution of our water supplies, the steady increase of radioactivity, and the

---

[1] O., professor of law at the U. of Zurich, had founded an association to combat noise ("Liga gegen den Lärm") and asked Jung for a contribution to be published in a reputable newspaper.

sombre threat of overpopulation with its genocidal tendencies have already led to a widespread though not generally conscious *fear* which *loves noise* because it stops the fear from being heard. Noise is welcome because it drowns the inner instinctive warning. Fear seeks noisy company and pandemonium to scare away the demons. (The primitive equivalents are yells, bull-roarers, drums, fire-crackers, bells, etc.) Noise, like crowds, gives a feeling of security; therefore people love it and avoid doing anything about it as they instinctively feel the apotropaic magic it sends out. Noise protects us from painful reflection, it scatters our anxious dreams, it assures us that we are all in the same boat and creating such a racket that nobody will dare to attack us. Noise is so insistent, so overwhelmingly real, that everything else becomes a pale phantom. It relieves us of the effort to say or do anything, for the very air reverberates with the invincible power of our modernity.

The dark side of the picture is that we wouldn't have noise if we didn't secretly want it. Noise is not merely inconvenient or harmful, it is an unadmitted and uncomprehended means to an end: compensation of the fear which is only too well founded. If there were silence, their fear would make people reflect, and there's no knowing what might then come to consciousness. Most people are afraid of silence; hence, whenever the everlasting chit-chat at a party suddenly stops, they are impelled to say something, do something, and start fidgeting, whistling, humming, coughing, whispering. The need for noise is almost insatiable, even though it becomes unbearable at times. Still, it is better than nothing. "Deathly silence"—telling phrase!—strikes us as uncanny. Why? Ghosts walking about? Well, hardly. The real fear is what might come up from one's own depths— all the things that have been held at bay by noise.

You have taken on a difficult task with this much needed noise-abatement, for the more you attack noise the closer you come to the taboo territory of silence, which is so much dreaded. You will be depriving all those nobodies whom nobody ever listens to of their sole joy in life and of the incomparable satisfaction they feel when they shatter the stillness of the night with their clattering motor-bikes, disturbing everyone's sleep with their hellish din. At that moment they amount to something. Noise is their *raison d'être* and a confirmation of their existence. There are far more people than one supposes who are not disturbed by noise, for they have nothing in them that could be disturbed; on the contrary, noise gives them something to live for.

Between this stratum of the population and the inertia of the authorities there is an unconscious *contrat social*[2] giving rise to a vicious circle: what the one doesn't want is welcomed by the other.

Modern noise is an integral component of modern "civilization," which is predominantly extraverted and abhors all inwardness. It is an evil with deep roots. The existing regulations could do much to improve things but they are not enforced. Why not? It's a question of morality. But this is shaken to its foundations and it all goes together with the spiritual disorientation of our time. Real improvement can be hoped for only if there is a radical change of consciousness. I fear all other measures will remain unreliable palliatives since they do not penetrate to the depths where the evil is rooted and constantly renewed.

Zola once aptly remarked that the big cities are "holocaustes de l'humanité," but the general trend is set in that direction because destruction is an unconscious goal of the collective unconscious at the present time: it is terrified by the snowballing population figures and uses every means to contrive an attenuated and inconspicuous form of genocide. Another, easily overlooked weapon is the destruction of the ability to concentrate—the prime requisite for operating our highly differentiated machines and equipment. The life of the masses is inconceivable without them and yet it is constantly threatened by superficiality, inattention, and slovenliness. The nervous exhaustion caused by the tempo leads to addiction (alcohol, tranquillizers, and other poisons) and thus to an even poorer performance and the premature wastage of the vital substance—another effective weapon for inconspicuous depopulation.

Excuse this somewhat pessimistic contribution to one of the less delectable questions of our time. As a doctor I naturally see more than others of the dark side of human existence and am therefore more inclined to make the menacing aspects the object of my reflections than to advance grounds for optimistic forecasts. In my view there are more than enough people catering to this already.

Yours sincerely, c. g. j u n g

---

[2] In his *Contrat social* (1762) Rousseau tried to show that all government should be based on the consent of the governed.

To Stephen Abrams

[ORIGINAL IN ENGLISH]

Dear Mr. Abrams,   21 October 1957

Your letter leads into the centre of a very complicated problem.[1] Being a scientist I am rather shy of philosophical operations, particularly of conclusions reaching beyond the limits of experience. F.i. I would not go as far as to say that the categories of space and time are definitely non-objective. I would rather ask, on which level or in which world are space and time not valid? In our three-dimensional world they are certainly and inexorably objective, but we have the definite experience that occasionally—presumably under certain conditions—they behave as if they were relatively subjective, that is relatively non-objective. We are not sure how far the relativity can go, so we do not know whether there is a level or a world on or in which space and time are absolutely abolished; but we remain within the limits of human experience when we accept the fact that it is the psyche which is able to relativize the apparent objectivity of time and space. This conclusion is fairly safe as we have, to my knowledge, no known reasons to assume that it is the action of time and space which enables the psyche to perform an act of precognition. They are in our experience, apart f.i. from parapsychology, unchangeable. However, Einstein's relativity theory[2] shows that they are not necessarily identical with our idea of them, f.i. that space may be curved and that time necessarily depends upon the stand-point and the speed of the observer. Such considerations support the idea of their relative validity. Parapsychological experience definitely shows their uncertain behaviour under psychic influence.

We conclude therefore that we have to expect a factor in the psyche that is not subject to the laws of time and space, as it is on the contrary capable of suppressing them to a certain extent. In other words: this factor is expected to manifest the qualities of time- and spacelessness, i.e., "eternity" and "ubiquity." Psychological experi-

---

[1] A. stated that "parapsychology can only be approached from the psychology of the unconscious." He asked if he was "correct in assuming that space and time do not have any objective existence in your view?"

[2] Einstein, in his theory of relativity, recognized that it is impossible to determine absolute motion, and that we have to assume a four-dimensional space-time continuum. This general theory of relativity leads to a new concept in which space is caused to curve by the presence of matter in space, thus setting up a gravitational field.

ence knows of such a factor; it is what I call the archetype, which is ubiquitous in space and time, of course relatively speaking. It is a structural element of the psyche we find everywhere and at all times; and it is that in which all individual psyches are identical with each other, and where they function as if they were the one undivided Psyche the ancients called *anima mundi* or the *psyche tou kosmou*.[3] This is no metaphysical speculation but an observable fact, and therefore the key to innumerable mythologies, that is, to the manifestations of unconscious fantasy. From *this* observation it does not follow that this factor is one and the same thing [inside] and outside the psyche, as it were. It may be, from a psychological point of view, a mere similarity and not a unity in essence. This question cannot be decided by ordinary psychology, but here parapsychology comes in, with its psi-phenomena that unmistakably show an essential identity of two separate events, as f.i. the act of prevision and the objective precognized fact. These experiences show that the factor in question is one and the same inside and outside the psyche. Or in other words: there is no outside to the collective psyche. In our ordinary mind we are in the worlds of time and space and within the separate individual psyche. In the state of the archetype we are in the collective psyche, in a world-system whose space-time categories are relatively or absolutely abolished.

This is about as far as we can go safely. I see no way beyond, since we are not capable of functioning in a four-dimensional system at will; it only can happen to us. Our intellectual means reach only as far as archetypal experiences, but within that sphere we are not the motors, we are the moved objects. Experiment in the ordinary sense therefore becomes impossible. We can only hope for occasional observations. From this argument it follows that we should expect an operative archetype. I have carefully analysed many parapsychological cases and I have been satisfied with the fact that there are indeed operative archetypes in many cases. I could not say: in all cases, I call them exceptions because they are very curious indeed. I don't want to enter into this point here. I only want to state my general experience: perhaps in most of the cases there is an archetype present, yet there are many other archetypal situations in which no parapsychological phenomenon is observable, and there are also cases of psi-phenomena where no archetypal condition can be demonstrated. There is no regularity between archetype and synchronistic

[3] = cosmic psyche.

166

effect. The probability of such a relation is presumably the same as that of the Rhine results.

I think you are correct in assuming that synchronicity, though in practice a relatively rare phenomenon, is an all-pervading factor or principle in the universe, i.e., in the Unus Mundus,[4] where there is no incommensurability between so-called matter and so-called psyche. Here one gets into deep waters, at least I myself must confess that I am far from having sounded these abysmal depths.

In this connection I always come upon the enigma of the *natural number*. I have a distinct feeling that Number is a key to the mystery, since it is just as much discovered as it is invented. It is quantity as well as meaning. For the latter I refer to the arithmetical qualities of the fundamental archetype of the self (monad, microcosm, etc.) and its historically and empirically well-documented variants of the Four, the $3 + 1$ and the $4 - 1$.[5]

It seems that I am too old to solve such riddles, but I do hope that a young mind will take up the challenge. It would be worth while.[6]

I have already heard some rumours about the foundation of a Parapsychology Club at the University of Chicago. I accept with pleasure and gratitude the honour of honorary membership. It is none too early that somebody in the West takes notice of synchronicity. As I have been informed, the Russians have already caught hold of my paper.[7]

Sincerely yours, C. G. JUNG

[4] Cf. Anon., 2 Jan. 57, n. 1.
[5] Cf. Wylie, 22 Dec. 57, n. 1.
[6] Since then, this subject has been taken up by M.-L. von Franz in her *Zahl und Zeit. Psychologische Überlegungen zu einer Annäherung von Tiefenpsychologie und Physik* (1970; tr., *Number and Time*, 1974).
[7] Jung had been told by a physicist who attended a congress in Japan, in either 1953 or 1954, that Russian physicists had expressed to him their interest in synchronicity. As a matter of fact they were working on problems of telepathy. According to a communication from A., Prof. Vasiliev of the Physiological Institute of Leningrad U. spoke in 1963 of his interest in synchronicity.

To Gustav Steiner

Dear friend,   30 December 1957

Your assumption that I already have more than enough to occupy me is only too true. I drown in floods of paper. You are quite right.

☐ (1878–1967) of Basel. He was a friend from Jung's student days; both be-

When we are old, we are drawn back, both from within and from without, to memories of youth. Once before, some thirty years ago, my pupils asked me for an account of how I arrived at my conception of the unconscious. I fulfilled this request by giving a seminar.[1] During the last years the suggestion has come to me from various quarters that I should do something akin to an autobiography. I have been unable to conceive of my doing anything of the sort. I know too many autobiographies, with their self-deceptions and downright lies, and I know too much about the impossibility of self-portrayal, to want to venture on any such attempt.

Recently I was asked for autobiographical information, and in the course of answering some questions I discovered hidden in my memories certain objective problems which seem to call for closer examination. I have therefore weighed the matter and come to the conclusion that I shall fend off my other obligations long enough to take up at least the very first beginnings of my life and consider them in an objective fashion. This task[2] has proved so difficult and singular that in order to go ahead with it, I have had to promise myself that the results would not be published in my lifetime. Such a promise seemed to me essential in order to assure for myself the necessary detachment and calm. It became clear that all the memories which have remained vivid to me had to do with emotional experiences that stir up turmoil and passion in the mind—scarcely the best condition for an objective account! Your letter "naturally" came at the very moment when I had virtually resolved to take the plunge.

Fate will have it—and this has always been the case with me—that all the "outer" aspects of my life should be accidental. Only what is interior has proved to have substance and determining value. As a result, all memory of outer events has faded, and perhaps these "outer" experiences were never so very essential anyhow, or were so only in that they coincided with phases of my inner development. An enormous part of these "outer" manifestations of my life has vanished from my memory—for the very reason, I now realize, that I was never

longed to the same student fraternity, "Zofingia," at Basel U. — Except for the two opening sentences and the ending, the letter is published in A. Jaffé's introduction to *Memories*, and the whole letter in an article by S., "Erinnerungen an Carl Gustav Jung. Zur Entstehung der Autobiographie," *Basler Stadtbuch* 1965 (1964), pp. 125f.

[1] Cf. Böhler, 14 Dec. 55, n. 2.

[2] Jung had begun to write down his recollections of childhood and youth, which formed the first three chapters of *Memories*.

really "in" them, although it seemed to me then that I was participating with all my powers. Yet these are the very things that make up a sensible biography: persons one has met, travels, adventures, entanglements, blows of destiny, and so on. But with few exceptions they have become phantasms which I barely recollect, for they no longer lend wings to my imagination.

On the other hand, my memories of the "inner" experiences have grown all the more vivid and colourful. This poses a problem of description which I scarcely feel able to cope with, at least for the present. Unfortunately I cannot, for these reasons, fulfil your request, very much to my regret.

With best wishes for the New Year,

Your old fellow Zofinger,[3] CARL

[3] See □ supra.

To Mrs. Otto Milbrand

[ORIGINAL IN ENGLISH]

Dear Mrs. Milbrand,   6 June 1958

I have often been asked the question you put to me: whether I have any reason to believe in a survival. As it means very little to me when somebody says "I believe this or that," I assume that it would be pretty futile to say "Yes, I believe in survival." I dislike belief in every respect, because I want to know a thing, and then I don't have to believe it if I know it. If I don't know it, it looks to me like an usurpation to say "I believe it," or the contrary. I think one ought to have at least some more or less tangible reasons for our beliefs. One should have some knowledge at least that makes a hypothesis probable. Your experience[1] f.i. is not a convincing reason, since we have no means of establishing whether it is a hallucinated piece of memory or a real ghost. In other words, I would dismiss neither the one nor the other possibility.

The only scientific approach to the question of survival is the recognition of the fact that the psyche is capable of extrasensory perceptions, namely of telepathy and of precognition, particularly the latter. This fact proves a relative independence of the psyche from time

□ Pompano Beach, Florida.
[1] M. reported that she "met" a friend of her husband's who had been killed in a motoring accident two weeks before. He smiled at her and vanished.

169

and space. This means that the two elements of time and space, indispensable for change, are relatively without importance for the psyche. In other words: the psyche is up to a certain point not subject to corruptibility. That's all we know. Of course one can have experiences of a very convincing subjective nature which need no support through scientific possibilities. But for those people not possessing the gift of belief it may be helpful to remember that science itself points to the possibility of survival.

I remain, dear Mrs. Milbrand,

Yours sincerely, c. g. j u n g

To Charles H. Tobias

[O R I G I N A L   I N   E N G L I S H]

Dear Sir,   27 October 1958

A bird has whistled to me[1] and told me that you have reached your 70th year of life. Although I do not know you, I assume you are quite satisfied with this achievement. It is something. I can talk with some authority, as I am in my 84th and still in passably good form and—looking back, as you probably do on this day of celebration and congratulation—I see following behind myself the long chain of 5 children, 19 grandchildren, and about 8 or 9 great-grandchildren. (The latter number is not quite safe as at frequent intervals a new one drops from heaven.) Mature youth begins, as one says, at seventy and it is in certain respects not so nice and in others more beautiful than childhood. Let us hope that in your case the latter part of the sentence will confirm itself.

My best wishes,

Yours cordially, c. g. j u n g

☐ Boston.

[1] T.'s son, completely unknown to Jung, asked him to write a congratulatory letter for his father's 70th birthday, since Jung was "one of the famous men and women whose accomplishments he [the father] has always admired."

To Mrs. C.

[O R I G I N A L   I N   E N G L I S H]

Dear Mrs. C.   3 November 1958

If power symptoms creep into the work that is done round you, then diminish your own power and let others have more responsi-

☐ England.

bility. It will teach you a very sound lesson. They will learn that more power and more influence bring more suffering, as you yourself are learning under the present conditions.

One should not assert one's power as long as the situation is not so dangerous that it needs violence. Power that is constantly asserted works against itself, and it is asserted when one is afraid of losing it. One should not be afraid of losing it. One gains more peace through losing power.

Cordially yours, c. g. j u n g

To A. Tjoa and R.H.C. Janssen

[ORIGINAL IN ENGLISH]

Dear Sirs,   27 December 1958

Your questions[1] remind me of a very wonderful discussion I once attended at a joint session of the Mind Association and the Aristotelian Society in London[2] about the question: are the individual minds contained in God or not? I must call your attention to the fact that I cannot possibly tell you what a man who has enjoyed complete self-realization looks like, and what becomes of him. I never have seen one, and if I did see one I could not understand him because I myself would not be completely integrated. Thus far your question is a scholastic one, rather like the famous "how many angels can stand on the point of a needle?" Integration in the empirical sense of this word means completion and not perfection. Being a doctor I have seen much of the profound misery of man in our days and of his dissociation. I had to help innumerable people to get a bit more conscious about themselves and to consider the fact that they consist of many different components, light and dark. That's what one calls integration: to become explicitly the one one has been originally. As Japanese Zen says: "Show me thine original face."

☐ Leiden, Netherlands.
[1] T. and J., both students of psychology, asked about the nature of integration: whether it would imply a saint-like quality expressed in "moral dominance over one's fellow men," or "only the inner freedom and firmness of structure . . . without any moral and characterological content . . . so that it would be possible even for a criminal to be integrated and individuated."
[2] The conference was held at Bedford College, London U., in 1914, at a joint meeting of the Aristotelian Society, the Mind Association, and the British Psychological Society. Cf. "Basic Postulates of Analytical Psychology," CW 8, par. 660.

171

To get integrated or complete is such a formidable task that one does not dare to set people farther goals like perfection. As f.i. the ordinary physician neither imagines nor hopes to make of his patient an ideal athlete, so the psychological doctor does not dream of being able to produce saints. He is highly content if he brings forth—in himself as well as in others—a fairly balanced and mentally more or less sound individual, no matter how far from the state of perfection. Before we strive after perfection, we ought to be able to live the ordinary man without self-mutilation. If anybody should find himself after his humble completion still left with a sufficient amount of energy, then he may begin his career as a saint. I never thought that I might be able to help him along far enough on this way. — In a case of criminality, I am sure that the process of completion would bring it to daylight that he is a wrong one, but these cases don't come to the doctor. They find their way all by themselves. But it is quite possible that a fellow wrongly believes he is a criminal and analysis makes it clear to him that he is no such thing. He would seek the doctor's help, but not the real criminal.

May I give you some advice? Don't get caught by words, only by facts.

Sincerely yours, c . g . j u n g

To H.A.F.

Dear Dr. F.,   16 January 1959

Many thanks for kindly sending me your very interesting dream.[1] I found it especially worthy of note that you obviously felt this dream to be highly significant right from the start. And so indeed it is, in so far as it pictures a phenomenon that is constantly recurring these days all over the world. The motif of being "carried off," for instance, occurs in widely believed reports in which the occupants of Ufos invite people to climb aboard in the friendliest manner and to make

☐ Switzerland.
[1] H.A.F. reported a dream in which he saw a large bird he wanted to photograph. But suddenly the bird—a swan—crashed to the ground, leaving a plume of smoke like an aeroplane. In the next scene an aeroplane appeared through clouds of smoke or fog. Then a contraption like a helicopter descended towards the dreamer to fetch him. He saw shadowy figures which he knew to be higher types of men, with greater knowledge and absolutely just, visitors from another world.

172

a round trip round the moon or to fly to Venus or Mars. The occupants of these contraptions are either very beautiful "higher" men
or else spiritual beings or angels. These fairytale reports have the
character of dreams of the same kind, such as yours. The bird sig-
nifies the aerial, volatile spirit (in the chemical sense "spirit" is
volatile, but it also designates the Spiritus Sanctus), whose physical
and spiritual meanings are united in the alchemical *spiritus Mercuri-*
alis. The bird is a messenger of the gods, an *angelus.* This image
hints at some activity "in the Beyond" relating to your consciousness, which is thereby to be raised to a "higher" level, transported
from the banal sphere of everyday life and wafted away from the
rational world of the intellect. In parallel dreams one is fetched into
the Beyond,[2] the "world of spirits," or experiences an illumination
akin to a *metanoia* through the intervention of "higher beings."

I myself recently dreamed that a Ufo came speeding towards me
which turned out to be the lens of a magic lantern whose projected
image was myself;[3] this suggested to me that I was the figure, himself deep in meditation, who is produced by a meditating yogi. The
yogi would be a transcendental figure comparable to the meditant
in the Chinese text of *The Secret of the Golden Flower.*[4]

The crash is an indication that something coming down to earth
from heaven, from the "Beyond," is felt as a catastrophe. According
to other parallels this is the fire which descends to earth, like the out-
pouring of the Holy Ghost in the form of tongues of fire. It produces
smoke or fog, i.e., a "fogging" and obfuscation of consciousness, a
disturbance of our orientation, turning eventually into panic and collective psychosis, a fall of the angels with apocalyptic consequences.
These symbolisms, which are cropping up everywhere nowadays,
paint a picture of the end of time with its eschatological conceptions:
destruction of the world, coming of the Kingdom of Heaven or of
the world redeemer.

Finally a question: would you allow me to publish your dream[5]
in the event of a second edition of my Ufo book?

With kind regards and again many thanks,

Yours sincerely, c . g . j u n g

[2] Cf. "Flying Saucers," CW 10, pars. 697ff. & Pl. I, at p. 404.
[3] As a matter of fact the images of the magic lantern and the yogi appeared in
two different dreams; both are reported in *Memories,* p. 323/298.
[4] Cf. CW 13, pp. 30–33.
[5] The dream was never published.

Anonymous

Dear N., 9 March 1959

I am sorry you are so miserable. "Depression" means literally "being forced downwards." This can happen even when you don't consciously have any feeling at all of being "on top." So I wouldn't dismiss this hypothesis out of hand. If I had to live in a foreign country, I would seek out one or two people who seemed amiable and would make myself useful to them, so that libido came to me from outside, even though in a somewhat primitive form, say of a dog wagging its tail. I would raise animals and plants and find joy in their thriving. I would surround myself with beauty—no matter how primitive and artless—objects, colours, sounds. I would eat and drink well. When the darkness grows denser, I would penetrate to its very core and ground, and would not rest until amid the pain a light appeared to me, for *in excessu affectus*[1] Nature reverses herself. I would turn in rage against myself and with the heat of my rage I would melt my lead. I would renounce everything and engage in the lowest activities should my depression drive me to violence. I would wrestle with the dark angel until he dislocated my hip. For he is also the light and the blue sky which he withholds from me.

Anyway that is what *I* would do. What others would do is another question, which I cannot answer. But for you too there is an instinct either to back out of it or to go down to the depths. But no half-measures or half-heartedness.

. . . .

With cordial wishes,

As ever, C. G. JUNG

☐ U.S.A. (a woman).

[1] = in an excess of affect or passion. Cf. "Synchronicity," par. 859.

To Erich Neumann

Dear friend, 10 March 1959

Best thanks for your long and discursive letter of 18.II. What Frau Jaffé sent you was a first, as yet unrevised draft,[1] an attempt to pin

☐ Parts of this letter were published in Jung and Jaffé, *Erinnerungen, Träume, Gedanken*, pp. 376ff. (not in *Memories*). The whole letter, together with Neumann's of 18 Feb., is in Jaffé, *Der Mythus vom Sinn im Werk von C. G. Jung* (1967), pp. 179ff. (not in tr., *The Myth of Meaning*).
[1] The first draft of ch. XII, "Late Thoughts," in *Memories*.

down my volatile thoughts. Unfortunately the fatigue of old age
prevents me from writing a letter as discursive as yours.

I

The question: *an creator sibi consciens est?*² is not a "pet idea"
but an exceedingly painful experience with well-nigh incalculable
consequences, which it is not easy to argue about. For instance, if
somebody projects the self this is an unconscious act, for we know
from experience that projection results only from unconsciousness.

Incarnatio means first and foremost God's birth in Christ, hence
psychologically the realization of the self as something new, not
present before. The man who was created before that is a "creature,"
albeit "made in the likeness" of God, and this implies the idea of
the *filiatio* and the *sacrificium divinum*. Incarnation is, as you say, a
"new experience."

"It has happened almost by accident and casually . . ."³ This sentence might well characterize the whole process of creation. The
archetype is no exception. The initial event was the arrangement of
indistinct masses in spherical form. Hence this primordial archetype
[mandala] appears as the first form of amorphous gases, for anything
amorphous can manifest itself only in some specific form or order.

The concept of "order" is not identical with the concept of "meaning." Even an organic being is, in spite of the meaningful design implicit within it, not necessarily meaningful in the total nexus. For instance, if the world had come to an end at the Oligocene period, it
would have had no meaning for man. Without the reflecting consciousness of man the world is a gigantic meaningless machine, for
in our experience man is the only creature who is capable of ascertain-
ing any meaning at all.

² = is the creator conscious of himself?

³ Paraphrase of a passage in *Memories* (which N. had read in MS form):
"Natural history tells us of a haphazard and casual transformation of species
over hundreds of millions of years of devouring and being devoured" (p. 339/
312). He objected to the "Darwinistic residue" in "haphazard and casual transformation" and suggested a different theory "in which your concept of the archetype and of absolute and extraneous knowledge will play a part." Concerning
N.'s concept of extraneous knowledge—a knowledge steering the life process and
in which the division between inner and outer reality, psyche and world, is
transcended in a "unitary reality"—cf. his "Die Psyche und die Wandlung der
Wirklichkeitsebenen," *Eranos Jahrbuch* 1952.

We still have no idea where the constructive factor in biological development is to be found. But we do know that warmbloodedness and a differentiated brain were necessary for the inception of consciousness, and thus also for the revelation of meaning. It staggers the mind even to begin to imagine the accidents and hazards that, over millions of years, transformed a lemurlike tree-dweller into a man. In this chaos of chance, synchronistic phenomena were probably at work, operating both with and against the known laws of nature to produce, in archetypal moments, syntheses which appear to us miraculous. Causality and teleology fail us here, because synchronistic phenomena manifest themselves as pure chance. The essential thing about these phenomena is that an objective event coincides meaningfully with a psychic process; that is to say, a physical event and an endopsychic one have a common meaning. This presupposes not only an all-pervading, latent meaning which can be recognized by consciousness, but, during that preconscious time, a psychoid process with which a physical event meaningfully coincides. Here the meaning cannot be recognized because there is as yet no consciousness. It is through the archetype that we come closest to this early, "irrepresentable," psychoid stage of conscious development; indeed, the archetype itself gives us direct intimations of it. Unconscious synchronicities are, as we know from experience, altogether possible, since in many cases we are unconscious of their happening, or have to have our attention drawn to the coincidence by an outsider.

II

Since the laws of probability give no ground for assuming that higher syntheses such as the psyche could arise by chance alone, there is nothing for it but to postulate a latent meaning in order to explain not only the synchronistic phenomena but also the higher syntheses. Meaningfulness always appears to be unconscious at first, and can therefore only be discovered *post hoc*; hence there is always the danger that meaning will be read into things where actually there is nothing of the sort. Synchronistic experiences serve our turn here. They point to a latent meaning which is independent of consciousness.

Since a creation without the reflecting consciousness of man has no discernible meaning, the hypothesis of a latent meaning endows man with a cosmogonic significance, a true *raison d'être*. If on the other hand the latent meaning is attributed to the Creator as part of a conscious plan of creation, the question arises: Why should the Creator stage-manage this whole phenomenal world since he already knows what he can reflect himself in, and why should he reflect himself at all since he is already conscious of himself? Why should he create alongside his own omniscience a second, inferior consciousness—millions of dreary little mirrors when he knows in advance just what the image they reflect will look like?

After thinking all this over I have come to the conclusion that being "made in the likeness" applies not only to man but also to the Creator: he resembles man or is his likeness, which is to say that he is just as unconscious as man or even more unconscious, since according to the myth of the *incarnatio* he actually felt obliged to become man and offer himself to man as a sacrifice.

Here I must close, aware as I am that I have only touched on the main points (so it seems to me) in your letter, which I found very difficult to understand in parts. It is not levity but my *molesta senectus*[1] that forces economy on me. With best greetings,

Sincerely yours, C. G. JUNG

[1] = burdensome old age.

To Joseph F. Rychlak

[ORIGINAL IN ENGLISH]

Dear Mr. Rychlak,   27 April 1959

The philosophical influence that has prevailed in my education dates from Plato, Kant, Schopenhauer, Ed. v. Hartmann,[1] and Nietz-

☐ M.D., then director of a mental health clinic connected with Washington State U., now professor of psychology at Purdue U., Indiana. — According to a letter from R., 16 Jan. 70, quoted with his kind permission, "the 'question' was essentially 'what role did Hegelian philosophy play in your education?' and then more indirectly 'what are your thoughts on the dialectic?' . . . It is my thesis that both Freud and Jung were instrumental in retaining the dialectical side of man (as metaconstruct) in this century of Lockean images of man (cybernetics, S-R psychology, etc.). As with most dialecticians in history Jung has had to bear the unfounded criticisms of being vague, mystical, and even sophistical—precisely because we have no appreciation of dialectical reasoning today." Jung's letter and R.'s thesis are published in his *A Philosophy of Science for Personality Theory* (1968).
[1] Eduard von Hartmann (1842–1906), German philosopher. His most important work is *Die Philosophie des Unbewussten* (1869).

177

sche. These names at least characterize my main studies in philosophy. Aristotle's point of view had never particularly appealed to me; nor Hegel, who in my very incompetent opinion is not even a proper philosopher but a misfired psychologist. His impossible language,[2] which he shares with his blood-brother Heidegger, denotes that his philosophy is a highly rationalized and lavishly decorated confession of his unconscious. The fact that I use the term "dialectical procedure"[3] or something of this sort exposes me to the misunderstanding that I envisage an intellectual procedure, which is not the case, but in truth a practical method of dealing with the very concrete propositions the unconscious presents us with. This is a very important chapter of psychotherapy. Since neurosis consists in a dissociation of personality, one is always confronted with an opposite or a *vis-à-vis* you have to reckon with; a fact which is unknown only to people who know of nothing else but the contents of their consciousness. Moreover the science of all moving as well as living bodies is based upon the concept of energy. Energy itself is a tension between opposites. Our psychology is no exception to the principle that embraces about the whole of natural science.

In the intellectual world in which I grew up, Hegelian thought played no role at all; on the contrary, it was Kant and his epistemology on the one hand, and on the other straight materialism, which I never shared, knowing too much about its ridiculous mythology. Hegel's dialectics, I can safely say, had no influence at all, as far as I know myself. The German term "Auseinandersetzung" was used by me in its colloquial sense. Being an empiricist and not a philosophical thinker, the terms I chose have their real source in experience; thus when I speak of "Auseinandersetzung" it could be just as well the discussion between Mr. A. and his wife. Another common misunderstanding is that I derive my idea of "archetypes" from Philo or Dionysius Areopagita, or St. Augustine. It is based solely upon empirical data, viz. upon the astonishing fact that products of the un-

---

[2] There is an anecdote according to which Hegel is supposed to have said: "Only one man has understood me, and even he has not."

[3] Cf. "General Problems of Psychotherapy," CW 16, pars. 1 & 7, where Jung describes psychotherapy as "a kind of dialectical process, a dialogue or discussion between two persons," and "the dialectical procedure as the latest phase of psychotherapeutic development." His practical therapeutic use of the term "dialectic" is completely different from Hegel's, to whom the dialectical method was a purely philosophical and abstract law of thought.

178

conscious in modern individuals can almost literally coincide with symbols occurring in all peoples and all times, beyond the possibility of tradition or migration, for which I have given numerous proofs.

I have never studied Hegel properly, that means his original works. There is no possibility of inferring a direct dependence, but, as I said above, Hegel confesses the main trends of the unconscious and can be called "un psychologue raté." There is, of course, a remarkable coincidence between certain tenets of Hegelian philosophy and my findings concerning the collective unconscious.

Hoping that I have answered your question satisfactorily, I remain,

Yours faithfully, C . G . J U N G

Anonymous

Dear Herr N.,   9 May 1959

While thanking you for your interesting offprints[1] I would also like to try to answer your questions to the best of my ability in writing.

A transference in the clinical sense does not always need a personal relationship as a bridge, but can take place via a book, a piece of hearsay, or a legend. In your case it is obvious that unconscious contents have forced themselves on you which have put you in the situation, so well known in the East, for instance in India, of the pupil who receives the necessary guidance from a guru (teacher). Since I was the nearest to hand, I have been assimilated to the East by this archetype.

It seems that one essential point at least—the concept of the archetype—has transferred itself to you. It may be a prejudice to think that the world of human ideas is conditioned by archetypes, but it is also a means of grasping something of the psychology of another organism. In this way a man can learn a good deal about the differences between this organism and himself, although in theory he will never succeed in forming a picture of the *Weltanschauung* of a salamander. "Teachings" are tools not truths; points of view that are laid aside once they have served their purpose. All systemizations are to be avoided. We would be going round every teaching in an end-

□ Switzerland.
[1] Of some of his zoological writings. N. was at the time a student.

179

less circle if we did not constantly find new ways of escaping from it. Thus the environment delivers us from the power of the archetypes, and the archetypes deliver us from the crushing influence of the environment.

Just like the animal, man too is caught up in the conflict between archetypal drives and environmental conditions. The solution is always a compromise. I am chary of all anticipatory generalizations. For me the archetype means: an image of a probable sequence of events, an habitual current of psychic energy. To this extent it can be equated with the biological pattern of behaviour. If exact observation—of the fright pattern, for instance—shows that the human and the animal pattern are identical, we have, in accordance with the principle *principia explicandi non sunt multiplicanda praeter necessitatem*,[2] no grounds for assuming (errors always excepted!) that another principle must be at work simply because we are dealing with an animal and not with a human being. It would be a prejudice to assume that the behaviour of a fish, for instance, necessarily cannot be compared with that of another organism. Cogent reasons would have to be offered for this.

If you isolate any way of looking at things, even one that has proved in practice to be the best, and then extend it to infinity you will end up with nonsense. This is a piece of morbid intellectualism which at most a philosopher can afford, but not an empiricist, who knows full well that all his views are provisional and cannot be valid for all eternity. It is therefore pointless to speculate about what would happen if all projections were withdrawn. Withdrawal of projections is obviously a truth whose validity is only of limited application. It is pretty certain that they can be withdrawn only to the extent that one is conscious. How far a man can become conscious nobody knows. We have as a matter of fact been able to correct a number of projections. Whether this amounts to much or little, and whether it is a real advance or only an apparent one, is known only to the angels. As to what absolute consciousness might be, this is something we cannot imagine even in our wildest dreams.

My remarks about the translation of the figurative language of alchemy into modern scientific terminology, and about this being yet another figurative language, were made partly *ad hoc* and partly as an expression of my doubt whether we have really conquered the final peak with our present achievements, which is highly unlikely.

[2] Cf. Frischknecht, 7 Apr. 45, n. 2.

As a rule it so happens that what passes for the profoundest knowledge and the ultimate truth on the first level is understood and derided as ridiculous ignorance on the next, and it is thought that now at last we have arrived at the right insights. When we reach the third level the same thing happens as before. We cannot see how we could ever attain to a universally valid view of the world in this way. You can, if you like, call these views an intellectual game with nature, but nature has the uncomfortable quality of occasionally playing a game with us, though we would scarcely have the nerve to call it a "game" any more.

Notwithstanding these doubts it would, however, be quite wrong to relapse into an impatient nihilism and, intellectually anticipating the worst, to write off all man's scientific achievements as nugatory. With science you really do get somewhere, even if you don't attain the ultimate philosophical insights. We don't attain any "ultimate truths" at all, but on the way to them we discover a whole lot of astonishing partial truths. You can call this progress, which indeed it is within the limited area of the drive for human knowledge. If we knew the meaning of the whole, we would know how much or how little progress we have made. But as we do not possess this knowledge we must be content with the feeling of satisfaction which is our reward for every increase in knowledge, even the smallest. With best greetings,

Yours sincerely, C. G. JUNG

To J. O. Pearson

[ORIGINAL IN ENGLISH]

Dear Dr. Pearson, 29 August 1959

The lack of dreams has different reasons: the ordinary reason is that one is not interested in the mental life within and one does not pay attention to anything of this kind. Another reason is that one has not dealt enough with one's conscious problem and waits for dreams so that the unconscious would do something about it; and the third reason is that the dreams have—as it were—emigrated into a person in our surroundings, who then is dreaming in an inordinate way.[1]

☐ Constantia (Cape Province), South Africa.
[1] Cf. the example of an 8-year-old boy "who dreamt the whole erotic and religious problem of his father," in CW 16, par. 106. "The father could remem-

A fourth reason, finally, can be a mental condition, in which dreams are redundant, inasmuch as compensations for the conscious attitude are not needed. A light sleep is certainly a favourable condition for the remembrance of dreams.

There is certainly a great difference between dreams. According to a primitive classification there are big dreams and small ones. The example you describe[2] is obviously a big dream of very particular importance. The small dreams are the ordinary stuff of unconscious fantasies which become perceptible particularly in light sleep.

Sincerely yours, C. G. JUNG

---

ber no dreams at all, so for some time I analysed the father through the dreams of his eight-year-old son."

[2] P. described a dream of "terrific intensity . . . one was everything, time, space, it was like being the hall, the audience, the players, the music, i.e., as if one could be each and every member of an orchestra at the same time. Marvellous, exciting, terrifying in that one felt what an atom must feel like before it is split." He asked why there appeared to be a dearth of such intense dreams.

To M. Leonard

[ORIGINAL IN ENGLISH]

Dear Sir,   5 December 1959

Mr. Freeman in his characteristic manner fired the question you allude to at me in a somewhat surprising way,[1] so that I was perplexed and had to say the next thing which came into my mind. As soon as the answer had left the "edge of my teeth" I knew I had said something controversial, puzzling, or even ambiguous. I was therefore just waiting for letters like yours. Mind you, I didn't say "there is a God." I said: "I don't need to believe in God, *I know*." Which does not mean: I do know a certain God (Zeus, Yahweh, Allah, the Trinitarian God, etc.) but rather: I do know that I am obviously confronted with a factor unknown in itself, which I call "God" in *consensu omnium (quod semper, quod ubique, quod ab omnibus creditur)*.[2] I remember Him, I evoke Him, whenever I use His name, overcome by anger or by fear, whenever I involuntarily say: "Oh

□ King's College, Newcastle upon Tyne.
[1] Cf. Brooke, 16 Nov. 59, n. 1.
[2] "What is believed always, everywhere, and by everybody." Cf. Anon., 6 Jan. 43, n. 3.

God." That happens when I meet somebody or something stronger than myself. It is an apt name given to all overpowering emotions in my own psychic system, subduing my conscious will and usurping control over myself. This is the name by which I designate all things which cross my wilful path violently and recklessly, all things which upset my subjective views, plans, and intentions and change the course of my life for better or worse. In accordance with tradition I call the power of fate in this positive as well as negative aspect, and inasmuch as its origin is beyond my control, "God," a "personal God," since my fate means very much myself, particularly when it approaches me in the form of conscience as a *vox Dei* with which I can even converse and argue. (We do and, at the same time, we know that we do. One is subject as well as object.)

Yet I should consider it an intellectual immorality to indulge in the belief that my view of a God is the universal, metaphysical Being of the confessions or "philosophies." I commit the impertinence neither of a *hypostasis* nor of an arrogant qualification such as: "God can only be good." Only my experience can be good or evil, but I know that the superior will is based upon a foundation which transcends human imagination. Since I *know* of my collision with a superior will in my own psychic system, *I know of God*, and if I should venture the illegitimate hypostasis of my image, I would say, of *a God beyond Good and Evil*, just as much dwelling in myself as everywhere else: *Deus est circulus cuius centrum est ubique, cuius circumferentia vero nusquam.*[3]

Hoping I have answered your question, I remain, dear Sir,

Yours sincerely, C. G. JUNG

[3] Cf. Frischknecht, 8 Feb. 46, n. 13.

To Eugen Böhler

Dear Dr. Böhler,   Bollingen, 1 January 1960

My first letter in this New Year, which opens a new decade, shall be to you, dear friend. It brings you my very cordial wishes not only for the coming year but also for this dawning decade 1960–70, in whose lap the black and white cards of our uncertain fate await us. The past decade dealt me heavy blows—the death of dear friends and

☐ (Handwritten.)

the even more painful loss of my wife, the end of my scientific activity and the burdens of old age, but also all sorts of honours and above all your friendship, which I value the more highly because it appears that men cannot stand me in the long run. Since I do not deem myself god-almighty enough to have made them other than they are, I must put it down entirely to my own account and lengthen my shadow accordingly. Your understanding and your interest have done much to restore my self-confidence, severely shaken by my incessant struggle with difficult contemporaries. It is indeed no trifling thing to be granted the happy proof that somehow one is "possible" and has achieved something whose meaning someone else, apart from myself, is able to see. Being well-known not to say "famous" means little when one realizes that those who mouth my name have fundamentally no idea of what it's all about. The gratification of knowing that one is essentially posthumous is short-lived. That is why your friendship is all the dearer to me in my grey old age, since it gives me living proof that I have not dropped out of the human setting into the shadowy realm of historical curiosities. Please accept this letter as a poor expression of my gratitude for the many kindnesses you have done me. Although the years hasten away more swiftly than ever, I still hope the New Year may bring a little more light and warmth.

Yours ever, c. g. jung

To Eugen Böhler

Dear friend,   25 February 1960

It is time I gave you some news of my existence. I am now well enough to write letters again. On Jan. 23rd I had a slight embolism followed by not too severe heart cramps. I was under house arrest for a month, forbidden all mental activity, i.e., active concentration. However, it didn't stop me from my long planned (renewed) reading of Buddhist texts, whose content I am leaving to simmer inside me. Thanks to my isolation I have been slipping away from the world and holding converse not with the men of today but with voices long past. On my return to the 20th century I discovered that I have heard nothing from you. Therefore I wanted to notify myself that it was I who was fetched out of the present and transported into the neigh-

☐ (Handwritten.)

184

bourhood of the Bardo,[1] which always happens when I hear such a distinct *memento mori.*

I am sufficiently restored to health to go, with luck, to Lugano this Saturday in the hope of heedless and deedless days in the blessed sun.

Hoping to see you again when I get back,

Yours ever, C. G JUNG

[1] Cf. Bertine, 9 Jan. 39, n. 1.

To Miguel Serrano

[ORIGINAL IN ENGLISH]

Dear Mr. Serrano,   31 March 1960

Thank you for your interesting letter.[1] I quite agree with you that those people in our world who have insight and good will enough should concern themselves with their own "souls" more than with preaching to the masses or trying to find out the best way for them. They only do that because they don't know themselves. But alas, it is a sad truth that usually those who know nothing for themselves take to teaching others, in spite of the fact that they know the best method of education is the good example.

Surely modern art is trying its best to make man acquainted with a world full of darkness, but alas, the artists themselves are unconscious of what they are doing.[2]

The very thought that mankind ought to make a step forward and extend and refine consciousness of the human being seems to be so difficult that nobody can understand it, or so abhorrent that nobody can pluck up his courage. All steps forward in the improvement of the human psyche have been paid for by blood.

I am filled with sorrow and fear when I think of the means of self-destruction which are heaped up by the important powers of the

☐ Then Chilean ambassador in New Delhi, later ambassador in Belgrade; student of mythology and yoga, Antarctic explorer. — The letter is published in S.'s *C. G. Jung and Hermann Hesse: A Record of Two Friendships* (1966), pp. 74f. Cf. also his *The Visits of the Queen of Sheba* (Bombay, 1960), with part of a letter by Jung, 14 Jan. 60, as foreword (published in CW 18, pars. 1769ff.).

[1] S. had written Jung 24 Feb. 60: "it would probably be better for the Westerners to recede into the background now and leave others to do the world's business, since the most urgent task for the Christian world today is to try to preserve Individuality . . ." (*Jung and Hesse*, p. 73).

[2] Cf. Jung, "Picasso," CW 15.

185

world. Meanwhile everybody teaches everybody, and nobody seems to realize the necessity that the way to improvement begins right in himself. It is almost too simple a truth. Everybody is on the lookout for organizations and techniques where one can follow the other and where things can be done safely in company.

I would like to ask Mr. Toynbee:[3] Where is your civilization and what is your religion? What he says to the masses will remain—I am afraid—sterile, unless it has become true and real in himself. Mere words have lost their spell to an extraordinary extent. They have been twisted and misused for too long a time.

I am looking forward to your new book[4] with great interest!

Hoping you are always in good health, I remain

Yours sincerely, c. g. jung

[3] The British historian Arnold Toynbee, whose visit S. had mentioned, had been lecturing in India on "A World Civilization," "A World Religion," and related subjects.
[4] *The Visits of the Queen of Sheba.*

Anonymous

[ORIGINAL IN ENGLISH]

Dear Sir,   7 May 1960

As your friendly letter has brought not only much amusement but also illumination to me, it deserves special consideration.[1] It is a model for the intelligent reader of today. It follows the excellent rule: Never read prefaces or introductions or footnotes as they are useless embellishments. Best begin reading in the end or at the most in the middle of the book. Then you see all there is about the twaddle. What an ass I have been not to see how simple things are: *God is Love*, that is the thing, and the whole of theology can go into the dustbin. Mineralogy is just stones, zoology simply animals, technology only how things are made to work, and mythology old fables of no consequence at all. I did not know that things are as simple to a joyous Christian. That is indeed an evangel, a Glad Tidings. To hell with all -logies. Why should anybody fuss with the history of symbols when everything is quite clear and can be summed up in the short

☐ Chicago, Illinois.
[1] N. wrote a long letter setting forth his reaction to *Answer to Job*. In his concluding paragraph he said: "The whole situation would be aired and simplified if we could stop imputing human characteristics to God, and accept the idea that God is Love."

formula "God is Love"? You seem to know it. I know much less about God, since whatever I might say about the supreme Unknown is arrogant anthropomorphism to me.

If you had cast a look into my preface and introduction you might have discovered that my little book is not interested in the least in what you or I believe about God, but solely and modestly in what the history of symbols has to say about it. Not having noticed this little difference you misunderstand the whole of my argument, as if I had discussed the nature of God. In reality I am dealing with anthropomorphic representations of the deity and thus walking through the dough at the bottom of the sea, as you aptly put it. This dough however is the human mind, as it has been for several thousand years. Being a physician I am concerned with the woes of the world and their causes, and I at least try to do something about them. But you are a joyous Christian way above the doughy bottom and you exult in your marvellous confession that God is Love, to which nobody listens. You are so little concerned with the "dough" that you do not even notice what I am preoccupied with. I have to help man, who sticks in the dough. In order to help his suffering I must understand his "dough." To me there is no high-handed dismissal of man's folly. It is your prerogative not to be interested in man but in your Love, which is God according to your statement.

Now, what about it? Since Love is your highest value, how do you apply it? It does not even reach as far as a compassionate interest in this insufferable dough, in which man is caught and suffering accordingly. The joyous Christian tells us how things ought to be, but he is careful not to touch things as they are. They are merely deplorable. This admirable superiority is almost enviable: one can leave things to themselves and let man wriggle in his comfortable mud.

Yes, what about your Love? On p. 2 of your letter you say: "What right had Job to go crying to God about his loss of mere things?" In case you should be married, please ask your wife how she feels about being considered as a "mere thing," a piece of furniture, f.i., somebody has smashed. She will certainly esteem such lovely appreciation. Your involuntary use of language throws a telltale light on the way in which your "Love" functions. Isn't it charming?

You deny the right of crying out to God. Does pain ever ask whether it has a right to cry out in its need and despair or not? Has the joyous Christian no right to cry out to his loving father or to the "God of Love" or "Love-God" for a certain amount of consideration or patience or at least of mere justice?

The "no right" for Job shows up your superior legalistic standpoint, but no human feeling.

I am weak and stupid enough to consider a certain amount of compassion, humility, love, and feeling as indispensable for the understanding of the human soul and its woeful dough, i.e., the slime and mud at its bottom, which seems to disappear when you look away from the old fables to the pleasant vistas of a simplified "reality."

I am much obliged to you for your benevolent honesty, which has allowed me to understand more and better why my *Answer to Job* is so thoroughly misunderstood. Please consider my letter as a further attempt to clarify the position of Job.

Sincerely yours, c. g. j u n g

To Pastor Oscar Nisse

Dear Pastor Nisse,   2 July 1960

It was actually through my therapeutic work that I began to understand the essence of the Christian faith. It became clear to me that the preoccupation with anxiety in psychoanalysis, where as you know it plays a considerable part, is not to be explained by the presence of religious teaching but rather by its absence.

With Freud personally—as I saw clearly over a period of years—anxiety played a great part. It is not hard to see that in him its source was the fear of Yahweh which is always present in the unconscious, particularly of Jews. In the Jewish mentality this imprint is so deep that the individual Jew can rarely get away from it. That is because he is Jewish, because he belongs and has belonged for thousands of years to a people characterized by their intimate connection with Yahweh.

With the Christian this anxiety is less important thanks to the fact that it was not until the day before yesterday that he rid himself of the gods, who represented the numinous aspects of the transcendent being as a plurality.

☐ (Translated from French.) Brussels. — In a letter of 16 June 60 N. had reported a lecture by a psychoanalyst who had maintained that anxiety (*Angst*) had to be regarded as the true root of religion and, in the discussion following, that Jung's writings did not allow the conclusion that Jung regarded himself as a Christian. N. had, on the contrary, formed the opinion that it was exactly through his psychological researches that Jung had arrived at his positive attitude to religion.

188

I assure you it was precisely through my analytic work that I arrived at an understanding not only of the Christian religion but, I may say, of all religions.

The Freudian idea that religion is nothing more than a system of prohibitions is very limited and out of touch with what is known about different religions.

To be exact, I must say that, although I profess myself a Christian, I am at the same time convinced that the chaotic contemporary situation shows that present-day Christianity is not the final truth. Further progress is an absolute necessity since the present state of affairs seems to me insupportable. As I see it, the contributions of the psychology of the unconscious should be taken into account. But naturally it is impossible for me to argue that point in a letter. With your permission, let me recommend my little book, *Psychologie et Religion* (Edition Corréa, Paris, 1958) or the introduction to my book *Psychologie und Alchemie* (Zurich, 1952, not yet translated into French).[1]

With highest regards, I am,

Yours sincerely, C. G. JUNG

[1] Tr. Henry Pernet and Roland Cahen (Paris, 1970).

To the Earl of Sandwich

[ORIGINAL IN ENGLISH]

Dear Lord Sandwich,   10 August 1960

It was a great pleasure to receive your kind letter and congratulations on my 85th birthday.

It is indeed quite a number of years since our interview in 1938, when I received an Honorary Degree at Oxford, while lecturing there at a Congress of Psychotherapists.[1] It was on the eve of war and I remember the air filled with forebodings and anxious anticipations. I remember vividly looking at the delightful buildings and lawns of the Universitas Oxonensis as if seeing them for the first and last time. Although Oxford has been spared barbarous destruction I *had* seen it for the first and last time. I have not been there again al-

☐ George Charles Montagu (1874–1962), of Huntingdon; member of the Committee of the British Council, Arts Section. — The letter was published in *Spring*, 1971.
[1] The 10th International Medical Congress for Psychotherapy, of which Jung was president. His presidential address is in CW 10, Appendix, pars. 1069ff.

though I always dreamt and hoped to delve more deeply into the treasures of alchemistic manuscripts at the Bodleian. Fate has decreed otherwise.

I had to follow the ineradicable foolishness which furnishes the steps to true wisdom. Since man's nature is temperamentally set against wisdom, it is incumbent upon us to pay its price by what seems foolish to us.

Old age is only half as funny as one is inclined to think. It is at all events the gradual breaking down of the bodily machine, with which foolishness identifies ourselves. It is indeed a major effort—the *magnum opus* in fact—to escape in time from the narrowness of its embrace and to liberate our mind to the vision of the immensity of the world, of which we form an infinitesimal part. In spite of the enormity of our scientific cognition we are yet hardly at the bottom of the ladder, but we are at least so far that we are able to recognize the smallness of our knowledge.

The older I grow the more impressed I am by the frailty and uncertainty of our understanding, and all the more I take recourse to the simplicity of immediate experience so as not to lose contact with the essentials, namely the dominants which rule human existence throughout the millenniums.

There are two sciences in our days which are at immediate grips with the basic problems: nuclear physics and the psychology of the unconscious. There things begin to look really tough, as those who have an inkling of understanding of the one thing are singularly incapable of grasping the other thing; and here, so it looks, the great confusion of languages begins, which once already has destroyed a tower of Babel.

I am trying to hold those two worlds together as long as my machinery allows the effort, but it seems to be a condition which is desperately similar to that of the political world, the solution of which nobody yet can foresee. It is quite possible that we look at the world from the wrong side and that we might find the right answer by changing our point of view and looking at it from the other side, i.e., not from outside, but from inside.

Thanking you once more for your kind letter, I remain, dear Lord Sandwich,

Yours very sincerely, C. G. JUNG

To Jolande Jacobi

Dear Dr. Jacobi,   25 August 1960

I was very impressed and pleased to hear that my autobiographical sketches have conveyed to you something of what my outer side has hitherto kept hidden. It had to remain hidden because it could not have survived the brutalities of the outside world. But now I am grown so old that I can let go my grip on the world, and its raucous cries fade in the distance.

The dream[1] you have called back to my memory anticipates the content and setting of the analysis in a miraculous way. Who knew that and who arranged it? Who envisioned and grasped it, and forcibly expressed it in a great dream-image? He who has insight into this question knows whereof he speaks when he tries to interpret the psyche. With cordial greetings,

Yours sincerely, C. G. JUNG

☐ (Handwritten.)

[1] J. retold a "big dream" of hers in 1927 which had the character of an initiation. It is reported in her *The Way of Individuation* (1967), pp. 76f.

To Herbert Read

[ORIGINAL IN ENGLISH]

Dear Sir Herbert,   2 September 1960

I have just read the words of a *Man*, that is, the statement of your views about my work.[1] Courage and honesty have won out, two qualities the absence of which in my critics hitherto has hindered every form of understanding. Your blessed words are the rays of a new sun over a dark sluggish swamp in which I felt buried. I often thought of Meister Eckhart who was entombed for 600 years. I asked myself time and again why there are no men in our epoch who could see at least what I was wrestling with. I think it is not mere vanity and desire for recognition on my part, but a genuine concern for my fellow-beings. It is presumably the ancient functional

☐ See Read, 17 Oct. 48 (in vol. 1). See pl. III.

[1] An essay published as a pamphlet in honour of Jung's 85th birthday, *Zum 85. Geburtstag von Professor Carl Gustav Jung, 26. Juli 1960* (Zurich, 1960). The original English version appeared in Read, *The Art of Art Criticism* (London, 1957).

191

PROF. DR. C. G. JUNG

KÜSNACHT-ZURICH
SEESTRASSE 228

Sept 2ᵈ 1960

Dear Sir Herbert,

I have just read the words of a <u>Man</u>, that is. the statement of your views about my work. Courage and honesty have won out, the two qualities, the absence of which in my hitherto critics has hindered every form of understanding. Your blessed words are the rays of a new sun over a dark sluggish swamp, in which I felt being buried. I often thought of Master Eckhart who was entombed for 600 years. I asked myself time and again, why there are no men in our epoch, who could see at least, what I was wrestling with. I think it is not mere vanity and desire for recognition on my part, but a genuine concern for my fellow beings. It is presumably the ancient functional relationship of the medicine man to his tribe, the "participation mystique" and the essence of the physician's ethos. I see the suffering of mankind in the individual's predicament and vice-versa.

As a medical psychologist I do not merely assume, but I am thoroughly convinced, that

Herbert Read, 2 Sept. 60, first page only

192

relationship of the medicine-man to his tribe, the *participation mystique* and the essence of the physician's ethos. I see the suffering of mankind in the individual's predicament and vice versa.

As a medical psychologist I do not merely assume, but I am thoroughly convinced, that *nil humanum a me alienum esse*[2] is even my duty. I am including "modern art"—and passionately— though I see you indulgently smiling. I have regretted very much not to have had the opportunity of a real talk with you about your book,[3] which has brought back to me all my thoughts about art. I have never been explicit about them because I was hampered by my increasing awareness of the universal misunderstanding I en- countered. As the problem is subtle, its solution demands subtlety of mind and real experience of the mind's functioning. After 60 solid years of field-work I may be supposed to know at least something about my job. But even the most incompetent ass knew better and I received no encouragement. On the contrary I was misunderstood or completely ignored. Under those circumstances I even grew afraid to increase the chaos of opinion by adding considerations which could not be understood. I have given a good deal of attention to two great initiators: Joyce and Picasso.[4] Both are masters of the frag- mentation of aesthetic contents and accumulators of ingenious shards. I knew, as it seems to me, what that crumpled piece of paper meant that went out down the Liffey in spite of Joyce.[5] I knew his pain, which had strangled itself by its own strength. Hadn't I seen this tragedy time and again with my schizophrenic patients? In *Ulysses* a world comes down in an almost endless, breathless stream of débris, a "catholic" world, i.e., a universe with moanings and out- cries unheard and tears unshed, because suffering had extinguished itself, and an immense field of shards began to reveal its aesthetic "values." But no tongue will tell you what has happened in his soul.

I saw the same process evolving in Picasso, a very different man. Here was strength which brought about the dissolution of a work. He saw and understood what the surge of depth meant. Almost con- sciously he accepted the challenge of the all-powerful spirit of the time. He transformed his "Können" ("Kunst" derives from "kön-

---

[2] "Nothing human is alien to me." Cf. Terence, *Heauton Timorumenos*, I.1.25: "Homo sum; humani nil a me alienum puto."
[3] Read, *The Form of Things Unknown* (1960).
[4] Cf. "Ulysses" and "Picasso," CW 15.
[5] Concerning the "light crumpled throwaway" drifting down the Liffey cf. "Ulysses," pars. 186ff.

nen") into the art of ingenious fragmentation: "It shall go this way, if it doesn't go the other way." I bestowed the honour upon Picasso of viewing him as I did Joyce. I could easily have done worse by emphasizing his falsity. He was just catering to the morbidity of his time, as he himself admits. I am far from diagnosing him a schizophrenic. I only emphasize the analogy to the schizophrenic process, as I understand it. I find no signs of real schizophrenia in his work except the analogy, which however has no diagnostic value, since there are plenty of cases of this kind yet no proof that they are schizophrenics.

Picasso is ruthless strength, seizing the unconscious urge and voicing it resoundingly, even using it for monetary reasons. By this regrettable digression he shows how little he understands the primordial urge, which does not mean a field of ever so attractive-looking and alluring shards, but a new world after the old one has crumpled up. Nature has a *horror vacui* and does not believe in shard-heaps and decay, but grass and flowers cover all ruins inasmuch as the rains of heaven reach them.

The great problem of our time is that we don't understand what is happening to the world. We are confronted with the darkness of our soul, the unconscious. It sends up its dark and unrecognizable urges. It hollows out and hacks up the shapes of our culture and its historical dominants. We have no dominants any more, they are in the future. Our values are shifting, everything loses its certainty, even *sanctissima causalitas* has descended from the throne of the axioma and has become a mere field of probability. Who is the awe-inspiring guest who knocks at our door portentously?[6] Fear precedes him, showing that ultimate values already flow towards him. Our hitherto believed values decay accordingly and our only certainty is that the new world will be something different from what we were used to. If any of his urges show some inclination to incarnate in a known shape, the creative artist will not trust it. He will say: "Thou art not what thou sayest" and he will hollow them out and hack them up. That is where we are now. They have not yet learned to discriminate between their wilful mind and the objective manifestation of the

---

[6] Perhaps the fantasy figure personifying the dark aspect of the unconscious, destructive and creative at once, described in Jung's earliest childhood dream (*Memories*, pp. 11ff./25ff., esp. p. 15/29). Many years later he encountered a parallel figure, "the pilgrim of eternity," in *The Candle of Vision* (1920) by the Irish poet "A.E." (George W. Russell), which impressed him profoundly.

psyche. They have not yet learned to be objective with their own psyche, i.e., [to discriminate] between the thing which you do and the thing that happens to you. When somebody has a happy hunch, he thinks that *he* is clever, or that something which he does not know does not exist. We are still in a shockingly primitive state of mind, and this is the main reason why we cannot become objective in psychic matters. If the artist of today could only see what the psyche is spontaneously producing and what he, as a consciousness, is inventing, he would notice that the dream f.i. or the object is pronouncing (through his psyche) a reality from which he will never escape, because nobody will ever transcend the structure of the psyche.

We have simply got to listen to what the psyche spontaneously says to us. What the dream, which is not manufactured by us, says is *just so*. Say it again as well as you can. *Quod Natura relinquit imperfectum, Ars perficit*.[7] It is the great dream which has always spoken through the artist as a mouthpiece. All his love and passion (his "values") flow towards the coming guest to proclaim his arrival.

The negative aspects of modern art[8] show the intensity of our prejudice against the future, which we obstinately want to be as we expect it. *We* decide, as if we knew. We only know what we know, but there is plenty more of which we might know if only we could give up insisting upon what we do know. But the Dream would tell us more, therefore we despise the Dream and we are going on to dissolve *ad infinitum*.

What is the great Dream? It consists of the many small dreams and the many acts of humility and submission to their hints. It is the future and the picture of the new world, which we do not understand

---

[7] = What Nature left imperfect, the [alchemical] Art perfects.

[8] Sir Herbert Read replied to Jung's letter on 19 Oct. 1960. With regard to fragmentation (par. 2 at n. 4) he said: "The whole process of fragmentation, as you rightly call it, is not, in my opinion, wilfully destructive: the motive has always been (since the beginning of the century) to destroy the conscious image of perfection (the classical ideal of objectivity) in order to release new forces from the unconscious. This 'turning inwards' . . . is precisely a longing to be put in touch with the Dream, that is to say (as you say) the future. But in the attempt the artist has his 'dark and unrecognizable urges,' and they have overwhelmed him. He struggles like a man overwhelmed by a flood. He clutches at fragments, at driftwood and floating rubbish of all kinds. But he has to release this flood in order to get nearer to the Dream. My defence of modern art has always been based on this realization: that art must die in order to live, that new sources of life must be tapped under the crust of tradition."

195

yet. We cannot know better than the unconscious and its intimations. *There* is a fair chance of finding what we seek in vain in our conscious world. Where else could it be?

I am afraid I never find the language which would convey such simple arguments to my contemporaries. Apologies for the length of my letter!

Sincerely yours, C. G. JUNG

To Ignaz Tauber

Dear Dr. Tauber, 13 December 1960

Many thanks for your kind suggestion that I write a commentary on my Bollingen symbols.[1] Nobody is more uncertain about their meaning than the author himself. They are their own representation of the way they came into being.

The first thing I saw in the rough stone was the figure of the worshipping woman, and behind her the silhouette of the old king sitting on his throne. As I was carving her out, the old king vanished from view. Instead I suddenly saw that the unworked surface in front of her clearly revealed the hindquarters of a horse, and a mare at that, for whose milk the primitive woman was stretching out her hands. The woman is obviously my anima in the guise of a millennia-old ancestress.

Milk, as *lac virginis*, virgin's milk, is a synonym for the *aqua doctrinae*,[2] one of the aspects of Mercurius, who had already bedevilled the Bollingen stones in the form of the trickster.[3]

The mare descending from above reminded me of Pegasus. Pegasus is the constellation above the second fish in Pisces; it precedes Aquarius in the precession of the equinoxes. I have represented it in its feminine aspect, the milk taking the place of the spout of water in the sign for Aquarius. This feminine attribute indicates the unconscious nature of the milk. Evidently the milk has first to come into the hands of the anima, thus charging her with special energy.

---

[1] The figures Jung carved in bas-relief on the outside wall of his Tower (see illus., p. 617). Cf. Jaffé, *From the Life and Work of C. G. Jung* (tr. 1971), p. 133.
[2] The water of doctrine, originally a Christian concept for the store of pure wisdom of the Church.
[3] Cf. Hull, 3 Aug. 53, and illustration; also Jung, "On the Psychology of the Trickster Figure," CW 9, i.

196

This afflux of anima energy immediately released in me the idea of a she-bear, approaching the back of the anima from the left. The bear stands for the savage energy and power of Artemis. In front of the bear's forward-striding paws I saw, adumbrated in the stone, a ball, for a ball is often given to bears to play with in the bear-pit. Obviously this ball is being brought to the worshipper as a symbol of individuation. It points to the meaning or content of the milk.

The whole thing, it seems to me, expresses coming events that are still hidden in the archetypal realm. The anima, clearly, has her mind on spiritual contents. But the bear, the emblem of Russia, sets the ball rolling. Hence the inscription: *Ursa movet molem.*[4]

There's not much more I can tell you, but as a sign of the times I would like to cite the opinion of one of my critics. He accuses me of being so uneducated that I don't even know that the sun moves into Pisces from Aquarius and not the other way round! Such is the level of my public. With best greetings to you and your wife,

Yours sincerely, C. G. JUNG

[4] "the she-bear moves the mass." Next to the female figure with the horse Jung carved two inscriptions: "Exoriatur lumen quod gestavi in alvo" (let the light that I have carried in my womb shine forth) and πήγασος πηγάζων ὑδροφόρου χοή (Pegasus leaping forth—a consecrating gush of the water-carrier). The latter involves a pun on the meaning of the name Pegasus, lit. "fount-horse."

To William G. Wilson

[ORIGINAL IN ENGLISH]

Dear Mr. Wilson,   30 January 1961

Your letter was very welcome indeed. I had no news from Roland H. any more and often wondered what has been his fate. Our conversation which he has adequately reported to you had an aspect of which he did not know. The reason was that I could not tell him everything. In those days I had to be exceedingly careful of what I said. I had found out that I was misunderstood in every possible way.

☐ (1896–1971), co-founder of Alcoholics Anonymous; he was known as "Bill W." His letter, dated 23 Jan. 61, and Jung's reply were published in the Jan. 1963 issue of AA *Grapevine* (monthly journal of Alcoholics Anonymous) and again in Jan. 1968. In his letter W. recounts how Jung's remark in 1931 to Roland H. (whom he was treating for chronic alcoholism), that his situation was hopeless unless "he could become the subject of a spiritual or religious experience—in short a genuine conversion," was instrumental in his own conversion and cure, and how as a result he came to found the organization in 1934.

197

Thus I was very careful when I talked to Roland H. But what I really thought about was the result of many experiences with men of his kind.

His craving for alcohol was the equivalent on a low level of the spiritual thirst of our being for wholeness, expressed in medieval language: the union with God.*

How could one formulate such an insight in a language that is not misunderstood in our days?

The only right and legitimate way to such an experience is that it happens to you in reality, and it can only happen to you when you walk on a path which leads you to higher understanding. You might be led to that goal by an act of grace or through a personal and honest contact with friends or through a high education of the mind beyond the confines of mere rationalism. I see from your letter that Roland H. has chosen the second way, which was, under the circumstances, obviously the best one.

I am strongly convinced that the evil principle prevailing in this world leads the unrecognized spiritual need into perdition, if it is not counteracted either by a real religious insight or by the protective wall of human community. An ordinary man, not protected by an action from above and isolated in society, cannot resist the power of evil, which is called very aptly the Devil. But the use of such words arouses so many mistakes that one can only keep aloof from them as much as possible.

These are the reasons why I could not give a full and sufficient explanation to Roland H. But I am risking it with you because I conclude from your very decent and honest letter that you have acquired a point of view about the misleading platitudes one usually hears about alcoholism.

You see, alcohol in Latin is *spiritus* and you use the same word for the highest religious experience as well as for the most depraving poison. The helpful formula therefore is: *spiritus contra spiritum.* Thanking you again for your kind letter, I remain,

Yours sincerely, C. G. JUNG

* "As the hart panteth after the water brooks, so panteth my soul after thee, O God" (Psalm 42:1).

198

Anonymous

[ORIGINAL IN ENGLISH]

Dear Sir, 14 February 1961

It is very difficult to answer your question.[1] I should give you the same answer as Shri Ramana Maharshi,[2] but I see too much the difficulty of the practical application.

If you want to do something useful, it only can be there where you live, where you know the people and circumstances. In nosing around among them you will find a possibility to help. It is certain that you will find one, but not rarely the unconscious blindfolds you, because it does not want you to find an application of your energies to external circumstances. The reason for such a resistance lies in the fact that you need some reconstruction in yourself which you would gladly apply to others. Many things should be put right in oneself first, before we apply our imperfections to our fellow-beings.

Thus, if you should find no obvious possibility, it means that you have to cultivate your own garden first. It is like water in a valley. It cannot flow and it stagnates, but if you have a lake on a hill you cannot keep it from overflowing. It may be that you need to raise your own level.

Sincerely yours, C. G. JUNG

☐ California.

[1] N., a man of "near sixty," asked if "there were some spot where I could make use of my knowledge in helping the world."

[2] Cf. Mees, 15 Sept. 47 & n. 2. N. quoted the Maharshi's answer to the same question he had asked Jung: "Help yourself and you help the world, for you are the world."

The Collected Works of C. G. JUNG

The Collected Works of C. G. JUNG

Editors: Sir Herbert Read (d. 1968), Michael Fordham, and Gerhard Adler; executive editor, William McGuire. Translated by R.F.C. Hull (d. 1974), except vol. 2; cf. vol. 6.

(*continued*)

* Published 1957; 2nd edn., 1970.   † Published 1973.

2 *(continued)*
   Further Investigations on the Galvanic Phenomenon and Respiration in
   Normal and Insane Individuals (by C. Ricksher and Jung)
   Appendix: Statistical Details of Enlistment (1906); New Aspects of Crim-
   inal Psychology (1908); The Psychological Methods of Investigation
   Used in the Psychiatric Clinic of the University of Zurich (1910);
   On the Doctrine of Complexes ([1911] 1913); On the Psychological
   Diagnosis of Evidence (1937)

*3. THE PSYCHOGENESIS OF MENTAL DISEASE
   The Psychology of Dementia Praecox (1907)
   The Content of the Psychoses (1908/1914)
   On Psychological Understanding (1914)
   A Criticism of Bleuler's Theory of Schizophrenic Negativism (1911)
   On the Importance of the Unconscious in Psychopathology (1914)
   On the Problem of Psychogenesis in Mental Disease (1919)
   Mental Disease and the Psyche (1928)
   On the Psychogenesis of Schizophrenia (1939)
   Recent Thoughts on Schizophrenia (1957)
   Schizophrenia (1958)

†4. FREUD AND PSYCHOANALYSIS
   Freud's Theory of Hysteria: A Reply to Aschaffenburg (1906)
   The Freudian Theory of Hysteria (1908)
   The Analysis of Dreams (1909)
   A Contribution to the Psychology of Rumour (1910–11)
   On the Significance of Number Dreams (1910–11)
   Morton Prince, "The Mechanism and Interpretation of Dreams": A Critical
   Review (1911)
   On the Criticism of Psychoanalysis (1910)
   Concerning Psychoanalysis (1912)
   The Theory of Psychoanalysis (1913)
   General Aspects of Psychoanalysis (1913)
   Psychoanalysis and Neurosis (1916)
   Some Crucial Points in Psychoanalysis: A Correspondence between Dr.
   Jung and Dr. Loÿ (1914)
   Prefaces to "Collected Papers on Analytical Psychology" (1916, 1917)
   The Significance of the Father in the Destiny of the Individual (1909/
   1949)
   Introduction to Kranefeldt's "Secret Ways of the Mind" (1930)
   Freud and Jung: Contrasts (1929)

‡5. SYMBOLS OF TRANSFORMATION (1911–12/1952)
   With Appendix: The Miller Fantasies

---

* Published 1960.   † Published 1961.
‡ Published 1956; 2nd edn., 1967.

(continued)

* Published 1971.   † Published 1953; 2nd edn., 1966.
‡ Published 1960; 2nd edn., 1969.   ** Published 1959; 2nd edn., 1968.

THE COLLECTED WORKS OF C. G. JUNG

* Published 1959; 2nd edn., 1968.   † Published 1964; 2nd edn., 1970.
‡ Published 1958; 2nd edn., 1969.

206

The Psychology of Eastern Meditation (1943)
The Holy Men of India: Introduction to Zimmer's "Der Weg zum Selbst"
(1944)
Foreword to the "I Ching" (1950)

*12. PSYCHOLOGY AND ALCHEMY (1944)

Prefatory note to the English Edition ([1951?] added 1967)
Introduction to the Religious and Psychological Problems of Alchemy
Individual Dream Symbolism in Relation to Alchemy (1936)
Religious Ideas in Alchemy (1937)
Epilogue

†13. ALCHEMICAL STUDIES

Commentary on "The Secret of the Golden Flower" (1929)
The Visions of Zosimos (1938/1954)
Paracelsus as a Spiritual Phenomenon (1942)
The Spirit Mercurius (1943/1948)
The Philosophical Tree (1945/1954)

‡14. MYSTERIUM CONIUNCTIONIS (1955–56)

AN INQUIRY INTO THE SEPARATION AND
SYNTHESIS OF PSYCHIC OPPOSITES IN ALCHEMY
The Components of the Coniunctio
The Paradoxa
The Personification of the Opposites
Rex and Regina
Adam and Eve
The Conjunction

**15. THE SPIRIT IN MAN, ART, AND LITERATURE

Paracelsus (1929)
Paracelsus the Physician (1941)
Sigmund Freud in His Historical Setting (1932)
In Memory of Sigmund Freud (1939)
Richard Wilhelm: In Memoriam (1930)
On the Relation of Analytical Psychology to Poetry (1922)
Psychology and Literature (1930/1950)
"Ulysses": A Monologue (1932)
Picasso (1932)

§16. THE PRACTICE OF PSYCHOTHERAPY

GENERAL PROBLEMS OF PSYCHOTHERAPY
Principles of Practical Psychotherapy (1935)
What Is Psychotherapy? (1935)

(continued)

* Published 1953; 2nd edn., completely revised, 1968.
† Published 1968.   ‡ Published 1963; 2nd edn., 1970.
** Published 1966.
§ Published 1954; 2nd edn., revised and augmented, 1966.

16 (*continued*)
  Some Aspects of Modern Psychotherapy (1930)
  The Aims of Psychotherapy (1931)
  Problems of Modern Psychotherapy (1929)
  Psychotherapy and a Philosophy of Life (1943)
  Medicine and Psychotherapy (1945)
  Psychotherapy Today (1945)
  Fundamental Questions of Psychotherapy (1951)
    SPECIFIC PROBLEMS OF PSYCHOTHERAPY
  The Therapeutic Value of Abreaction (1921/1928)
  The Practical Use of Dream-Analysis (1934)
  The Psychology of the Transference (1946)
  Appendix: The Realities of Practical Psychotherapy ([1937] added, 1966)

*17. THE DEVELOPMENT OF PERSONALITY
  Psychic Conflicts in a Child (1910/1946)
  Introduction to Wickes's "Analyse der Kinderseele" (1927/1931)
  Child Development and Education (1928)
  Analytical Psychology and Education: Three Lectures (1926/1946)
  The Gifted Child (1943)
  The Significance of the Unconscious in Individual Education (1928)
  The Development of Personality (1934)
  Marriage as a Psychological Relationship (1925)

18. THE SYMBOLIC LIFE
  Miscellaneous Writings

19. COMPLETE BIBLIOGRAPHY OF C. G. JUNG'S WRITINGS

20. GENERAL INDEX TO THE COLLECTED WORKS

See also:

C. G. JUNG: LETTERS
Selected and edited by Gerhard Adler, in collaboration with Aniela Jaffé.
Translation from the German by R.F.C. Hull.
  VOL. 1: 1906–1950
  VOL. 2: 1951–1961

THE FREUD/JUNG LETTERS
Edited by William McGuire, translated by
Ralph Manheim and R.F.C. Hull

C. G. JUNG SPEAKING: Interviews and Encounters
Edited by William McGuire and R.F.C. Hull

C. G. JUNG: Word and Image
Edited by Aniela Jaffé

Appendix: Biographical Notes

BIOGRAPHICAL NOTES

Helton Godwin Baynes, M.D. (1882–1943), English psychotherapist, author and translator of several of Jung's works. Cf. his *Mythology of the Soul* (1940); *Germany Possessed* (1941); *Analytical Psychology and the English Mind* (1950). ("Peter" is a friendly nickname.)

Eleanor Bertine, M.D. 1887–1968), American analytical psychologist. Cf. her *Human Relationships* (1958); *Jung's Contribution to Our Time* (1967). Jung's foreword to the former is in CW 18.

Eugen Böhler (1893–1977), professor of economics at the Swiss Federal Polytechnic (E.T.H.), Zurich, 1924–1964. In July 1955 he was one of the speakers at a celebration when Jung received an honorary degree in natural science at the Polytechnic. (Cf. Hug, Meier, Böhler, Schmid, *Carl Gustav Jung*, Kultur- und Staatswissenschaftliche Schriften, no. 91, 1955.) B.'s growing interest in the psychology of economics led to friendly personal relations between the two men. Cf. his "Conscience in Economic Life," in *Conscience* (Studies in Jungian Thought, 1970; orig. 1958), and "Die Grundgedanken der Psychologie von C. C. Jung" *Industrielle Organisation* (Zurich), no. 4, 1960.

Sandor Ferenczi, M.D. (1873–1933); Freud's closest friend and collaborator, founder of the Hungarian Psycho-Analytical Society.

Jürg Fierz, student in 1942, later Ph.D., journalist, since 1950 editor of the Zurich *Tagensanzeiger*.

Josef Goldbrunner, Ph.D., Roman Catholic priest. In Munich in 1941; now professor of theology at the U. of Regensburg, Germany.

Hermann Hesse (1877–1962), German/Swiss novelist and poet. He then resided at Montagnola, in Canton Ticino. Received Nobel prize for Literature, 1946.

Jolan (later Jolande) Jacobi, Ph.D. (1890–1973), analytical psychologist, originally of Budapest and Vienna, later Zurich. Cf. her *The Psychology of C. G. Jung* (6th edn., 1962), *Complex/Archetype/Symbol* (1959); *The Way of Individuation* (tr., 1967); *Frauenprobleme/Eheprobleme* (1968); *Vom Bilderreich der Seele* (1969); *Psychological Reflections, An Anthology of Jung's Writings* (2nd edn., 1970). Around 1928, as leader of the Kulturbund, she brought Jung to Vienna to lecture.

Dr. Paul Maag was superintendent of a sanatorium in Thurgau, Switzerland.

213

P. W. Martin (1893–1971), founder of the International Study Centre of Applied Psychology, Oxted, England. Cf. his *Experiment in Depth* (1955).

John Weir Perry, M.D., analytical psychologist in San Francisco. Cf. his *The Self in Psychotic Process* (1953); *Lord of the Four Quarters* (1966); *The Far Side of Madness* (1974).

Sir Herbert Read (1893–1968), English poet, novelist, art critic, co-editor of CW.

Upton Sinclair (1878–1968), American writer.

Ignaz Tauber, of Winterthur, a general medical practitioner who also made use of analytical psychology, was treating Jung in 1953.

J. H. Van der Hoop, M.D., Dutch psychotherapist, President of the Dutch group of the International Medical Society for Psychotherapy. Cf. CW 10, Appendix, pars. 1048, 1055.

R. J. Zwi Werblowsky, lecturer at Leeds U. and at the Institute of Jewish Studies, Manchester in 1951; now professor of comparative religion at the Hebrew U. of Jerusalem.

Father Victor White, O.P. (1902–1960); Dominican priest; in 1945 he was professor of dogmatic theology at Blackfriars, Oxford. Cf. his *God and the Unconscious* (1952, with a forward by Jung, now in CW 11), and *Soul and Psyche* (1960).

Frances Gillespy Wickes (1875–1967), American analytical psychologist. Cf. her *The Inner World of Childhood* (1927, rev. 1965); *The Inner World of Man* (1938/ 1950); *The Inner World of Choice* (1963). Jung's foreword to the first book is in CW 17; to the second, in CW 18.

Heinrich Zimmer (1890–1943), German Indologist (U. of Heidelberg), later at Columbia U., New York. Cf. Jung, "Heinrich Zimmer," in *Erinnerungen, Träume, Gedanken*, pp. 385f. (The American/English edn. does not contain this tribute.)

Index of Correspondents

INDEX OF CORRESPONDENTS

217

218